Remembering IÑIGO

Glimspes of the Life of Saint Ignatius of Loyola

The *Memoriale* of Luís Gonçalves da Câmara

Remembering
IÑIGO

Glimpses of the Life of
Saint Ignatius of Loyola

The *Memoriale* of
Luís Gonçalves da Câmara

Translated with introduction, notes and indices by
Alexander Eaglestone *and*
Joseph A. Munitiz, S.J.

Gracewing Publishing | The Institute of Jesuit Sources
Leominster, England | Saint Louis, USA

No. 19 in Series I: Jesuit Primary
Sources in English Translation

©2004 The Institute of Jesuit Sources
3601 Lindell Boulevard
Saint Louis, MO, 63108.
Tel.: 314-977-7257
Fax: 314-977-7263
e-mail ijs@slu.edu
website www.jesuitsources.com

Library of Congress Control Number 2004107003
ISBN 1-880810-51-4

CLARAE

CONIUGI ET AMICAE
CLARISSIMAE

CONTENTS

INTRODUCTION

In 1553, on the Tuesday after Whit Sunday (23 May), a weary 33-year old Portuguese Jesuit[1] arrived after a long journey (via Spain and Paris) at the residence in Rome of Ignatius Loyola.[2] However, despite his tiredness he must have felt very excited, as he had been waiting over many years for the chance to meet the General Superior of the Society of Jesus. Moreover, he now came with an important, if delicate, mission: to report on the state of affairs of the Portuguese province, which had been plunged deep in crisis under the erratic government of a close personal friend of Ignatius, Simão Rodrigues. Rather to his chagrin he was greeted politely, and even affectionately, by Ignatius, but "without the kind of celebration and warmth that we here [in Portugal] are used to show towards our guests" (§109). And many months were to pass before Ignatius finally had a long conversation with him. However from then on, their relations grew ever more intimate. Ignatius recognized in da Câmara a man to whom he could open his heart, something that had occurred previously only with the first companions and a few exceptional men—like Nadal and Polanco. It would be da Câmara to whom he would finally consent to recount his autobiographical reminiscences. It was also da Câmara whom he selected to look after the material running of the residence as "minister" of the house, even if financial affairs were entrusted to someone else. In a couple of years da Câmara had been included in the innermost circle of close collaborators, regularly dining with Ignatius and having daily contact with him.

[1] Luis Gonçalves da Câmara must have been born in 1519 or 1520, and began his M.A. studies in Paris in 1535 or 1536; by 1544 he was in Coimbra engaged in graduate theology studies, and the following year he joined the young Society of Jesus. Given his aristocratic family connections it was thought best to send him away from Portugual for his novitiate (in Valencia), and he was ordained priest already in 1546, and shortly after appointed rector in Coimbra. A year later the provincial (Fr. Rodrígues) decided that a little mortification would be good for him and from being rector he was sent to work in the kitchen. Between 1548 and 1553 he was asked to undertake pastoral work in Portugal and North Africa (in the liberation of captives), but principally at the Portuguese court (though he explicitily refused to hear the confessions of the Royal family). In 1553 he was invited to make his final solemn profession in the Society, and despite reluctance—he put forward his inadequacy—he finally agreed and his vows were received by Francis Borgia in March. He then left for Rome.

[2] Ignatius had been living in rooms here since 1544; the building had been acquired the previous year and then expanded. Further reforms were needed, e.g. in 1551, and the *Memoriale* refers to additonal work in the construction of the infirmary.

In this way da Câmara now found himself in a situation of which he had dreamed: he could note in minute detail the actions, words and even thoughts of the man he most admired in the world. He felt that he had the duty to record for the benefit of other Jesuits the tiny, insignificant aspects of the person that he believed should serve as the living pattern of other Jesuits.

He was singularly gifted for the task: possessed of a remarkable memory, which offset his poor eye-sight, fluent in several languages (Italian, French, Latin, Spanish) apart from his own, quick on the uptake (to the point that Ignatius would constantly be reprimanding him for his impulsiveness),[3] acquainted with the "ways of the world" through his earlier contacts at Court, and an affectionate, humble, friendly man. Early in 1555 it occurred to him that the best course to follow would be to jot down daily memorandum notes concerning matters that had occurred, and so he took to carrying round with him a note-book and portable ink-well and pen. Ignatius knew what he was doing, and was willing to oblige by pausing in his speech to allow his amanuensis time to catch up. For almost a year the note-book was in constant use.

Thus one part of the *Memoriale* came into existence,[4] written in Spanish (though peppered with Latin phrases)[5] and striving to be factually correct and accurate: da Câmara was aware that by nature he was too sensitive and over-impulsive—"He [Ignatius] said he had noticed that I greatly exaggerate things, and that was bad when I was reporting on a matter, because it destroyed my credibility. . .[§291]." A little too lively a Boswell for the measured self-control of an Ignatius! There is also no denying that he loved a good gossip: he can spot when Ignatius is pulling somebody's leg,[6] or when he enjoys a rare joke.[7] But his veneration for Ignatius means that he holds up a mirror in which his hero is truly reflected: da Câmara records without questioning, and he probably felt that his memorandum notes were more for his own personal use than for general publication. This would explain the time that elapsed before the second part of the *Memoriale* came into existence, the Portuguese commentary,[8]

---

[3] See §289.

[4] Printed in larger type and with full margins in this edition.

[5] The Spanish of da Câmara would repay philological study; despite occasional Italianisms it is mainly correct. It is significant that when he writes in Portuguese he rarely introduces Latin words and his style flows more easily.

[6] As when Ignatius suggests that Bobadilla and Salmerón of all people are hypocrites: §23.

[7] "Two popes against one abbot...!" referring to Abbot Martinengo's double interruption of his Spiritual Exercises to cope with papal demises.

[8] Printed in smaller type and with indented margins in this edition.

that would be written nearly two decades after da Câmara's departure from Rome in October, 1555. Even then all the indications are that the public envisaged by da Câmara was restricted to an in-house audience of fellow-Jesuits: these were the men he hoped to encourage by recalling close personal contact with the Iñigo he so admired.

In any case, to understand the *Memoriale* it is essential to bear in mind the different nature of the two parts—or elements, because they are so closely intertwined—of which it is composed. By the year 1573 da Câmara was in his early fifties but already troubled with ill health. He had made one return journey to Rome, in 1558, when the First General Congregation met to elect a successor after the death of Ignatius (31 July 1556), and the plan then had been that he should stay in Rome as Assistant to the new General, Laínez. However, pressure from the Portuguese court forced his return to Lisbon and to the unenviable task of acting as tutor to the boy-king, the self-willed Sebastian I, who came to respect and love this kindly, prudent man. Eventually he was able to retire from the court and was living at the Jesuit college in Evora. He was persuaded to prepare his original Spanish note-book for publication; he would do so by writing a commentary on the different entries, explaining their relevance to the new generation of Jesuits. Both his rector and the new General, Everard Mercurian, encouraged him warmly in the task and he began with enthusiasm. But it is clear from the unequal length of the comments added to each month—copious for the first three, then trailing off, and finally very meagre for the last three—that his energy soon began to wane. By 1574 his health had become so uncertain that in August he returned to Lisbon and died seven months later, on 15 March 1575, without having put the finishing touches to his work.

This second part, the commentary, must be seen as written with the perspective of nearly twenty years of hindsight, and with a new purpose in mind: the Society had undergone great changes—external expansion to a degree that would never have been expected—and internal developments (involving the training of younger Jesuits, the form of government, the norms of spirituality). To some extent da Câmara restricts himself to clarifying phrases, identifying people, explaining events. But there are also comments that clearly display dissatisfaction with certain developments: e.g. with the growing formality of the novitiate (in contrast, in Ignatius's time, "the novices . . . lived in greater freedom—I mean without so many rules and external ceremonies, thanks to which now each one can cover up any spontaneous reactions" [§257]); and also with the new prohibition in Portugal against reading lives of the saints ("It was with reading stories of the saints of other religious orders that Fr. Ignatius prepared himself for Our Lord to do with him what he did" [§370]). But most important, da Câmara expatiates at length, in a moving way that has a personal ring to it, on how government in the Society was to be conducted (§§269-72): he insists on the need for true delegation of responsibility, so that local superiors can act with freedom and confidence in their personal judgement:

> ... God gives special assistance to the immediate superior and his subordinate in particular cases, such as pertain properly and immediately to his office. Therefore, to seek to limit such cases, or govern by general rules, would be to remove from him his essential role as superior, and consequently to impede co-operation with the special grace of God, which is more efficacious, as applying to a particular agent, than anything else. (§271)

However, even when the original notes of da Câmara and their subsequent commentary are seen in their context, the *Memoriale* remains something of a conundrum.[9] The heart of the puzzle lies in the personality of Ignatius himself. In some ways a gigantic figure who towers in sanctity and vision above all the other Jesuits of his day: da Câmara evokes this awe when he compares the impression made on him by the saintly Pierre Favre and then later by Ignatius:

> ... in Madrid ... I made my confession to him [Fr. Favre] and had long discussions with him. I was so astonished by what I saw in him, I felt there could not be any man in the world more filled with God ... However, when I got to know him [Fr. Ignatius] in Rome and talked with him, the feelings I had experienced for Fr. Favre lost their force, and in the end he seemed to me a child in comparison with our Father. (§8)

And yet in the *Memoriale* there are times when it is difficult to recognize this person as the same Ignatius. Perhaps particularly difficult to understand is his attitude in imposing mortifications, both mental and physical, on others; but there are other repellent aspects: his authoritarianism, his controlled anger which inspired such fear in his most devoted followers, the deviousness of procedures adopted to ensure that others would incur censure rather than he himself.

---

[9] So uncertain were the Roman authorities about allowing the publication of the *Memoriale* that only a few contemporary individuals were allowed access to it (such as Ribadeneira, Leczyski [Lancicius], Nadal, Romei, and Santiago Jiménez), and when Aquaviva became General he turned down a request from the Castilian Province for a copy: "non expedit omnium manibus circumferri" (MHSI, vol. 66, p. 511]. The text had to wait until 1904 for a first edition, but was given the honour of a full critical edition in 1943.

It would be tempting to undertake in this Introduction a defence of Ignatius, and previous editors (particularly the French and the Spanish) have made valiant efforts to do this.[10] Instead a different policy has been followed here. Much time has been devoted to drawing up a detailed Index to the text. This seemed particularly necessary as the *Memoriale* is something of a rag-bag, with items collected higgledy-piggledy as they happened to occur during the course of the ten months during which da Câmara noted his memos, and with his commentary following that chaotic order, or even adding to the inconsistencies. There is much to be gained from a continuous perusal of the *Memoriale*, but readers may find that with the Index in hand it is possible to see much more in these random notes. It would be a pity if the freshness of their approach were to be impaired by the application of coloured lenses before they began. Instead readers are invited to take the entries listed in the Index under different lemmas, especially those under "Ignatius", but also e.g. "Câmara", "Nadal", or themes like "obedience", "penances", "vocation", and build up their own impressions.

A directive from the Spiritual Exercises may be helpful at this point: ". . . it must be presupposed that every good Christian should be readier to justify than to condemn a neighbour's statement" (§22). The enormous cultural and religious differences that separate the sixteenth century from our own raise great barriers to our understanding of these texts. Any simplistic interpretation, that would defend a literal transfer of outmoded practices, can only be misleading. The very vividness and actuality of da Câmara's narrative can be deceptive. One may feel drawn into a false proximity to persons and ways of thought that are in fact very distant and foreign to later readers. The *Memoriale* is basically only one fragment in the mosaic of historical evidence. However it cannot be overlooked. First, because of the first-hand evidence it provides about Ignatius himself and the early Jesuits, in particular about the admission and dismissal of applicants, who cause so much preoccupation to da Câmara. But also because of what the *Memoriale* implies about the international ramifications of this small group, in both the ecclesiastical and the political sphere; not only popes and cardinals, but also kings and emperors form a constant background to the notes. Moreover it is also clear that the Society itself is a meeting-point of different nationalities, each with a marked character:

---

[10] Both of these editions are provided with excellent detailed Introductions, well worth consulting. A more critical approach is suggested by J.M. Granero, "El 'Memorial' de Cámara", *Manresa* 39, 1967, pp. 75-78, in which he reviews the French edition.

Portuguese warmth met with Castilian courtesy, German strength with Italian diplomacy.

More generally, the strength of the document is that it presents a stream-of-consciousness account of life with Ignatius, which means that difficult issues in the Society's way of life are powerfully illuminated, but not resolved.

*   *   *

In undertaking the translation, our policy has been to reflect as faithfully as we could in English the Spanish and Portuguese text so carefully edited in the *Monumenta Historica*. Thus we resisted the temptation to paraphrase and streamline da Câmara's often twisted sentences. The original text began as a series of notes, and by the time he came to write his commentary, da Câmara was ill and prematurely aged. Readers should be warned that at times the resulting English may not make easy reading, and it may be significant that the most recent Spanish edition of the text provides a twentieth-century Castilian version in parallel columns with the original sixteenth-century text; once the translator had provided a version of the Portuguese into modern Spanish, he felt that his readers would need a modern version of the original Spanish as well.

One of the pleasures of producing this book has been to see the goodwill of those who helped us. Not all can be mentioned, but we hope that those omitted by name will feel included in our general expression of thanks. Particular thanks must be given to the following: our two publishers, Mr. Tom Longford (*Gracewing*) and Fr. John Padberg (*Institute of Jesuit Sources*); Fr. Billy Hewett, the Director of Inigo Enterprises; Fr. Josep Vives in Barcelona; Fr. Philip Endean, *corrector eximius,* and Mrs Joyce Adams, our typist. Finally, we would like to dedicate this book to Clare (the Clara of the dedication), whose discreet presence made the whole thing possible.

GLOSSARY

Assistant
the General Superior originally had four Assistants, elected by the General Congregation that elected him, to be constantly with him and provide advice and help both on a personal basis, and on a broad regional basis (e.g. Italy); moreover if necessary they were to arrange for his replacement: cf. *Constitutions* IX, 779ff. [Ganss, pp. 320-21]; as time went on their number increased and the allocation of their duties was altered.

brother
see "coadjutor" and §22 with note; novices are also referred to as brother Novices, and in the *Memoriale* the term "brother" can be used for anyone who is not a priest, or even (in the plural, "brethren") for all members of the community.

coadjutor
a full member of the Society, but one who is not professed; he can be a "Brother" (technically a "temporal coadjutor") or a priest ("spiritual coadjutor").

consolation
the term used by Ignatius along with "desolation" to designate "situations in which the deep influences of good and bad spirits manifest themselves through the interplay of feelings, thoughts and imaginations" (Ivens, *Understanding the Spiritual Exercises*, p. 137).

consult-(ors)
a meeting of those appointed to advise a superior; Ignatius would sometimes summon a consultation without being present himself.

discipline
a form of corporal mortification involving the use of a small whip of knotted cords which are swung over the shoulders.

Doctor
a university title indicating that prescribed post-graduate studies have been successfully completed; it is rarely used here to denote medical qualifications.

experiment
cf. §253.

first companions
the original group that gathered round Ignatius in Paris and then in Venice, before proceeding to Rome to ask for papal approbation.

First Probation

In 1541, when the Society was beginning, this First Probation lasted about three months; it was lengthened to six months for a few years (1545-49), then reduced to about a fortnight, "during which the candidate was a guest, examining the Society and being examined by it"; cf. G. Ganss, *Constitutions,* p. 76, note 9. The term "Second Probation" refers to the novitiate proper, which usually lasts two years. At the end of all the training a Third Probation" (tertianship) was devoted mainly to pastoral work and spiritual reflection (see §73).

First Vows

the traditional religious vows (the evangelical counsels) of poverty, chastity and obedience; from the beginning "First Vows" in the Society were classified as perpetual (as distinct from the temporal first vows common in many religious orders).

General

the over-all (and therefore "general") superior as opposed to the other superiors who have more restricted obligations (cf. provincial).

General Congregation

the highest legislative body in the Society, which ordinarily meets only to elect a new General or if some special need arises: cf. *Constitutions* VIII, 2-7 [Ganss, pp. 294-306].

indifference

cf. §120 note, and Index.

little table

a form of public penance which required the penitent to kneel for his meal while his fault was made public, by himself or by someone else, with or without a public reprimand.

Loreto

pilgrimage site near Ancona in Italy, where the house of the Virgin Mary is said to have been transported from Nazareth.

Master

the university title ("magister") granted on completion of the graduate course; further post-graduate studies could lead to acquiring the title of "doctor".

Micer

frequently used by da Câmara as an honorific title.

minister

person in charge of the material running of a house.

modesty	*modestia* has a special meaning in these texts and is roughly equivalent to "good manners as befitting a religious": see §20.
novice	someone wishing to join the Society and accepted initially for a two-year trial period; he becomes a full member only after taking his First Vows, which can be taken either as a Brother (coadjutor), or as a scholastic (training for the priesthood).
ours	Jesuit jargon for "members of the Society of Jesus."
probation	cf. First Probation.
procurator	treasurer or bursar, responsible for financial arrangements.
professed	a professed priest in the Society is one who has taken both the three religious vows, and a number of further vows, notably one to go wherever the Pope (through the General) wishes to send him; the grade of profession, conferred at the end of the full period of formation to those priests judged suitable, makes one eligible to hold certain administrative posts in the Society.
provincial	the superior put in charge of a region: e.g. Spain was divided into various provinces, while Ireland formed one province.
residence	the main house in Rome used by Ignatius, then next to the small church of Our Lady of the Way (*Santa Maria della Strada*), which was subsequently replaced by the Jesuit-built church of the Gesù (built 1568-99); technically it was a "professed house", i.e. not permitted to own capital and relying on alms.
scholastics	Jesuits who have taken their First Vows and are in training to become priests.
Stations	cf. §§209, 237.
second table	the second session for meals, mainly for the benefit of those serving at the first.
syndic	an admonitor or corrector; Ignatius appointed such officials to supervise domestic observance, but later their role was taken over by the minister: cf. G. Ganss, *Constitutions*, p. 160, n. 11.

Vicar   the office of Vicar-General, held by someone while the
                               General is indisposed or absent.

villa (house)   a secondary residence generally outside the city with a
                               healthy climate used for relaxation or recuperation.

Visitor   a Jesuit sent by the General from Rome to a province to
                               act on his behalf if action is needed or to report back.

BIBLIOGRAPHY

Abbreviations

Autobiography	cf. Munitiz, Joseph A., and Endean, Philip
Constitutions and *Examen*	cf. Ganss, George E.
Constitutions and Complementary Norms	cf. Padberg, John
Exercises	cf. Munitiz, Joseph A., and Endean, Philip
Ignace: Écrits	cf. Giuliani, Maurice

MHSI   *Monumenta Historica Societatis Iesu:*
      Epist.   = Letters of Ignatius, vols. I-XII.
      Fabri Mon. = Fabri Monumenta (vol. 48 of MHSI, Madrid 1914)

Inigo: Letters	cf. Munitiz, Joseph A.
Select Letters	cf. Munitiz, Joseph A., and Endean, Philip
Spiritual Diary	cf. Munitiz, Joseph A., and Endean, Philip

Critical edition

Fontes Narrativi de S. Ignatio de Loyola et de Societatis Iesu initiis, vol. 1, *Narrationes scriptae ante annum 1557*, ediderunt Dionysius Fernández Zapico, S.I., et Candidus de Dalmases, S.I., cooperante Petro Leturia, S.I. [MHSI vol. 66, Monumenta Ignatiana, Series Quarta, Scripta de S. Ignatio, altera editio, Tomus I, Fontes Narrativae de Sancto Ignatio de Loyola et de Societatis Iesu initiis, vol. 1] Rome 1943, pp. 508-26 Praefatio, pp. 527-752 *Textus.*

Translations

FRENCH *Louis Gonçalves da Câmara, Memoriale 1555, traduit et présenté par Roger Tandonnet, s.j.* [Collection Christus No. 20, Textes], Paris, Desclée de Brouwer, 1966 [the first translation of the *Memoriale:* the translator acknowledges his constant debt for his Introduction and Notes to the MHSI Editors; these accompany an excellent translation].

GERMAN   Luis Gonçalves da Câmara, *MEMORIALE, Erinnerungen an un-
seren Vater Ignatius,* übersetzt von Peter Knauer, S.J., Frankfurt am Main,
1988 [privately printed; a careful translation, but there are no notes and only
a short Vorwort].

SPANISH   *Recuerdos Ignacianos: Memorial de Luis Gonçalves da Câmara,
Versión y comentarios de Benigno Hernández Montes, S.I.* [Colección
MANRESA 7], Bilbao and Santander, Ediciones Mensajero and Editorial Sal
Terrae [1992] [the original Spanish text is accompanied by a modern Spanish
paraphrase; the Portuguese texts are translated into Spanish].

Secondary Literature

Bangert William V. (ed. and completed by Thomas M. McCoog), *Jerome Nadal,
S.J. 1507: Tracking the First Generation of Jesuits,* Loyola University Press,
Chicago, 1992.

Bernard, St., ed. J. Leclercq et alii, *Opera omnia* (vol. 3, *Treatises*), Rome, 1957-
77.

Caraman, Philip. *The Lost Empire: The Story of the Jesuits in Ethiopia, 1555-1634*
London 1985.

Favre, Pierre, *The Spiritual Writings: The Memoriale, and selected Letters and
Instructions,* St. Louis, Institute of Jesuit Sources, 1996.

Ganss, George E. *Saint Ignatius of Loyola: The Constitutions of the Society of
Jesus,* St. Louis, Institute of Jesuit Sources, 1970.

García-Villoslada, Ricardo, *San Ignacio de Loyola, Nueva Biografía* [Biblioteca de
Autores Cristianos, Maior, 28], Madrid, 1986.

Gilmont J.-F, *Les écrits spirituels des premiers jésuites,* Rome (Institutum
Historicum S.I.), 1961.

Giuliani, Maurice, ed., *Ignace de Loyola: Érits* [Collection Christus 76], Paris,
Desclée de Brouwer, 1991.

Ivens, Michael, *Understanding the Spiritual Exercises, Text and Commentary: A
Handbook for Retreat Directors* [Inigo Texts Series: 4], Leominster, Gracewing
and Inigo Enterprises, 1998.

Munitiz, Joseph A., ed., *Inigo: Letters Personal and Spiritual* [Inigo Texts Series 3]
Leominster, Inigo Enterprises, 1995.

Munitiz, Joseph A. and Endean, Philip, eds., *Saint Ignatius of Loyola: Personal Writings—Reminiscences* [= Autobiography], *Spiritual Diary, Select Letters, including the text of the The Spiritual Exercises* [Penguin Classics], London, 1996.

O'Malley, John W., *The First Jesuits*, Cambridge MA, Harvard Univ. Press, 1993.

O'Reilly, Terence "Saint Ignatius Loyola and Spanish Erasmianism", *Archivum Historicum Societatis Iesu*, 43, 1974, pp. 300-21.

[Padberg, John W. ed.], *The Constitutions of the Society of Jesus and Their Complementary Norms*, Institute of Jesuit Sources, St. Louis, 1996.

Palmer, Martin E., ed. and transl., *On Giving the Spiritual Exercises: The Early Jesuit Manuscript Directories and the Official Directory of 1599*, Institute of Jesuit Sources, St. Louis, 1996.

Rotsaert, Mark, *Ignace de Loyola et les renouveaux spirituels en Castille*, Rome [Centrum Ignatianum Spiritualitatis] 1982, pp. 128-45.

Schurhammer, Georg, trans. M. Joseph Costelloe, *Francis Xavier: his life and his times,* 4 vols., Rome, Jesuit Historical Institute, 1973-81.

Walsh, J. P. M., "Work as if everything depends on—who?" *Way Supplement* (Ignatian Horizons 1491-1991), 70, 1991, pp. 125-36.

NOTES[1]

of Fr. Luís Gonçalves

concerning some things about the life of our Father Ignatius

The main text[2] of these notes is written in Castilian,

because that is how he wrote them in Rome

at the time when he was dealing with our Father;

and to provide more clarity, some annotations

by way of a gloss have been added in Portuguese,

because this same Father Luís Gonçalves wrote those here in Portugal.

---

[1] This title, written in Portuguese, was added to the main codex, *Lus. 109*, now in Rome.

[2] Printed in slightly larger type, while the annotations are in slightly smaller and are more indented; both the title and the Prologue are in Portuguese.

1

PREFACE
by
Fr. Luís Gonçalves da Câmara

1 Since religious orders are nothing other than particular ways of living according to Christ's precepts and counsels, ways that differ not only from the common obligation and rule applying to all in respect of the perfection of observance which is professed in these orders, but that differ also among themselves because of the specific ends and the means, which each order has chosen to obtain those ends, I have always considered that just as God called Bezalel, son of Uri, as scripture says,[1] and filled him with a holy spirit of wisdom, understanding, and knowledge, to design and execute perfectly everything that could be worked in gold, precious stones, silver, copper, marble, and every kind of wood, and gave him Oholiab as his companion to construct the tabernacle, the ark of the covenant, the propitiation, and all the other objects God had ordered Moses to make, so also for the foundation and building of any religious order which God our Lord wanted to found and build in the world, his custom has been to call and choose particular craftsmen, and to fill them with the grace and spirit which they specially needed to be the immediate founders of these living tabernacles and arks of the covenant, dedicated to keeping the law and the perfect observance of the divine cult.

2 And for this reason, just as the other craftsmen, who were occupied in the construction of that work, would have been much more perfect the more they strove to imitate Bezalel and Oholiab, in the same way I thought it absolutely necessary for members of religious orders, who aspire to perfect themselves in each one's way of life, to be very diligent in keeping the spirit of its immediate founder, and that a religious order would maintain the purity in which it was instituted as long as the imitation of the one God chose as the first founder persisted.

[1]Exod.31:2ff.,35:30ff.

3 For this reason, as soon as I entered the Society[2] at Easter, 1545, I always greatly desired to see and have dealings with our Father, Ignatius of Loyola, whom our Lord gave us as an example and head of this mystical body, of which all sons of the Society are members. Among other more particular motives which increased this desire in me, there were two that moved me especially: one was the desire to exercise that obedience of the understanding, of which I heard so much in the Society, and I thought that in order to reach this virtue it would be good to hear this doctrine from him whose ideas about the conduct of the Society must be considered like those first principles of a particular science which it is not customary, and indeed impossible, to demonstrate. The other motive was the very high opinion which I held of the personal holiness of our Father, which I deduced not only from what was told about him by those who had dealt with him, but also from the great perfection which already I observed in the Society and in its way of proceeding. I recall, then, thinking these things over and arguing with myself: if the fruit and the work are like this, what must the tree and the craftsman be like?

4 It was not my intention simply to acquire a general and common knowledge about Fr. Ignatius, because I was well aware that such aspects of his life must be written down some day, as has always usually been done for the founders of religious orders. Rather my wish above all was to get to know through direct experience—by having dealings with him— his special and particular characteristics, since I thought that from these the perfect imitation of our Father, to which we all should aspire, depended. I can understand this very well when I recall that holy friar, whom St. Francis called from the plough, and took as his brother and companion; he was called N.[3] The chroniclers of the order say that he imitated St. Francis, copying his every movement and gesture in such a naive way, even in his bodily movements and postures: for example, if St. Francis raised his hands in prayer to God, Friar N. would raise his; if St. Francis lifted up his eyes to heaven, or fixed them on the ground, Friar N. did just the same; if St. Francis got down on his knees and prayed moving his lips, the Friar immediately did the same; if St. Francis got up, he got up; if St. Francis spat out or hawked, he spat out or hawked. So in every respect Friar N. did not want to be anything other than a shadow of the Saint whom the Lord had given him for his head.

---

[2] The catalogues of the Portuguese province testify that Fr. Gonçalves da Câmara entered on 27 April, during the Easter season (Easter Sunday fell on 4 April that year).

[3] Although da Câmara does not give the name there seems no doubt that this was Friar John the Simple mentioned in the *Vita secunda* of Thomas of Celano.

5   It seemed to me most important that we should act in exactly the same way as our Fr. Ignatius, especially in matters touching the government of the Society and its essential qualities, and in order to achieve this it would be very necessary to have a knowledge of him not only in a general sense, but also from the concrete examples that could be observed, by means of which we could really see how he behaved, as much in pros- perity as in adversity, how he treated the perfect and how the imperfect, how he dealt with someone who was tempted, and how with those at fault, whether he tolerated what was bad and how greatly he cherished what was good, how he would administer punishment, and how he gave signs of love, how he formed novices and how he treated those who were old and tired.

6   And I considered worthy topics of investigation, to be known, written up, and preserved among us as of great value, not only these things and similar matters, which are absolutely necessary for both the general and the particular government of any religious congregation, but even all the other things, such as knowing in detail how he prayed, how he celebrated Mass, how he put questions, how he answered them, what topics pleased him in conversation, what he reprehended, how he ate, how he dressed, and finally everything else that could be found out about him. For just as an excellent tree is valued not just for its fruit, but also for its foliage, its branches, even the leaves that fall to the ground and the tiny little husks that the wind bears away, because every part of it has its own value, so I thought we should not rest content until we knew even the most insignificant things about our Father. In all these details we should search for the great value and virtue they have as a remedy and example for us.

7   But to return to what I was relating before, I wrote twice[4] to our Father in Rome about these desires I had to see him, earnestly asking him to order me to go there in order to fulfill them. He sent the reply to these letters to Fr. Master Simão,[5] placing everything in his hands (as was his

---

[4] These letters have not been preserved, and on the other hand two letters were sent from Rome directly to Fr. da Câmara (MHSI *Epist.* III, pp. 357, 377) in 1551, so his memory may have played him false here.

[5] Simão Rodrigues (1510-79), one of the first companions in Paris, and the first provincial of the newly created province of Portugal (1546); his idiosyncratic style caused many problems, and he was recalled to Rome, 1551 (see §152); a short period as provincial in Aragon was also unsuccessful (1551-2), and eventually (1554) he came to Rome and was forbidden to return to Portugal, until 1573.

custom in other individual matters, which he always wanted should go through the immediate superior).[6] And since Fr. Simão was not of the opinion that I should go, the visit was postponed until the arrival of Fr. Dr. Miguel de Torres in the province as Visitor, which was in 1552.[7] He took my wishes into consideration and also the need for someone to go and report to Fr. Ignatius on the affairs of this province, and sent me to Rome, where I arrived on 23 May 1555. I then discovered so much about our Father that, truly, what I had previously heard seemed very little, as will be quite clear from what I am going to say now.

8 On the way back to this province of Portugal in 1546 with Fr. Gonçalo (afterwards called Urbano) Fernández[8]—he was the fourth rector of the college at Coimbra—we left Valencia and arrived in Madrid on 20 January, the feast of St. Sebastian. There we found Fr. Pierre Favre,[9] whom I had known before I entered the Society, first in Paris,[10] a year before he had gone to Venice with the nine other companions to wait for Fr. Ignatius, who at that time had gone to Spain,[11] and later while I was a student in the University of Coimbra.[12] We stayed there in Madrid for some days with Fr. Favre, during which I made my confession to him and had long discussions with him. I was so astonished by what I saw in him, I felt there could not be any man in the world more filled with God; so much so that when later I heard people say how far Fr. Ignatius surpassed everyone, I believed this only by an act of faith, and for the reason I

[6] This is explained more fully in §§269-272.

[7] Miguel de Torres (c. 1507-1593), a former professor in Alcalá, became friendly with Ignatius in Rome (1545), but entered the Society only in 1547, being sent almost at once to found the new college at Salamanca; his visitation to Portugal was traumatic (as many had to be expelled from the young Society) but effective; he spent much of his life in Portugal, where he was provincial, but was also provincial in Andalusia and died in Toledo when over eighty.

[8] This Portuguese Jesuit was a novice with Fr. da Câmara in Valencia (1545); he died on the way to India in 1553.

[9] Pierre Favre (1506-1546), a Savoyard, the only priest among the first companions; after the foundation of the Society (1540) he travelled extensively (in Germany, Spain, and Portugal), gaining a reputation for sanctity and attracting many into the Society; he died in this same year in Rome while preparing to assist at the Council of Trent. For his published works, cf. Bibliography.

[10] Thus da Câmara met Favre on three occasions: Paris, probably 1535; Coimbra, 1544 or 1545; Madrid, January 1546.

[11] There is some inaccuracy here: Favre accompanied eight (not nine) of the first companions to Venice, and it was Ignatius who waited for them there, rather than the contrary; Ignatius left Paris in 1535 and after travelling diagonally across Spain (Azpeitia-Valencia) reached Venice in 1536; the others arrived in 1537.

[12] His studies in Coimbra, which finished with his entry into the Society in 1545, may

mentioned, that he was the head and starting point of the Society. However, when I got to know him in Rome and talked with him, the feelings I had experienced for Fr. Favre lost their force, and in the end he seemed to me a child in comparison with our Father. And already then, knowing better the conclusion of my old reasoning,[13] I turned it into a first premise, and arguing more validly, where I had previously said, "How great must Fr. Ignatius be, because he was the means of founding the Society," I now drew the conclusion that since the spirit and graces of God were so great in Fr. Ignatius, the founder of the Society, great had to be its perfection and excellence.

9 I stayed in Rome until 23 October 1555,[14] and in September 1554 our Father appointed me minister[15] of the residence. It was at that time, as much for the greater efficiency of my office as for my private consolation, that I took the trouble of noting down matters of some importance that our Father said, or did, or ordered. And as I thought that such notes might help this province, and especially its superiors, I began in the following month of January to record them as a sort of memorandum, writing them down immediately on the same day on which they occurred. And I brought these jottings with me and have always kept them until now, among other things that have remained with me. And as I judged that just as it consoled me to read them, so it would give pleasure to other members of the Society to know them, since they record things that concern us and things about our Father, I tried at times to put them in order and make a fair copy, so that they might be communicated to this province. But because of so many tasks and obstacles this could not be completed until now, this being the year 1573 in Evora, when Fr. Manoel Alvarez,[16] the superior of the college, greatly encouraged me in this task, so that I considered it appropriate to take a little time each day to complete it.

---

have been at the doctoral level as he already had a master's degree from Paris.

[13] See §3, end.

[14] The last entry is dated 18 October 1555.

[15] See Glossary.

[16] Manoel Alvarez (c. 1526-1583) joined the Society in 1546, and became the author of a famous Latin grammar that was frequently reprinted. In addition to this encouragement, da Câmara also received a letter from the General, Fr. Mercurian (12 January 1574), urging him to complete the work and he replied saying that he hoped to have it ready by Whit Sunday (30 May 1574), but his death intervened (15 March).

10 Because I have decided to do no more than simply relate and explain the events which I witnessed and experienced, as I say, with our Father, I thought the best system would be first to put in order what I had noted in Rome, using the same language and words that I had done, putting the same date on which they happened, and the other circumstances that had a part. And later, as some things would need to be explained more explicitly, because at the time they were notes I made to help my own memory, I thought it would be good to add what seemed necessary for their better understanding, adding some further examples of the same kind on the same themes to serve the same purpose.

11 In order that everything should receive due faith and authority, I will keep the additions in the same order as what I had brought from Rome, as is noted below.[17] However, in the margins of the first notebook there are three or four marginal notes that Fr. Pedro Ribadeneira[18] added, which I thought proper to leave in this copy, as will be seen below, because they cover the same material and are so reliable.

---

[17] §12.
[18] The notes are to be found in §§31, 46, 67, 91-92; and see §31 for an account of Ribadeneira himself.

MEMORANDUM

OF OUR FATHER'S REPLIES TO ME CONCERNING MATTERS OF THE HOUSE BEGINNING ON THE 26th JANUARY 1555

12 It should be noted that all those chapters prefixed by a number[1] are replies that Father gave me on *a date that is indicated;*[a] all the others are also replies of his[2] but given on different occasions and for different reasons.

(a) *a date that is indicated*

> I use the term "date that is indicated" for those dates on which I heard our Father say, or saw him do, the things that are related here, because only those dates are mentioned, and not the dates on which they were written, because sometimes I could not rewrite them in a fair copy until some day after the event, although I always noted them at once in a notebook, which I carried with me together with a small inkwell, in order to put each thing in its place. When the Father saw me writing in his presence, he stopped talking while I was writing.

26 January

13 1. *As to the teaching*[b] of doctrine by Fr. Vitoria, our Father proposes that *two things should be considered:*[c] the first, whether there will

---

[1] These are numbers in the text prefixed to certain paragraphs, as distinct from the §§ numbers next to the left margin (supplied by the MHSI editors); they are not entirely consistent, especially towards the end of the *Memoriale*. The abbreviation [n.d.] stands for [not dated].

[2] In fact remarks by others are also recorded, but da Câmara wants to establish the broad distinction between remarks that are strictly dated and those that are not.

[3] Juan Alfonso de Vitoria or Victoria, born in Burgos, joined the Society in Rome (25 March 1549) and later held high posts—Rector in the college of Vienna and Procurator General in Rome—as well as teaching and preaching; he died in Naples, 22 March 1578.

be a competent audience; the other, *if it will be possible to persevere*[d] in what has been started; and if, after considering these points it is decided that he should teach doctrine he wishes that he should give three lectures in private, which those who are to judge the matter should attend.

[b] *As to the teaching*

14 At that time there was no reading-service of Scripture in our church, as was the custom there [in Rome] for the people in the evening, as a sort of sermon. Some thought it would be a good idea if Fr. Vitoria undertook to do it, and so I proposed this to Father Ignatius and he replied, as I say here.

[c] *two things should be considered*

15 In everything that he arranged our Father used great circum-spection with regard to the means employed, to the ends that should be pursued, and to the problems that might arise, especial-ly when public affairs were involved, open to the sight and judge-ment of outsiders. I recall that a few days after my arrival in Rome, Cardinal de la Cueva[4] asked him for a preacher for La Goleta, where a relative of his was Captain General.[5] As Fr. Polanco[6] thought that Fr. Mendoza[7] could cope with this assignment, our Father gave instructions exactly as is told here about Fr. Vitoria, that he should preach three times in the refectory and that those three persons whom he [the Father] had consulted about sending him, should hear him so as to give their opinions with as full a knowledge as possible.[8]

---

[4] The son of the Duke of Albuquerque, Bartolomé de la Cueva was a cardinal from 1544 until his death in 1562.

[5] This was Alfonso de la Cueva, a brother of the Cardinal; the fort of La Goleta was near Tunis, and was held since 1535 by the Emperor Charles V.

[6] Juan Alfonso de Polanco (1517-1576), born in Burgos. He entered the Society (15 August 1541) and from 1547 was secretary to Ignatius and became his right-hand man until his death; he continued as secretary to two successive Generals and was a key figure in the early history of the Society.

[7] Cristóbal de Mendoza, a Spanish Jesuit who arrived in Rome in 1554 and was appointed military chaplain as indicated, but was unable to get beyond Naples, where he was made Rector of the college for nine years; later he worked in Sicily and Spain where he died (30 April 1578).

[8] This "examination" is recounted in full later; see §193.

(d) *the other, if it will be possible to persevere*

16 Many people both inside the residence and outside were astonished by the great constancy our Father showed in pursuing those objectives which he was convinced were in the service of God and for the spiritual advantage of one's neighbour. I frequently thought that the origin of this lay in the lengthy communication and discussion he had with God before deciding on any particular business: since he proceeded like one who had already attained the end that the affairs could have, and according to that end he found means that were unusual and very different from those that anyone else might have found.

Pope Julius III [1550-55] wanted to found in Rome a seminary for German youths who, after having studied doctrine and become thoroughly imbued with Catholic practice, would be able to serve the churches in Germany for which there were no priests. Houses suitable for college life were sought, and once some students had been assembled, the Pope entrusted their spiritual direction and the management of the house to Father Ignatius. Material needs were to be provided for by the alms which Julius III himself gave, as well as those from the cardinals who saw how pleased the Pope was with the project.[9]

17 But it so happened that after his death [23 March 1555] and that of Marcellus II [30 April 1555], Paul IV [23 May 1555 - 18 August 1559], who succeeded to the pontificate, did not like this project, and therefore did not grant it any favours or alms, such as had previously been given; and so the cardinals also stopped giving their alms, with the exception of Cardinal Morone.[10] It was he who had proposed the setting up of the college in the time of Julius III, since he had spent a long time in Germany as Nuncio, and he always gave ten *cruzados* every month.

[9] The Papal Bull establishing the German College is dated 31 August 1552; the idea of founding this college came in fact from Cardinal Morone (mentioned in the next paragraph), and the names of twenty-two cardinals appear in the lists of those who contributed alms originally.

[10] This Italian cardinal, former bishop of Modena, had served as Nuncio in Vienna, taking part in many of the religious discussions that were held in Germany (1540-42) and becoming a cardinal in 1542; he will be mentioned below (§153) when named Papal Legate (1555) to the Diet in Augsburg; he was to play a key role in the Council of Trent's third period (1562-63), and died in 1580 at the age of seventy-one.

But as this was not enough to provide for the maintenance of the resident students, many people tried to convince our Father that he should dissolve the college until a better opportunity arose. But none of this was enough to make him desist, and because it was humanly impossible to maintain all those who were already in Rome, he ordered the students to be distributed among the Society's colleges in Italy and Sicily, where they could live at our expense, and that two or three should remain in Rome under the same conditions (if it could be done no other way), in the rented house, so that the ownership and government of the college might be preserved. And so it was done.[11]

Once the previous facilities had been re-established, they [the students] all returned to Rome; the college began to grow and to gain so good a reputation that it has continued until now. It has, in addition to the German students for whom it was instituted, some 200 resident students, the majority of whom are sons or relations of noblemen of nearly all nationalities. It is popularly called "the German College."

The reason why our Father accepted so many resident students in addition to the German students (for whom the College had been founded) was so that with the fees they paid each month, it was possible to pay the rent of the house, which was large, and contribute to the upkeep of the Germans themselves.[12]

18 At the time of Paul IV [1555-59], when the problems of maintaining the college grew worse, something happened that it is appropriate to mention here. When Father Ignatius took upon himself the responsibility for that operation, he began immediately to take every possible step to ensure that candidates suitable for the task, for which the college was set up, should come from Germany and all those regions, and he therefore wrote and recommended the college strongly to members of the Society who were active there. This was the reason why, precisely at the time in which because of the shortage of funds described above, the project could not be sustained, nine young men, nearly all from

---

[11] The dispersion took place in the autumn of 1555.

[12] The MHSI editors note that the idea of widening the scope of the German College and admitting lay boarders who had no intention of becoming priests came from Laínez: in this regard see §138.

Bohemia, arrived,[13] for whom moreover, I believe, members of our Society there had negotiated alms from Emperor Ferdinand for the voyage.[14]

19 Our Father received them in our residence with every sign of charity and as guests of honour, and since he saw the difficulty there was in achieving the purpose for which they had been sent to Rome, he decided to attract them to the Society, because in it they could contribute to the conversion of their own countries just as much or even more than in the new college. It is worth mentioning the devices and means he adopted for this purpose. On the one hand he treated them very well, and made as much a fuss of them as he could; he sent them at their table fresh fruit and other delicacies, he asked me to be with them at mealtimes, to make them feel happy and to treat them hospitably, urging me to bring them back "converted,"[15] and on the other hand he made them understand the difficulty they would meet in any other way of life they might want to follow in Rome. In short, he dealt with them in such a way that all nine sought admission to the Society and entered it with such good intentions that only two did not persevere.

20 But returning to the constancy which our Father showed in the things he undertook, before the Society had become so widespread, he concerned himself with certain pious works of special service to God, such as the founding of the houses for catechumens[16] and for repentant women,[17] and other things of the same

[13] Peter Canisius (1521-97), who joined the Society in 1543, was responsible for sending these to Rome in August, 1555.

[14] Strictly speaking Ferdinand, brother of Charles V, was King of Bohemia and Hungary, and had the title of King of the Romans in 1555; he became Emperor in 1556 on the abdication of his brother.

[15] This is a loaded term that will recur later, when the problem that originates here comes to a head (see §345). The French translator (p. 59, note 1) feels the need to justify the conduct of Ignatius, claiming that he is simply using legitimate human means to attract vocations to the Society; any candidates who did apply for entry would have to show that their choice was completely free (as required by the *Constitutions:* see *Examen* 3, 14 §51 [Ganss, p. 91]).

[16] Ignatius always showed great interest in the Jews and worked hard to convince them of the truth of the Catholic faith, to the point of establishing a special house in Rome where those who wished to become Christians could gather for instruction (catechizing), and so was called the House of Catechumens: cf. James W. Reites, "St. Ignatius of Loyola and the Jews", *Studies in the Spirituality of Jesuits*, 13, no. 4 (1981), pp. 1-48.

[17] Another personal apostolate of Ignatius was that to help prostitutes change their lives; he founded the House of Saint Martha as a place where they could take refuge and be cared for.

kind. The custom in Rome is for such works to be entrusted in a special way to a cardinal, so that as patron he can oversee the administration of those who undertake them. Often, then, Fr. Ignatius wanted to undertake or continue works of this kind, manifestly in the service of God, but because the cardinals, who had accepted the oversight for such works, were not seriously concerned with them, conflicts arose; but he did not desist because of this in completing the tasks which he considered to be for the honour of God, even if they were not to the liking of men. But because the cardinals were who they were, it was important to retain their good will towards the affairs of the Society, so our Father necessarily had to take a hand in these matters, even though he would have preferred to keep out of them, because he could not continue them without considerable detriment to us. I learnt of all this because the Father himself, as well as other members of the Society, recounted it to me. Indeed we can agree that Cardinal di Carpi,[18] our own protector, was quite right when he applied to him the saying, "He has driven the nail home!", as if to say that once the Father had formed a judgement in such matters it was as sure and constant as a nail well driven in.[19]

21 2. The rules *of modesty*[a] which the Father has drawn up must be the subject of exhortations,[20] and in general this policy should be followed: those who have most need of such rules should read them out or explain them to others, and similarly, the same should be done with regard to other faults.

---

[18] Rodolfo Pio di Carpi (1500-64) served as pontifical legate in France (1535) and was then made a cardinal (1536). Ignatius mentions a visit to his house in the *Spiritual Diary* 25 February 1544 (§23, p. 86), and as di Carpi had become Dean of the Cardinal Inquisitors by 1555, he suggested asking his help to avoid accepting responsibility for the Inquisition in Portugal (see §354 below, and *Select Letters* No. 36, p. 272).

[19] This phrase, which became well known among Jesuits as characterizing Ignatius, is given by da Câmara as, " *Ya ha fixo el chodo,*" viz. in a mixture of Italian and Portuguese; but the Italian cardinal probably used the Italian proverb that says of someone who comes to a firm decision, " *aver fisso il chiodo.*"

[20] The translation here is controversial: the Spanish read *Platíquense en casa*, and the MHSI editors suggest that this is a typical 16th century confusion between the two verbs *platicar* (meaning "to talk about" or in this context "to give exhortations [pláticas] about") and *practicar* (meaning "to put into practice"); they opt for the second sense because in his later Portuguese commentary da Câmara says that Ignatius "ordered me ... to ensure their observance." However the rest of the original memo makes it clear that it is the "talking about" which has caught da Câmara's attention; Ignatius wants those who have need of the rules to hear about them. Moreover in the commentary (§23) da Câmara also uses

(a) *of modesty*

22 Our Father had a high regard for modesty and external composure in members of the Society. In order to help us to maintain such standards he set himself with great energy to the writing of the following rules and he ordered me, as I say here, to ensure their observance in the house with penances and by all other means that are in use for the other rules.

[Rules of Modesty²¹]

[This is what the brethren²² of the Society should observe in their public appearances: in general one may say briefly about our brethren that there should be visible in their outward features a modesty and religious manner and a good example and edification for the benefit of all who see them; but more in particular the following points should be observed:
* *he should not turn his head lightly from side to side, but with maturity and happiness as is proper; and when there is no other need, he should hold his head slightly inclined forward from the neck, leaning neither to one side nor to the other.*
* *the eyes should usually be turned down, not raising them much nor turning them from one side to the other; when talking,* maxime *[especially] when with persons to be respected, they should not stare fixedly at the faces of such persons, but rather look usually below their faces.*
* *wrinkles in the forehead are to be avoided, and much more in the nose, so that an outer serenity²³ may display that which is possessed within.*
* *The lips neither very shut nor very open.*

---

the Portuguese word *pratica* (MHSI ed., p. 541, line 69) in the sense of an exhortation or sermon, and then to signify "conversation."

²¹ From the previous remark (§22) and that at the end of §23 it is clear that da Câmara wanted these rules to be transcribed here, but they are missing in the Roman manuscript. The MHSI editors have inserted them in their footnotes using the text of the earliest Spanish version preserved in the Roman archives.

²² The term *hermanos* is used at times by Ignatius and da Câmara to refer to Jesuits in general and is then translated as "brethren"; at other times it has a more technical sense, a "Brother" being a lay coadjutor, and this is made clear in the translation with the use of a capital letter.

²³ The MHSI text reads *sinceridad* ("sincerity"), but Benigno Hernández suggests that this is an error, and the later Latin versions confirm that Ignatius wrote *serenidad* (as translated above).

• *All of the face and countenance should show happiness rather than sadness or any other less ordered affection.[24]*

• *The top garment should cover all that is underneath, in such a way that only the top part of the neck is visible.*

• *All should wear clean clothes.*

• *The hands, if not occupied in raising the hem, should be held in a proper way and still.*

• *The walk should be at a moderate pace without notable haste, unless there is some urgent need, preserving due decorum as much as possible.*

• *Finally, all one's gestures and movements should be such that they show forth humility and incite to devotion all those who might be looking at them.*

• *When they go out of the house several at a time they should keep in pairs or threes, in the way that they are told to do so.*

• *If they happen to converse, they are to keep modesty in mind, both in their words and in the manner of speaking.*

• *Nobody of the residence or of the Society will dare to say anything insulting or scandalous to another of the Society, nor to anyone from outside, under penalty of eating only bread and wine and soup, and nothing else, both at morning and at night, during three weeks, three days per week.]*

And in order that everyone should understand these rules of modesty Father Ignatius ordered Fr. Laínez[25] to make them public in a sermon given for this purpose, to which he made everyone in the residence attend, without exception, both the older and the newly arrived.[26] The theme was the text of the canonical epistle of St. James, chapter 4, "Behold now, you who say, 'Today or tomorrow we will go to that city and spend a year there, and do business and make profit,' yet you are ignorant of what tomorrow will

[24] Another error, this time corrected by the MHSI editors: the text reads *efecto* ("effect") instead of *afecto* ("affection").

[25] Diego Laínez (1512-1565), a Spaniard with Jewish ancestry and a companion of Ignatius from 1534 when they met in Paris; he became one of his closest associates. As a competent theologian he took part on behalf of the Papacy in all three periods of the Council of Trent, and was involved in the discussions with the Protestants (e.g. at Augsburg and Poissy); he also undertook constant pastoral activities, while occupying important posts in the Society, and finished his life as the second General. His name occurs frequently in the *Memoriale* (see Index).

[26] The date of this sermon/exhortation (and of the incident mentioned in §23) is given by Ribadeneira (MHSI *Font. Narr.* II, pp. 362-3) as mid-August, even if an order to

bring,"[27] etc. On these words he spoke at length about the great importance God attaches to things which are humanly thought to be very small.

23 I remember also that at that time something occurred that seemed to all of us mysterious. It was that while the exhortation [*pratica*] was being given the roof fell in on a certain part of the residence where the Fathers and Brothers usually assembled at that hour. If they had not been all together listening to the sermon in the other place it would certainly have caught many of them underneath.

Some of us were at table one day with our Father, and the conversation touched upon what was being said in Rome, that we were all hypocrites; our Father replied that he would like us to have more of that kind of hypocrisy. He added, "I have gone over in my mind all the members of the Society, and I have not found any hypocrites except for Bobadilla and Salmerón."[28] Both of these Fathers were there and both have a very cheerful appearance, quite the opposite of hypocrisy. And I recall that after this had happened, the Father wrote the rules that are copied out above.

They were to be read in the refectory during meals, and at the same time were to be explained, as was the custom with other readings, if something occurred to the reader.

observe the rules was issued by Ignatius to da Câmara, as minister of the residence, on 26 January.

[27] James 4:13-14; the quotation is in Latin in da Câmara's text.

[28] An interesting example of Ignatian irony, as the pair mentioned were notoriously straightforward and unpretentious. The episode is recounted once more below, §374, and as Simão Rodrigues is mentioned there as having been present, it must have occurred before 4 June 1554, when he left Rome. As for the men mentioned, they are (along with Laínez) among the earliest companions, both having joined Ignatius in Paris in 1534; Bobadilla (c. 1511-1590), whose full name was Nicolás Alonso Pérez, but who was always known by his birthplace, a village in Spain, had been destined for India, but had to be replaced by Francis Xavier when he fell ill; he showed considerable theological talent, taking part in the religious discussions of his day, but was known for his outspoken, ebullient, pugnacious character, which caused no small problems on the death of Ignatius as he objected to the election of Laínez as second General. Ignatius teases him both here and at other times (see §§292, 333), but probably got as good as he gave; e.g. Bobadilla described the *Constitutions*, over which Ignatius had laboured so much, as a "prolix labyrinth—no one will be able to understand it!" (MHSI 27, *Mon. Nadal* 4, p.101). On the other hand,

24 [n.d.] Sometimes, in order to correct someone in a fault, our Father is accustomed to appoint him as a *syndic*[29] for that fault; as *syndic* he can correct everyone and *everyone can correct him.* [a] He is also accustomed for the same purpose to make a person examine himself for that fault many times each day, and tell someone that he has examined his conscience the number of times he has been told to do so before supper or before going to bed. And our Father himself does this each time the clock strikes during the day (as well as at night when he is awake), if he is not occupied with a visitor or in some other important business. When this happens he makes up the time in the following hour. He once wished to cure himself of the habit of laughing, that is to say that *when he saw someone*[b] he immediately began to laugh to himself, and after the examination of conscience he gave himself as many strokes of the discipline as were the times he had laughed.

[a] *everyone can correct him*

25 This second course he adopted very few times, but the first, that is to say, that the one who was accused of a fault should be its corrector, very often.

[b] *when he saw someone*

Whenever our Father met one of the brethren, he used to think of the value of his soul and of Christ Our Lord who had redeemed it. He received so much consolation from this thought that he always expressed it through smiling and outward joy.[30]

Alfonso de Salmerón (1515-85) was the most straightforward and imperturbable of men, with an enormous capacity for work (his publications run to sixteen folio volumes); he served as papal diplomat, beginning (unsuccessfully) in Ireland and later visiting Poland and Belgium, usually as adviser to papal legates; as a theologian he also attended Trent with Laínez, and taught in various universities, apart from filling several administrative posts in the Society.

[29] The term *syndic* is explained in the Glossary.

[30] This commentary by da Câmara has puzzled the editors: probably one should distinguish involuntary laughter (of the type described by Ribadeneira in his *Life of Ignatius* in the early years of his conversion, from which he wanted to correct himself, as he kept bursting into laughter when he met people) and the later more controlled joyful smile that he continued to have later in life, and which he recommended to others.

26 [n.d.] As in laughter so in all external manifestations reflection always seems to come first for the Father; thus he shows himself sometimes to be angry or cross, without being so at all, at other times happy and affectionate toward someone, without really having so much affection for him. To sum up, as far as one can tell from those with whom he deals, he is so much *a master of his interior passions*[a] that he only uses them in so far as reason demands.

[a] *a master of his interior passions*

27. One of the things that shone forth most in our Father was this mastery of both interior passions and outward manifestations. With this he so edified and impressed those he dealt with that by this alone he won many distinguished people for the Society. In this way he won over the father, Dr. Miguel de Torres,[31] having invited him to meals occasionally in Rome. He also gained Frs. Nadal[32] and Madrid[33] and many others by no other means of persuasion than by his behaviour at table, eating and talking with them.

28 Fr. Pierre Favre[34] used to distinguish three kinds of words: *verba verborum, verba cogitationum,* and *verba factorum.*[35] According to this division he understood the third kind to be the good example of the deeds one performs, which is the most efficacious and intelligible of all. I mention this so that it may be understood that it was this third sort that was most frequently used by our Father,

---

[31] See §7.

[32] Jerónimo Nadal (1507-80), from the island of Majorca, had met Ignatius in Paris (1534) and reacted against him; only in 1545 did he undergo a change of heart and enter the new order; he became a key player in its expansion: rector of the first Jesuit college (Messina), official promulgator of the newly written *Constitutions* all over Europe, Vicar General when Ignatius was ill, and holder of important positions after his death. He is mentioned frequently in the *Memoriale.*

[33] Cristóbal de Madrid, a friend and adviser to Ignatius (see §116 note) before entering the Society (1555); he was, even while a novice, given charge of certain works (see §251) and indeed appointed along with Nadal and Polanco to take charge of the Society when Ignatius became gravely ill the following year (1556); he was one of the few present while Ignatius breathed his last; he went on to become Adviser ("Assistant") to the second General (Laínez) and superior of the Roman residence; he died in 1573.

[34] See §8.

[35] One might say, "the language of (mere) words, the language of thoughts (put into words), and the language of deeds."

though he sometimes used the second type of speaking.

29 3. *Petronio*[a], [36] must not speak to his brother Fabio until twelve days have passed, unless it seems that Fabio wishes to join the Society; after the twelve days he can talk to him because Petronio will be that much more certain of his vocation.

Our Father is usually very strict in requiring that novices should not talk to people from outside, least of all to relations and friends.

[a] *Petronio*

This Petronio was a nobleman, born at Pesaro in Italy: he entered the Society after his father's death and he brought with him into the Society three younger brothers.

30 4. *Bernardo, the Japanese,*[b] should go to serve in the college, but first he should be told that he ought to find out what best suits his health, and if he thinks it suits him to undertake some domestic tasks, he should be told to do them, but making him promise that whenever he feels under strain or in need of something, he should say so.

[b] *Bernardo, the Japanese*

Bernardo,[37] born in Japan, was one of the first converts of Father Master Francis Xavier[38] in those islands. After his conversion he was always his faithful companion in all his undertakings and travels in those parts. Then at the orders of that same father

---

[36] The first of several references to a family of five brothers: Petronio, the eldest, Cincinnato, Lancillotto, Job, and Fabio. All but the last came to Rome (November, 1554) with the declared intention of joining the Society. However, da Câmara is mistaken in his comment (written much later) that their father was already dead, as he is mentioned elsewhere as having been alive in August, 1558.

[37] Born in Kagoshima, this convert was baptised in 1549 and then accompanied Xavier to Japan, and also in India. Arriving in Portugal in 1553 (with a letter from Xavier in Goa dated 8 April 1552), he applied to enter the Society and after two years went to Rome, where he stayed for about ten months (January to October). He died shortly after his return to Portugal in 1557.

[38] Francis Xavier (1506-52), one of the earliest companions (Paris, 1534, see §306), left Rome for the Far East in 1540 and after extensive missionary work in India reached Japan in 1549. He died while preparing to enter China.

he came to this kingdom [Portugal] to study its customs, and from here to go to Rome to visit the holy places, to see the Pope, and to meet Fr. Ignatius and other members of the Society. He was a most exemplary man both in the East and here. He told a number of edifying stories about Father Francis and bore a remarkable witness to his great virtue. He was especially devout in respect of those customs and practices of the Church which are denied by the heretics of our days, such as confession, use of other sacraments, obedience to the Pope, etc. And he spoke about all of this with such enthusiasm and fervour that he seemed to have received special understanding and exceptional grace and light from God. When he went to Rome our Father welcomed him warmly and always treated him with great affection, which he really felt for him. And since, even though he was of delicate health, he wanted to work at the college in domestic tasks, our Father did not want to allow him to do so, except under the conditions explained here. After he had been about a year in Rome I brought him back with me when I returned to this province in 1555, and he died here in the college at Coimbra, showing the same edification and giving the good example he had shown in his life.

31 [n.d.] Our Father always takes the greatest care of the sick so that they can get better, and also for the healthy that they maintain their health;[39] for this reason, in spite of there being some seventy men and more in the college, there are very seldom any sick and then only with light ailments.

Marginal Note: Fr. Pedro Ribadeneira[40] wrote in the margin the following lines about what he had seen our Father do,

[39] The French translator notes that there is evidence of this care for the sick in the *Constitutions* III, 2, 6, §§303-4 [Ganss, pp. 169-70].

[40] Pedro Ribadeneira (1526-1611) was a mischevious page in the household of Cardinal Farnese when he first met Ignatius and was completely won over; he joined the Society in 1540 and undertook extensive studies; ordained in Rome, 1553, he left in October 1555 and travelled extensively in Europe, teaching, preaching, and occupied in administration; however his great life-work was the composition of a massive biography of Ignatius written (1569) in Latin (publ. 1572) and translated by him in a distinctive personal Castilian style (publ. 1583) that had great success.

and then when this notebook[41] was copied for me in Rome—
because mine had been lost—it was included in the text with the
remainder.

There are many *indications*[a] of this: asking the buyer of food to tell
him every day if he had given the infirmarian everything he had asked
him for; selling *the pewter plates*[b]; taking *lots on the blankets,*[c] the
penances which were given for any slackness in regard to the sick, as can
be seen in the case of *Micer Bernhard,*[d] who was minister, whom he
wished to throw out of the house at night; the sending of someone to see
how the vein was when someone was being bled; ordering the rector to
let him know immediately when someone had fallen ill; the fact that he
used to say that only one thing made him tremble, namely, that members
of the college should become ill, and he used to say that he greatly feared
the assault from that quarter. *One must note here the obedience*[e] that our
Father shows to the doctors, once he has put himself in their hands, even
if he judges that something else would be better for him. Similarly the
obedience he wishes the sick to show, *ut patet* [as is seen] in the case of
Don Silvester[42] and others, whom he wanted to send to the hospital or
expel from the Society because of this.

[a] *indications*

32 All that follows, to the end of this paragraph, Fr. Ribadeneira
had added for me in the margin of my notebook.

[b] *the pewter plates*

Our Father ordered the pewter plates to be sold in order to buy
necessities for the sick, for which there was no other money in the
residence.

---

[41] da Câmara must have left a copy of his original Memorandum notes in Rome when
he left in 1555; he then had a copy sent to him c. 1574 when he was urged to write up the
Portuguese commentary, and found that Ribadeneira had added some paragraphs, which
he was happy to include (as he says in his Prologue, §11).

[42] Silvester Landini was an Italian Jesuit already ordained in 1547 when he fell ill; he
was such a bad patient that Ignatius had sent him home, though without dismissing him;
subsequently he proved to be an excellent pastoral worker, dying in Corsica in 1554; it is
not clear why the title "Don" appears (unusually) here.

(c) *lots on the blankets*

33 There were no more blankets in the house than were necessary for the brethren. And since everyone needed those they were using, our Father ordered lots to be cast for those that should be sold if there were need to do so in order to care for the sick.

(d) *Micer Bernhard*

34 I do not remember the details of this case, which happened before my arrival in Rome and which Fr. Ribadeneira recounted to me, nor the other events related in the added paragraph. Father *Micer* Bernhard[43] was Flemish by birth; he was minister in the house in Rome before I went there; he died in Flanders, having spent his life fruitfully in the reconciliation[44] of those provinces.

(e) *One must note here the obedience*

35 In his illnesses our Father obeyed the doctors with the same perfection with which he wished members of the Society to obey their superiors. He seemed in this respect like a man who has lost all personal judgement regarding the things he was being ordered, and all care for himself and his health. While he was in Rome, he fell quite gravely ill; he was taken care of by a young man, only slightly qualified, who was the house doctor;[45] he mistook the cause of the sickness, and applied hot remedies, which did a lot of harm. This was in the summer and at a time of great heat in Rome. The doctor ordered him to wrap himself up with many blankets, and the doors and windows to be shut, so that no air could come in; he ordered him to drink only unmixed, very strong wine, because he thought his stomach pains were caused by the cold.

---

[43] Bernhard Olivier (1523-56) made a pilgrimage to Rome, 1546, and joined the Society in 1549; already as a novice he was made minister of the residence (1550) and on taking his First Vows rector of the German College (1551); he eventually returned to Flanders and was due to become Provincial of one of the German Provinces, but died before he could do so.

[44] The Portuguese word is *redução* (literally, "reduction"), and a similar Spanish word is used by Ignatius in similar circumstances (e.g. with reference to the "reconciliation" of England, §230, and when writing about the "conversion" of the Ethiopian Christians to the Roman Catholic Church: cf. *Inigo Letters*, No. 63 [MHSI *Epist.* VIII, 680-90, No. 2 in Appendix]).

[45] See §143.

Father was burning with thirst, but never asked for a drop of water to drink: he was melting away with sweat, caused by the intense pains and a raging fever, which burned him up so that the sweat soaked through the mattresses of the bed, and he did not complain. At last he felt himself weakening, but said nothing, demonstrating in every way how much he esteemed and submitted himself to the doctor, as if he were a famous specialist in medicine, although it was quite clear to the Father on the other hand that his knowledge was more than insufficient. At last the situation reached such extremes that he began to prepare himself for death, which we realised when he ordered that no one should go to speak to him in his room except the infirmarian, handing over to the Fathers all the Society's affairs, like one who has already resigned himself to death. We the professed fathers in the house then gathered together, and all decided that we were obliged to call another doctor to visit him and to see if he could still live. Dr. Alessandro[46] came, and as soon as he saw him and had been told of what had happened in the course of his treatment, he started to cry out that they had been killing him through the excess of heat. He immediately ordered them to take away the excess clothing, to open the windows and to give him as much cold water as he wanted, and in this way he was cured and recovered his health in a very short time.

36 5. *The days of fasting*[a] which Bernardo has vowed to keep are to be commuted to some other penance, and a consult should be held about what it should be.

[a] *The days of fasting*

This Bernardo was the Japanese man I spoke about above;[47] he had made a vow to fast on certain days and Fr. Ignatius commuted them because Bernardo had a weak and delicate constitution.

37 *The minister can report*[b] to Fr. Nadal about everything which according to his rule should be referred to his superior (and with that he fulfills the rule) "except for matters concerning the sick."

---

[46] Dr. Alessandro Traiano Petronio (later described as "the principal doctor in Rome," cf. §135) became a good friend of Ignatius and assisted him when dying.

[47] See §30.

(b) *The minister can report*

After I had become minister our Father named Fr. Dr. Jerónimo Nadal, who had already finished his first visitation,[48] as Vicar General of the whole Society. In the rules and duties of the minister there were many matters to be referred to the superior for decision; in these matters I always referred to Fr. Ignatius. I then wondered if it would be all right to consult Fr. Nadal about them, so that our Father should have less to occupy him. I asked him, and as he replied yes, I did so from then on in all matters. At this time one of the brethren fell sick, and, as one of the matters reserved to the minister was the sickness of the brethren, I went straightaway to tell Fr. Nadal without first telling the Father. He learned about it later, and immediately summoned me and asked me why I had not told him immediately that the brother was ill. I replied that I had told Fr. Nadal in accordance with the order his Reverence had given me. In spite of everything he made me do a good penance for it. When I discussed this case later with Fr. Polanco I remember that he said that when our Father imposed this penance, he wanted to make it clear that he made an exception in the instruction he had given me for the sicknesses of the brethren. For this reason I have described the matter in detail here, along with his general reply to my question, even though he was more specific about it only when he reprimanded me.

The Father gave penances and rebukes with great ease in light matters, even if there were no blame, and likewise he was often heard to say, "In giving penances it is good to be liberal."

38 7. The rule that novices should continue to wear the same clothes that they brought from the world can be dispensed, when it is thought that the cold will do someone serious harm, even if one cannot find other clothes similar to those he brought with him, e.g. by giving a heavy coat to someone who came with an old jacket, since one could not protect him from the cold in any other way.

---

[48] Nadal returned from Spain in 1554 (see §196); he was appointed Vicar General, elected unanimously by all the professed fathers in Rome, in November, but had to leave Rome once more in February 1555 (see §152).

39 While I was minister, two Spanish soldiers joined the Society in Rome. One of them, Juan Roiz,[49] copied out for me some of the passages contained in this notebook. They came wearing very light doublets, and on top some clothes worn to shreds, with yellow stockings and caps on their heads. Besides this they had only capes, in which they could not do domestic work, and they went about dressed like this for part of the summer. When winter came they suffered a great deal in the intense cold of Rome. I was afraid they might get ill, and was especially sorry for the one who acted as a secretary for me in my room. I asked our Father if he would like us to give them some clothing, and he then replied as I have written here. In the observance of this rule he was so strict that he allowed a dispensation only for reasons of health. Fr. des Freux[50] wore silk clothes for the whole of his novitiate, until he had worn them out in lowly domestic duties about the house.

The same thing happened to Fr. Araoz,[51] who walked around Rome begging alms with a sack on his back wearing his silk jerkin. He washed bowls in the street dressed in the same way on the Father's orders, and as his velvet shoes wore out before his clothes, he wore hemp shoes, such as we wear, to go with his silk.

40 The captain[52] of the principal castle of Naples joined the Society, and other noblemen from outside came to visit him and talk to him. Fr. Ignatius ordered him to be called from the kitchen, and he appeared with an apron on top of the velvet suit he had brought from the world and always wore.

---

[49] Perhaps Brother Juan Rodríguez (as this surname was often abbreviated as "Roiz"), who in 1556 was in Perugia, where he edified people by his death.

[50] André des Freux joined the Society as a priest in 1541, and was soon recognized as an accomplished classicist; in the winter of 1546-47 Ignatius asked him to translate into reasonably elegant Latin the Spanish text of the *Spiritual Exercises*, even though a rough Latin version already existed; the new translation was presented for official approval by the Pope (Paul III), who granted this along with permission to print it in 1548. (For the problems that arose over this translation, see §322). Fr. des Freux was appointed rector of the German College in 1552 and held this post until his death at the end of October, 1556.

[51] Antonio de Araoz (1515-1573), a relative through an in-law of Ignatius, had joined, while in Rome, the first companions as early as 1539; he was accepted into the nascent Society and sent back to Spain; he was to occupy key administrative posts in Spain, during most of his life, and had very friendly relations with the court of Philip II, which brought both advantages and disadvantages to the Society.

[52] Juan de Mendoza, commander of the Castel Nuovo in Naples, suddenly decided to enter the Society in February, 1556, and presented himself at the Jesuit college in that city; he was sent to Rome and put to work in the kitchen; his health broke down and he was sent back to Naples but died en route in September.

I recall that in the old days we made so much of this exercise here in our own province, that it was a generally agreed idea that the best novice was the one whose suit, which he had brought with him into the Society, lasted longest. And it was noted that the clothes of those who were less careful lasted less time. And as Fr. Bras Gómez[53]—whom the Lord now has in His glory—kept his clothes for a long time, the Fathers said they understood from that he would turn out to be as we all knew him.

Fr. Don Gonçalo,[54] martyred at Monomotapa, told me once in the College at Coimbra that one of the things that most helped him was a black satin doublet, which he had when he joined the Society and which he wore in the house until it was completely worn out, since every time he put it on or took it off he thought to himself, "The world believes I am now another man, but I'm so much the same that I haven't even changed my clothes."

What I have said above about Fr. des Freux happened long before I was in Rome, but I learnt of it from a reliable source. For Fr. Araoz, I knew about it from a companion of his, a Brother coadjutor, who greatly edified all of us in this province, and he put it in writing for me with other things that Fr. Araoz had told him. He was called Inigo of Ochandiano,[55] born in Vizcaya, and came from Madrid. As for what happened to the captain of the castle of Naples, this occurred after my first stay in Rome and I learned about it from the Fathers there on my second visit when I went to the First General Congregation in 1558.[56]

---

[53] Bras Gómez (1535-70) had joined the Society in 1556 and was clearly much admired before his early death.

[54] Gonçalo Silveira (1526-1561) was a pupil at the Jesuit college in Coimbra, joined the Society and went out to India in 1556, where he was appointed provincial by Ignatius; however his missionary work later took him to East Africa, where he was martyred.

[55] A village in Vizcaya: this Brother, known (like Bobadilla) by the name of his birthplace, became a Jesuit in Medina del Campo, and spent much of his life as secretary and travelling companion of Fr. Araoz. He died in Madrid in 1575.

[56] This was the delayed meeting of professed fathers (held up by the declared state of war between the Papacy and Spain), which elected Diego Laínez as second General of the Society.

27 January

41 1. *To the petition*[a] of Cardinal Viseu,[57] who requests a preacher, our Father replied that he must be excused from getting involved in these matters, and that we should speak to Fr. Nadal who takes his place.

[a] *To the petition*

This paragraph will be understood better in the light of what follows. The cardinal was Don Miguel, Bishop of Viseu.

42 [n.d.] When a request is made which our Father cannot grant, he usually likes to keep out of the matter, in order to maintain his friendship, which it is important to keep in relation to the head rather than to any of the members.

43 [n.d.] *As for the brother*[b] who is tormented by the devil over his vocation because someone had spoken to him and worried him while he was out begging for alms, *the Father ordered,*[c] firstly that no one should go begging for alms without special permission, and then he referred the whole case to Fr. Nadal. When I spoke to him later about it the Father said there was nothing more to be said or done, since the matter had been referred to Fr. Nadal; if it had not been referred to Fr. Nadal he would have suggested three courses of action which might help in such cases: first, the order should be given that someone should talk to him, so that just as he had many devils inciting him to leave the Society, there would be many ministers of God on the other side; second, if he did not wish in any way to stay, he should be told that since he has been kept for four months because he requested this, he should stay for a fortnight at our request, without being bound to anyone by obedience; third, if neither of these courses helped, all the Brothers and Fathers should assemble and ask him to give the reason why he wished to leave, in front of them, and that each one should reply according to his own opinion. Our Father added something else in another conversation on this subject: it would be a good idea to ask someone to sleep in his room, and our Father would himself make him[58] promise that every time he woke up he would

---

[57] Miguel da Silva, Cardinal Bishop of Viseu, was then Ambassador of the King of Portugal to the Holy See; he died in Rome shortly before Ignatius; see *Sup.* 1n.

[58] Although there is ambiguity here, the most likely interpretation is that it is the one tempted who should wake the "volunteer" sleeping in the same room; however the Spanish could mean that the latter is to keep on eye on the person tempted and call out to him when he saw him waking up.

call his companion and not give the devil a chance, because the strongest temptations come when one is waking up, if the devil is involved in the affair; and if the experiences are from God, they are also very powerful.[59]

(b) *As for the brother*

44 He was a novice from Siena, who had joined about four months before; when he went begging for alms in the street he was tempted by a relation whom he met there. I think our Father felt it particularly strongly because I had ordered him to go out and undertake that test, when he had not developed sufficient strength for such a task. And for this reason he gave orders that in future no one should do this without his approval, and used so many means to make him return to the right path.

(c) *the Father ordered*

45 This way of begging for alms[60] exposed someone who was weak in virtue to the dangers of temptation too easily, as it was not the custom then for two brothers to go together to each house, as it is now in São Roque;[61] rather, each one took a separate stretch of the street with his sack on his back begging from door to door; and thus it was often necessary for one of the two to be on his own at some distance away, hoping for alms, as do other members of other religious orders who beg in this way. This was how the brother novice had time to listen to the relation who talked to him while he went begging.

In spite of this exercise being linked to such adversities, however, and although our Father had been particularly affected by this case, I observed, even so, that he did not make it a general rule that no novice should in future beg alms. He simply gave orders that no one should do so without his approval. For, in general, it was not in the spirit of our Fr. Ignatius to make general laws for

---

[59] The importance of the waking moments is noted in the *Exercises:* "When I wake up I turn my attention at once (so as not to leave room for stray thoughts) to the subject I am about to contemplate. . ." (§74).

[60] There are further similar reflections on the system of begging for alms later in the *Memoriale*, see §253.

[61] The Jesuit residence and church in Lisbon were dedicated to São Roque (English "Roch", Italian "Rocco"), the 14th century healer of the plague-stricken.

particular evils; rather, he took great care to remedy these, resort-
ing especially to the dismissal of the corrupt members who caused
them, but not by making universal rules that bind or impede those
who are good.

46 [n.d.] The Father usually treats very sweetly novices who are tempted, as he did last year *a Fleming*[a] who had no educational qualifications,
and little academic ability, whom he welcomed warmly. In contrast, he is
accustomed to be very rigorous with some who have been members of
the Society for a long time, and who should already have acquired spiritual strength, *maxime* [above all] *if it is a case of not wanting to obey*[f]
or give up their own judgement when asked to do so, and equally when
they lead other members of the Society astray. Then he treats them very
severely, even expelling them: an example of the first case would be what
he did *with a father*[b] in December 1554, and of the second how he
expelled Antonio Marino,[c] professor of logic in the College, and one of
the best for that task in the arts faculty of the College, in July 1553.

> *Marginal Note by Fr. Ribadeneira:* How he ordered him to
> leave that very night, although he would have preferred to
> stay till the following morning. About Marín, one should
> explain how he was thrown out. *Item*, Jacob,[62] *Soldevilla,*[d]
> *Zapata,*[e] and others.[g]

[a] *a Fleming*

47 This Fleming was from Holland[63] by birth, a young man of

[62] Several of the comments that follow (§§50-60) deal with the incidents mentioned by
Ribadeneira; however da Câmara makes no further mention of this Jacob Aldenard, who,
so Ribadeneira himself mentions in some biographical notes on Ignatius, *de actis P.N.
Ignatii*, 99 [MHSI *Fontes Narrativi* II, p. 387], was a learned young man, also from
Flanders like the person described in §47; Polanco in his *Chronicon* (the history of Ignatius
and the early Society) confirms Ribadeneira's information (cf. MHSI *Polanci Chronicon*
for 1553, §29, vol. III, p. 20); and the MHSI editors note here that elsewhere he mentions
the same person, and supplies the family name.

[63] The name of this Fleming is not known. In 1555 the province of Holland was still
part of Burgundy, although in this year, with the abdication of Emperor Charles V, it was
included in the Spanish Netherlands under Philip II. As no house for novices existed there
at this time many Dutch/Flemish candidates came to Rome.

about 19 or 20. He was still in his First Probation.[64] As soon as our Father heard of his temptation he ordered the older fathers to speak to him, and as this was not sufficient he went himself, as is related here. He told us afterwards that when he embraced him he had to give a little jump so that his arms could reach his neck, because he was very tall, but not even this moved the Fleming to want to stay in the house.

(b) *with a father*

48 This father was Francisco Marín,[65] who had already been in the Society three or four years when I arrived in Rome for the first time. He was a native of Andalusia, already going grey, and very well educated, who in the world had held a post in the administration of justice. He was minister in Rome before me for about a year more or less, and after he had been removed from this position, he continued to deal with people outside on our Father's orders in matters concerning the Society, and he often had to pay visits to cardinals and noblemen in the carrying out of this duty. This father was always obstinate, especially in those matters in which, from his studies and the posts he had held, he believed he had superior knowledge. He showed little submissiveness and would not put aside his own judgement in matters where obedience required this. In order to cure this fault, our Father ordered that he be given the Exercises, and I remember that Fr. Nadal said to me that he feared the Exercises would be discredited, for the little good they would do him. He finished them with a slight shadow of amendment, but once he had returned to his own occupation, he returned also to his own opinions and his own wishes. As he persisted in this our Father expelled him forthwith from the Society.

---

[64] See Glossary.

[65] This identification is a mistake by da Câmara, who has misunderstood the mention of Fr. Marín in the note added by Ribadeneira. The latter is referring to two different cases: the first was that of the Flemish novice mentioned in §47, who according to Ribadeneira wanted to leave at all costs, and said he would go the following morning, at which point Ignatius insisted that he should go at once, even though it was night-time (the story is told by Ribadeneira before his mention of Jacob Aldenard, reference given in the note to §46); the second case is that of Francisco Marín, and this is correctly described by da Câmara except that the expulsion took place at a later date, October 1555 (instead of December 1554) and not at night. A further complication arises from the possible identification of this Fr. Francisco with the one mentioned below, §360.

In the marginal note to this passage, Fr. Ribadeneira wrote to tell me that Fr. Marín was expelled at night in spite of his wish to stay until the morning. I cannot recall the reason why his departure was so sudden. And even though I was the minister I do not know the reason; because this happened in December and as I started writing these notes beginning in the following January, if I had known so striking a reason it seems logical that I would have recorded it here. But the Father may have acted according to his custom of not communicating faults except to those he could not avoid telling.

[c] *Antonio Marino*

49 Antonio Marino,[66] a Spaniard by birth with an M.A. from the University of Paris, was regarded, both within the residence and outside, as a man of much talent with great literary gifts. Father Ignatius chose him to lay the foundations for the teaching of philosophy in our Roman College, and he began the first course ever taught there and lectured most successfully.[67] Among his students were Fr. Benedetto Palmio,[68] who has been for so long an Assistant[69] for the Society in Rome, and Fr. Pedro Ribadeneira, who wrote the life of our Father Ignatius.[70]

Marino began at this time to be disturbed himself, and to perturb others. In particular he showed that his opinions and judgements on certain matters of the Society were very different from those usually held in it, and he passed on these opinions to others. Fr. Ignatius called for him and strove to bring him back to the right way, but when he saw how little he amended his ways, he expelled him. This happened at a time when it was necessary to replace him to give the course with a Flemish brother, who had been a novice for only a few months, but was a man of great humility and virtue. There was such a shortage of suitable people that the course had

---

[66] Two brothers, Antonio and Francisco Marino, joined the Society early in 1552, and both left shortly afterwards; however Antonio re-applied for entry in 1553, only to leave once more some three months later, his second period as a novice coinciding with the early part of da Câmara's stay in Rome (he arrived 23 May 1553).

[67] The MHSI editors note that his name does not figure in the list of professors, but suggest that this is because officially lectures began only in October, 1553.

[68] A Sicilian who reached Rome with Fr. Nadal in 1553; by 1559 he had been appointed Provincial of Lombardy and in 1565 the Italian Assistant; he reappears frequently in the *Memoriale*.

[69] See Glossary.

[70] See §31 with note.

to be given by ten lecturers [one after the other] after Marino had been expelled, as there was no one who was satisfactory. I was so distressed by this incident, that even though I had arrived only a short time before in Rome, I could not resist interceding with our Father on his behalf, when I learned that they wanted to expel him. I recall that he replied to me laughingly saying, "Well, you go and convert him!"

(d) Soldevilla

50 Soldevilla,[71] a priest and theologian, was a Catalan by birth, and had the reputation among our fathers in Rome of being a spiritual and devout man. This father adopted his own way of dealing with spiritual matters, one different from the Society's usual method, and he passed it on secretively to other members of the community. His fabrications were pernicious not only to the soul, because they detached subjects from their obedience, but also to the body. I recall Peter Silvius, a Fleming, who was at that time a simple brother, a man of extraordinary humility, obedience and gentleness, and blessed with many other natural and acquired virtues. He later became a great worker and doctor of theology, and lived and died in the Society, giving great edification. Fr. Soldevilla, however, drove him to such extremes with his doctrine that, as a result of the enormous and prolonged violence which he imposed on his imagination, he was unable to speak for a long time and became completely befuddled, so that there was no hope that he would live.[72] "When our Father heard of what had happened he applied the following remedy: he ordered the priest [Fr. Soldevilla] as penance, both in the residence and in the College, to go to the refectory stripped to the waist, and to discipline himself wearing angel wings on his shoulders, which Father ordered to be made especially for this occasion, while repeating the words, "No flying without wings!" or these (since I do not actually recall well), "I ask pardon of all of you, because I wanted to fly without wings." And after he had given this satisfaction, he expelled him immediately.[73] Then, when he recognized his fault and found himself in

---

[71] Antonio Soldevilla had entered the Society in Valencia, 1551, as a diocesan priest (in Tarragona) and came to Rome in 1553; after having worked in Genoa, he was sent, as mentioned below, to Naples, where he died in 1601.

[72] Other sources speak of his illness in similar terms; he had recovered by early 1554. Later in life he worked in Germany, dying there in 1571.

[73] No other sources refer to this (temporary) dismissal, and the chronology of these incidents may have become confused in da Câmara's memory (note the MHSI editors).

the world, he decided, as in other ways he was a good man, to ask mercy of our Father, so that he would re-admit him. To prove his amendment he went to work in a hospital, and for the four or five months he was there gave such edification and showed such signs of repentance, that at the end of this period he was freshly admitted to the Society and from then on our Father placed more trust in him than before. So much so that a few days later he appointed him minister of the house. I succeeded him in the same post. Our Father sent him to give instruction in cases[74] of conscience in Naples: I thought it very appropriate to record here the rigour with which he treated the culprit, and the benign spirit which he showed to the contrite.

(e) *Zapata*

51 Francisco Zapata,[75] born in Toledo, joined the Society in Rome. He was well known there and rich, since he held an honoured public office: when he saw that Fr. Nadal was going to preach at the Banchi[76] (a demeaning exercise because usually charlatans preached there) he formed a bad opinion of this mortification, and he criticised it accordingly in the house. Father Ignatius heard of this one day at night when everyone was already in bed, and immediately, without any further discussion of the matter, he ordered him to be got up and given back the clothes he had brought, and landed him in the street.[77] He then became a Franciscan friar and has acquired a great reputation for his virtue and religious life in that order, continuing to be a great friend of the Society, and Father Ignatius and the other fathers relied much on him.

---

[74] Casuistry, described in the *Oxford Dictionary of the Christian Church* as "the art or science" of bringing general moral principles to bear on particular cases, was a regular feature of the teaching of the time.

[75] Even before joining the Society this priest, employed in Rome as a Vatican secretary, volunteered to accompany Frs. Broët and Salmerón on their papal mission to Ireland (1542); in 1546 he applied for admission as a coadjutor.

[76] This was the name for an area of several streets named after banks (e.g. via Banco S. Spirito) near the Ponte de Sant' Angelo; Ignatius had also taught children at the church of San Celso in this area.

[77] Although the exact date of this dismissal is not certain (1547 or 1548), there are documents that establish clearly the justification for his expulsion, the criticism mentioned being only the final straw (cf. MHSI *Scripta* I, pp. 630-645). Ribadeneira confirms that he had a good reputation as a Franciscan.

(f) *if it is a case of not wanting to obey*

52 Our Father castigated and deeply regretted the lack of obedience, not only in essential matters, such as those mentioned in the examples I have related apropos of Fr. Ribadeneira's marginal note, but also in any other circumstances, even if they were not of great importance in themselves. An example is the penance he gave me before appointing me minister of the house, which I think I should relate at this point.

In 1554 our Father sent from Rome Fr. Master Andrés de Oviedo and Fr. Master Melchior Carneiro,[78] already designated as bishops and companions of Fr. João Nunes, the Patriarch of Ethiopia, to be consecrated here [in Portugal] and to embark for India. Giovanni Tomaso and Master Jan,[79] a Fleming, came with them. Further, since the four were travelling with horses, at the expense of the King of Portugal [João III], our Father wanted another fourteen to travel with them, as together with Fr. Laínez they were going to found the college in Genoa, so that the weaker members might receive help at stages from the mounts. They all left one day in the morning [19 September 1554]; the fourteen destined for Genoa went ahead, because they were going on foot, intending to wait for the others at a place five leagues from Rome, where they had arranged to eat all together.

53 For both their consolation and ours we asked and obtained our Father's permission that Frs. Olave[80] and Ribadeneira, who were in the College, and I myself, who lived in the residence, should accompany the five who were left for a small part of the journey. In order to do this we requested some mounts on loan, and departed all together, intending to return and eat in the residence. When we had ridden a distance that seemed to me enough, we started discussing our return journey and both the Fathers that we were accompanying, as well as my two companions, began to persuade

[78] Both of these, and Fr. João Nunes, are described below §§120-23.

[79] Giovanni Tomaso Passitano, a Neapolitan, and his companion, Jan Boukyau, had taken their vows as professed fathers in Rome in 1554.

[80] Mentioned frequently in the *Memoriale*, Fr. Martín de Olave had met Ignatius while still a student in Alcalá de Henares (1526) and had then helped him financially; he joined the Society in 1552 and after a short novitiate took his vows in 1553, being put in charge at once of the nascent Roman College, where he was also a professor; he died very shortly after Ignatius on 18 August 1556.

me that we should reach the place of the meal, where the other fourteen were waiting for us, saying that since we had already arrived so far, this would be what our Father wanted. Even so I demurred, fearing what might happen, saying that it was already time, and that afterwards it would be very late, etc. But in the end, bearing in mind the authority of my companions—Fr. Olave, superintendent[81] of the Roman College, and Fr. Ribadeneira, who was very familiar with our Father's views since he had been brought up by him since his youth—I followed their advice, and we arrived at the place where the other fourteen were waiting for us. After having eaten together and said good-bye to the pilgrims, we began the return journey. The days were short and the journey long: above all, the mount I had was an old mule which even if beaten with a stick did not budge. I remember Fr. Olave kept saying to me, "Flog it, father, flog it!" and I replied, "It's useless, she seems to think that we agreed she should carry me out here on condition that I carried her back." So it took me a great deal of trouble to get home. After all this, we did not arrive back in Rome until an hour and a half after sunset.[82] As I wanted companions at my first meeting with our Father, I asked that we should go straight to the residence, and I thought we were going that far, but they took me to the door of the College, planted me at the door, dismounted, and offered me lodging for the night if I wanted.

54 I was by then quite exhausted, but so that "the end might not be worse than the beginning"[83] I set off home by myself. I arrived dying of hunger and thirst (and to crown everything it was a fast day, being the Wednesday of the Ember days of September), completely worn out with dragging both myself and the mule on my back. I had hardly thrown myself on to my bed when I received a message that our Father was calling for me. He received me with a very severe expression and, not even asking me the reason for the delay, said, "You don't want to be obedient, and I don't know what to do with you! Don't come to see me any more! Go to the College and we shall see if you can be obedient there. Don't eat or drink anything today, and tell your companions to do the same."

---

[81] Cf. §217.

[82] Nearly 8 o'clock at night.

[83] A play on the sentence in Ecclesiastes (7:8): "Better is the end of a thing than its beginning."

Saying no more, the Father dismissed me from his presence and from the residence.

55 I went straightaway to the College, and so that the penance might be perfect, I passed by the Piazza de Altieri,[84] which at that time was full of holes and ditches that were being dug to extract pieces of sculpture from the ancient ruins. And as I was alone and the night was dark and I was half blind,[85] if I missed one hole it was only to fall into another. In this way I arrived at the College, where my companions welcomed me with much jollity. I relayed our Father's words to them and the penance he had given me and told them they too were obliged not to eat or drink that day as part of the penance. But since they had already had supper, I alone must needs pay the price for all. After eight days of banishment from the residence, our Father decided to welcome me back and restore me to his favour.

(g) and others

56 One of the brethren went into the lavatory, and he got ready and undressed himself with less care and more haste than was proper; when someone else, who was already inside, saw him like that, he gave him a spank on the buttocks. This happened before I arrived in Rome. Our Father Ignatius told me about it, and I clearly grasped from the way he told the story that it was nothing more than a prank, but he said that only because of this he had ordered him to be dismissed at once.

57 We had a Brother in the residence in Rome who had been nine or ten years in the Society; his behaviour was very edifying, and for most of this time he had held the office of infirmarian, showing great humility, patience, and charity towards the sick. He was so good at this that when Dr. Arce[86] fell seriously ill in Rome (though a wealthy man, he had no one in his house to look after him or who could help him to get better, and the Society was under some obligation to him, having received favours from him in times of

---

[84] The site of the present Piazza del Gesù, which is near the former residence of the General.

[85] The poor sight of Fr. da Câmara was an affliction ever since his entry into the Society; see §251.

[86] Jerónimo de Arce was a Spaniard, doctor in theology, who had supported Ignatius on various occasions, most notably in 1543 when he gave a large sum (200 *escudos/ecus*).

need). Father Ignatius ordered this brother to stay at the doctor's house in order to care for him. He was there for a month, without anyone else from the Society. I remember that this happened at a time when we had many sick in the house (their health was so important to the Father that he put it before anything else), and when I went to him and explained the great need we had of an infirmarian, he only wanted the brother to care for the doctor. I was greatly amazed at the extraordinary virtue of gratitude that the Father showed on this occasion.

58 After my departure from Rome, it happened that one day when this Brother was washing the feet of a sick man, he put his hand a little higher than was necessary. The sick man was a foreign Brother, whom he had not known or had any familiarity with previously, which might have given rise to some suspicion that the action was ill-intentioned. Nevertheless, as soon as our Father heard of it, he ordered him to be expelled. The fathers came to him and begged him insistently to punish him in some other way, but not to expel him completely. The Father was not willing, but finally, after many requests, he granted them that he should be allowed to make a pilgrimage of 400 leagues,[87] and that if he proved satisfactory by his good example he could be admitted in any house of the Society outside Rome. This was one of the last acts of Father Ignatius, because a few days later Our Lord called him to Himself [31 July 1556]. The Brother performed his penance and stayed a long time in the Society outside Italy, returning to Rome only long after the death of our Father.

But when I was in Rome for the second time for the First General Congregation [May 1558], he was no longer in the Society and then I learned of what had passed between Father and him from the accounts of Frs. Laínez and Madrid (it was they who had interceded for the Brother), and also perhaps from Fr. Polanco, although I am not certain of this third one. To sum up, in matters concerning chastity our Father had a most perfect zeal.[88]

[87] The "league" varied in length in different countries; the Iberian league at this time was just over 4 miles or nearly 7 kilometres.

[88] The MHSI editors, clearly somewhat scandalized by the severity, apparently arbitrary, of Ignatius in some of these stories, suggest that he is perhaps more to be admired than imitated, but also point out that the account of da Câmara is necessarily incomplete (see §51 note). As da Câmara refers to the Brother's staying in the Society and returning to Rome "a long time" after 1556, although not more than two years could have elapsed if he had left the Society by 1558, there seems to be some inaccuracy here.

59 A very elderly Father went to hear the confession of a woman in her house and succeeded in placing his companion in such a way that he could not be seen by the companion during the confession. Our Father heard of this and although the priest concerned was one whose great virtue and age could not, morally or naturally, give grounds for any suspicion, he imposed a penance on him for this: he should discipline himself for the duration of seven Psalms. However he asked me to tell him to find some of the shorter psalms, and thus all was done properly.

These things should not surprise anyone who considers how much the saints valued the eminent virtue of perfect chastity and how they punished the contrary vice. Even though it is not my intention to give examples of this, I thought I should give one here which is narrated in volume 2 of the *Councils* concerning the Tenth Council of Toledo:[89] it reads as follows.

DECREE WITH REGARD TO BISHOP POTAMIUS

60 We could have taken up a singing flute to celebrate so great a Fraternal joy, since divine kindness convened our gathering to encourage our efforts for concord, and it was appropriate to avoid sadness as we seemed to have renovated paternal rulings with the presence of disciplined order. However, in fact we take up the melancholy rattle instead of the cymbal, and our song is a lament instead of a paean; we say, groaning with the lamentations of Jeremiah, "The joy of our hearts has ceased; our dancing has been turned to mourning" [Jeremiah, Lamentations 5:15]. Thus we gaze on woe, for we see how the crown has fallen from our head now that such nobility, which stood as the sublime pinnacle of sanctity, has sunk so low.

[89] There were some thirty ecclesiastical Councils held in Toledo, between the 5th and the 16th centuries, some of which had national importance (e.g. against Priscillian [in 400], and establishing the primacy of Toledo [in 681]); the Tenth Council (in 656) passed a series of canons, and also dealt with the case of Bishop Potamius, who had confessed to sins of fornication; the Council decided to depose him, appointing an administrator (the Bishop of Duma) in his place, but allowing him to keep his episcopal title. The text that da Câmara had copied out at this point is in Latin, taken from an early edition of the Council's *Acta*.

Behold, while we were debating peacefully about ecclesiastical rulings, a sort of letter was presented to our gathering, filled with a confused confession and bearing a signature that should have been deleted, which Potamius, the bishop of Braga, had written down about his own doings and in his own words and phrases. When this was opened, the tearful assembly discussed, more in tears than in words, what the page—which should have been destroyed—and the various written letters—which should have been deleted—made public.

Then, when the bishops of God had gathered in secret session, we had the aforementioned bishop appear on his own before us. Addressing him with sobs rather than words we laid open before him that written account of his deformity and cause of our confusion. He picked up the document and re-read it, and when we enquired if it was evidence of his action and of his statement, he asserted that it was his doing, that the words were from his mouth, and the writing the effect of his fingers, something that was before his eyes as he re-read it. Once again, adjuring him to call on the divine Name, we asked him to declare if he had uttered some lie about himself of his own accord, or if he were under threat from some violence and therefore said these things out of terror. But he, with tears in his voice and his eyes overflowing in weeping and choking with sobs, he cried out, swearing in the name of the one God, that he truly confessed these evil things about himself, and that he had not been obliged by any violence to make this confession. For this, he said, during almost nine months he had of his own accord abandoned the government of his church and shut himself up in some prison cell to do penance for the crime he admitted.

So, once it was known and recognized by his trustworthy confession that he had besmirched himself with female contact, even if paternal antiquity stipulates by sacred canons that such a person should be demoted from his honour, nevertheless we, respecting the rights of mercy, do not remove from him his title of honour, a punishment he himself in the confession of his crime had already assumed, but we have decreed with valid authority that he should apply himself in perpetual penance to duties and hardships, for *we foresee that, by following the painful and thorny path of penitential solitude, he will be better directed to reach one day the mansion of rest, rather than being left to the broad laxity of his own will to be hurled over the precipice into eternal damnation.*

Therefore we have appointed, by unanimous vote of all, the venerable Fructuosus, bishop of the church of Duma, to take charge of governing the church of Braga, so that assuming the rule of the whole metropolis of the province of Galicia, with all the bishops, people and monasteries, and taking spiritual care of all the persons of the church of Braga, he may so dispose and conserve it as both to give glory to Our Lord by the uprightness of his conduct, and assure us the joy of that church's integrity. And as one should look to the future, lest in the midst of peace the disturbance of some legal appeal should arise, our vigilant care should ensure that the sentence of the fathers which rightly condemns the said Bishop Potamius is joined to this decree.

61 [n.d.] The method for dismissing members from the Society which our Father normally uses is to send them on pilgrimage: and he prefers, even when someone certainly ought to go, to expel him, rather than let him leave on his own account, and he does this so that such a one can go with love. He acted in this way *with Lazcano*[a] in October 1553; he wanted to leave, and the Father asked him to wait for him [to tell him], and because he [the Father] judged that he was not suitable for the Society, he arranged matters in such a way that he stayed very friendly towards the Society, and went back to Spain.[90] This was how he wanted to treat *the Calabrian,*[b] who left a few days ago and also departed as a great friend. And *breviter* [in brief], Father does everything possible so that they do not leave embittered.[91]

[a] *with Lazcano*

62 The case of Lazcano was like this: Lazcano was from Vizcaya, a soldier, a nobleman, and of a certain age. He had been ordained deacon when very young, before he joined the Society, more on

[90] Sebastiano Lazcano (or Lescano) reached Naples in 1553, with letters of recommendation for Fr. Salmerón and other Spanish Jesuits there.

[91] At other places in the *Memoriale* there are similar comments on the policy followed by Ignatius over dismissals (see §348); he deals with the topic expressly in the *Constitutions* II, 3 (§§218-230), cf. Ganss, pp. 146-149.

account of his nobility than his learning, since he could not even read at this time, although he was over forty. I remember that there, in front of Father Ignatius, he was given a book to read, and he held it upside down, and then started rubbing his eyes saying that the humidity affected his sight. He joined the Society in Rome in my time, and I shall say here something about obedience that I first heard from Father Ignatius when Lazcano joined. It was another Basque gentleman who brought Lazcano, a man of great authority, and out of respect for him and because of his insistence the Father received Lazcano. Our Father went to talk to them, and since they were standing, he told the novice that those who joined the Society had to enter on two feet, that is to say, with a right and a left foot: the right he called "obedience of the understanding," and the left "obedience of the will." And he said that those who simply had the same wish, without having the same feelings and judgements about things as the superior, had only a left foot in the Society. Some months after Lazcano had been received, it happened that he fell into temptation against this very same obedience and vocation. The Father did a great deal to calm him, not to keep him in the Society, because he was quite unsuitable, but rather in order to expel him with his conscience at peace. In order to bring this about, seeing that he wanted to go regardless, he ordered him to be locked in a room. He was there five or six whole days refusing to eat anything, so that they would expel him. But at the end of this time he quietened down, and then our Father dismissed him with many tokens of affection and love, and he left consoled and happy.

(b) the Calabrian

63 This Calabrian[92] was a professor of grammar, already a man of mature age. I remember that when Fr. Polanco spoke to him before receiving him into the Society, he replied in a very assured manner, "Take me on my word. You will not regret it." After he had been received into the Society he was never able to understand why he, a professor of grammar, should have to wash the pots and pans. He was not satisfied even when he saw professors of theology and the superiors of houses also washing them, or even when we told him that Fr. Francis [Borgia], who had been the Duke of Gandía, had done the same. But the chief reason for his temptation was

---

[92] Nothing further is known about this candidate.

that the Father ordered him to get rid of a bottle of oil from his room, which he would use to rub on his temples to refresh his memory; this was something he simply could not stand, and for this reason he left.

29 January

64 1. Neither the doors of the College nor of the residence are to be opened to the relations of *Mario.* [a] When the Father learned later that Mario's relations *went with him to lectures,* [b] books in hand, he told the teacher to order them to repeat the lessons and to go to confession according to the custom of the college. [93]

[a] *Mario*

65 Mario Beringucci [94] was a young nobleman from Siena, whom I brought with me [October, 1555] to this province [of Portugal]. Here he followed the Arts course of Fr. Pedro da Fonseca. [95] His relatives regretted his entry into the Society in Rome, and since they tried to worry him about his vocation, our Father ordered the action I describe here.

[b] *went with him to lectures*

66 When they were not admitted by the porters of the residence or the College they pretended to be students and went to Class One, which Brother Mario attended, in order to be able to talk to him there.

67 [n.d.] In such cases our Father is accustomed to take great pains lest the novices should be disturbed. One can see an example of this in the case of Tarquinio; [96] *though he was so constant* [c] in his vocation, our Father sent him to Spain, saying that he did not want him to be disturbed

---

[93] All the external students attending the Roman College were strongly encouraged to confess their sins at least once a month.

[94] His father, who had the same name, was professor of law in Naples (Polanco mentions this in his *Chronicon,* IV, 186); the son entered the Society in 1554 and, after completing his studies in Portugal, took his final vows in Brescia in 1569.

[95] A famous philosophy lecturer in his day at the Jesuit college in Coimbra, Pedro da Fonseca (1528-1599) had joined the Society in 1548; he later held a number of administrative posts (e.g. Assistant to the General in Rome, 1573-81).

[96] Tarquinio Raynaldi (1533-1571) was born in Rome, the son of a distinguished legal figure who vigorously opposed his entry into the Society (in 1553); to escape paternal pressure he was sent to Florence and later to Valencia; eventually he took his vows and was rector of several colleges but died young.

by the least thought. This was how the Father replied to the consult, who
thought that Tarquinio would certainly persevere. Other examples of the
same kind are *Ottoviano the Neapolitan,* [a] *Lucio Croce,* [b] and *Giovanni
Ricasoli,* [d] the Florentine.

> *Marginal Note by Fr. Ribadeneira:* Explain here the
> Father's custom of ordering that they themselves should
> write. Similarly, what he told me about the good example
> that in this respect there is in the Society particularly in the
> case of Ottaviano, with the judgement of Cardinal
> Carpi,[97] and in the case of *Master Polanco.* [c] Similarly,
> what was done in the case of Lucio Croce, whom I took to
> Sicily.

[c] *though he was so constant*

68 Tarquinio was a young man about twenty-one years old, more
or less, the son of a judge in Rome. His father loved him dearly,
and was very upset when he joined the Society. He said it was a
dishonour for him that his son should be in it. He soon went to see
Father Ignatius and did everything he could to get his son back,
both personally and through Cardinals and other noblemen,
whom he used as intermediaries. But as he had no success, he
turned to all sorts of tricks and ruses to drag him out of the house
by force.

69   Father Ignatius thought this man would calm down if
Tarquinio left Rome, and so he sent him to Florence (in the company of Fr. Caspar Rodrígues,[98] who was still a brother, and had
arrived a few days earlier from Portugal to be my assistant, and is
now in Rome), where Father Laínez was superior of four or five
members of the Society. Tarquinio's father tried hard to make our
Father bring him back to Rome, where he could continue studies
not available in Florence. As our Father would not grant this, he
wrote to Florence to some nobles who had influence with the
Duke[99] to get the young man back in any way they could. He finally realized he would achieve nothing through letters, and went to

---

[97] See §20 with note.
[98] Probably the Portuguese Gaspar Roiz (or Rodrigues), born in Evora, who joined the
Society in 1552 and later taught casuistry in Evora with great success.
[99] Cosimo I de Medici (1519-1574).

Florence himself in person. Once in the city he arranged with the Duke that he should send a message to Fr. Laínez telling him that the Duke would be pleased to see the brother, and therefore begged him to send him to the palace.

70 Fr. Laínez granted his request, far from suspecting what might happen. No sooner had the brother entered the door of the palace, than he was seized by I don't know how many soldiers, posted there by his father for this purpose. They took him away to the house where his father was staying. They dressed him very richly in silk clothes, with feathers and brooches on his hat and with all the other worldly decorations they had prepared expressly. They then tried hard through numerous parties and coaxing to make him forget the religious life. But it drew nothing from him other than the reply, "You can do what you like with my clothes and my body, but as for my soul and will, you cannot change these for me."

In the meantime Fr. Laínez exerted himself with the Duke to order his release, but all in vain, because the Duke depended totally on the Marquis of Marignano,[100] who was in Florence as Captain General of the Emperor [Charles V] at his special command, and he greatly favoured the judge. But at last, as the brother showed himself so unmoved by everything they offered him and so alien to the desire to remain in the world, his father himself, quite jaded by now, let him return freely to our house.

When the storm had passed, our Father, thinking they would not bother him any further, ordered him to return to Rome to study; but his father, hoping he might yet achieve something, sent his servants, dressed as students, to our lectures, so that they could talk to Tarquinio and upset him. When our Father learned of this he called a consult and acted as is related in this paragraph.

(a) Ottaviano the Neapolitan[101]

I do not recall the details of this case.

---

[100] Jacobo Medici, from a Milanese family not related to the Florentine Medicis; his brother, Cardinal Giovanni Angelo Medici, became Pope Pius IV.

[101] Ottaviano Cesari was the son of the Duke of Monte Leone in Naples; his entry into the Society, against the wishes of his parents, caused endless trouble and complex negotiations between 1553 and 1556. Eventually he left the Society.

(b) *Lucio Croce[102]*

71 Lucio Croce was a young nobleman, from Tivoli. When he entered the Society he was pursued by his relations, who, in order to make him return, used the influence of cardinals, and nobles, and even of the Pope, to whom also they complained, in addition to other means. Our Father resisted all this, and finally in view of the situation sent him to Sicily with Fr. Ribadeneira, as he told me and noted in the margin of this passage.

(d) *Giovanni Ricasoli[103]*

72 This brother was a native of Florence, of a very noble family and very gifted, both virtuous and intelligent. He joined the Society in my time and his relations followed and tempted him in the same way. I remember that our Father acceded to the request of a cardinal, and sent him home with a father, so that he could talk to them in his presence, and for this visit he ordered him to dress like a student of the Society, for until then he had dressed (and later continued to do so) in the clothes he had brought with him. He convinced his relations and persevered in the Society, giving edification and good example. I have heard that he taught theology in our schools in Padua.

(e) *Master Polanco—with reference to the marginal note of Fr. Ribadeneira[104]*

73 The way our Father proceeded in the case of Fr. Polanco, which Fr. Ribadeneira noted for me here, can be seen from a passage of a letter Fr. Bartolomeo Ferrão[105] wrote at that time on the orders of our Father to Fr. Dr. Miguel de Torres about some matters concerning the Society. The passage reads as follows:

---

[102] A nephew of the bishop of Tivoli; he entered the Society in 1549 and despite all the opposition stayed in it until his death in Rome in 1596; for a letter of Ignatius to his father, cf. *Select Letters*, No. 25, pp. 238-240 [= MHSI *Epist.* II, No. 958, pp. 603-06].

[103] He entered in 1554, and Ignatius had to appeal to the Pope to intervene on behalf of his choice; he continued in the Society, dying in Rome in 1581.

[104] See §67; da Câmera added these words in the margin.

[105] See §126: a version (slightly more authentic) of this letter is available in MHSI *Epist.* I, 467-70 No. 154; it is dated March 1547.

Master Juan de Polanco,[106] *having been in the Society for six years, and having completed his studies at Padua, began the customary year of probation.*[107] *He preached for nearly four months [end of 1546 and start of 1547] in Bologna and Pistoia with great benefit to souls, both in hearing confessions and in lectures, sermons, and spiritual direction. When he had completed half the year he left Padua and went to Florence with the intention of continuing the same work there. He met one of his brothers,*[108] *who was rich and favoured by the Signoria, who then with his followers tried hard to persuade him to go to Burgos to join his parents and leave the life he had started. When our Father heard this, he wrote to him telling him either to go to the Council [of Trent], where our fathers were, or to come back to Rome. But his brother, suspecting that he wished to leave, kept him prisoner in a house to stop him. Nevertheless he contrived ingeniously to escape, and went to the house of the Bishop of Pistoia,*[109] *having forced open a door and jumped out of a window with a rope.*

74 Even this did not prevent his brother, who was a powerful man, from dragging him by force from the Bishop's house and taking him back to his own house, as we learned from Polanco's own letter and from the Bishop himself. Matters had reached this point, when Fr. Lunel,[110] *who was General of the Franciscans, and a Dr. Sandoval*[111] *came to ask Father Ignatius to give Fr. Polanco permission to go to Burgos and visit his relations as his brother wished. However Fr. Ignatius replied that Fr. Polanco should come*

---

[106] As noted above (see §15), became a Jesuit in 1541; he had already studied in Paris before this, but was sent to Padua for further theological studies, 1542-46; after the year of pastoral experience mentioned here he was called to Rome to become secretary to Ignatius and the whole Society; his *Chronicon* covers the early history of the Society.

[107] Apart from the First Probation (see Glossary) and the novitiate (or Second Probation) it is customary for Jesuits to have a year of probation (the so-called "tertianship") after the completion of their studies and prior to Final Vows; this custom was introduced as early as 1541; cf. Glossary.

[108] Luis de Polanco, a younger brother.

[109] Pietro Francesco Galigari [sic in the Spanish translation, "Gallianus" in the MHSI edition], bishop of Pistoia from 1547 to 1559.

[110] Vicente Lunel, the O.F.M. Minister General from 1535 to 1550.

[111] He was involved in the administration of the Roman College and had much to do with the Jesuits.

> *first of all to Rome, to gain wider knowledge of the Society,*
> *and as for the permission to go to Burgos, he would put the*
> *matter in the hands of two persons, one being Fr.*
> *Lunel himself,*[112] *and he would not do it any other way. They were*
> *fairly satisfied with this reply and wrote immediately to*
> *Florence on the matter. But Father Ignatius, to make sure*
> *and without letting them know, arranged for Don Juan de*
> *Vega*[113] *to write to the Duke of Florence, and for de*
> *Marquina*[114] *to [write to] Don Pedro de Toledo,*[115] *who was*
> *staying in his house, so that His Excellency would free Fr.*
> *Polanco, whose brother had taken him prisoner violently.*
> *With the letters he sent Master André [des Freux] and*
> *Gerolamo, the one from Bassano.*[116] *Two or three days after*
> *their arrival Fr. Polanco left Florence and came here, put-*
> *ting himself and the whole affair into the hands of our*
> *Father.*

75   2. [29 January] *Job and Cincinnato,*[a] although very young, should be
received into the Society, but not be enclosed.

[a] *Job and Cincinnato*

These were two younger brothers of Petronio;[117] the third,
whom I shall mention later, was called Lancillotto. Petronio

---

[112] The decision, drawn up (in Latin) by Fr. Lunel and Cristóbal de Madrid (see §27), has been published [MHSI *Polanci Complementa* I, 33-34]; it states that Polanco is under no obligation to visit his parents in Spain before making his profession, but this should not be done before a full year has passed, and in the meanwhile he should write frequently to his father, doing his best to persuade and console him.

[113] All the family of this Spanish nobleman were close friends of Ignatius (cf. *Select Letters* No. 27, pp. 243-4 [MHSI *Epist.* III, 326-27] for a letter of consolation to the daughter on her brother's death in 1551); in this year (1547) the father, Juan de Vega, was moved from the post of Imperial Ambassador to the Vatican to that of Viceroy of Sicily.

[114] Pedro de Marquina was a secretary at the Spanish Embassy who helped Ignatius with correspondence on other occasions; however da Câmara's text here is none too clear, as the French translator points out, and it may be significant that the version of the letter published in MHSI *Epist.* omits the name of de Marquina.

[115] This may be the Marquis of Francavilla and Viceroy of Naples, the father-in-law of Duke Cosimo, married to Leonora de Toledo, but the MHSI editors of the *Memoriale* think it suspicious that his titles are not mentioned here, and suggest he may be a homonym of the same family.

[116] On Fr. André des Freux, see §39; Fr. Gerolamo (1520-81) came from the town of Bassano, his family name being Otello: he entered the Society in 1544 and had made his profession by 1552, becoming a noted preacher in Rome (see §95) and then in Sicily; his death took place in Verona.

[117] See §29.

studied in Rome with the intention of joining the Society, and in order to encourage the same vocation in his younger brothers, he frequently sent them to bring messages and gifts to Father Ignatius. Father talked to them, and invited them in, and made much of them for the same reason. I remember he ordered me to keep a box of Pesaro figs, such as we keep in baskets, which Petronio had sent by his brother Job, and telling me in front of him that he would give them all to him when we received him into the Society. The reason why they were not strictly enclosed when they entered was that they should not have as severe a First Probation as is usual.

76 Of these four brothers only Petronio persevered and died in the Society,[118] where he gave great edification as rector of a college. I took Lancilloto with me to Portugal, but left him sick in Genoa; and in his place I took Wolfgang, born in Bohemia; he is now in Prague, and was one of the nine who came for the German College and entered the Society.[119]

77 3. *As for accepting Guillaume*[120, (a)] the Frenchman, and the philosopher,[121] Father put the matter to the consult and did the same with the Fleming.

(a) As for accepting Guillaume

I remember nothing in particular about this case.

78 [n.d.] *In the meantime the Father called*[(b)] the brother who was troubled, and spent two hours with him to make him say why he wished to leave. He suspected the reason was some sin he might have committed in the world, and in order to make him feel less ashamed Father told him something about his own life, *etiam* [even] *the bad things he himself had done*[(c)] and *in this way he confessed to him the reason,*[(d)] which was a

---

[118] The information here is faulty: Cincinnato also died as a Jesuit (in Pesaro, 1564).

[119] See §18-19; however the MHSI editors suspect that da Câmara's memory may be faulty here or his information inaccurate, as no "Wolfgang" quite fits with his remarks.

[120] In 1573 there is reference to a French Brother coadjutor called Guillaume, who had been a Jesuit for seventeen years and therefore could have joined in 1555; later in the *Memoriale* the French novice is said to be ill (see §144).

[121] His name is uncertain, but later (§144) da Câmara speaks of "the two novices in their First Probation," one being the Frenchman, Guillaume, and the other Alonso, a Spaniard, who may be "the philosopher."

very small thing. Beforehand the Father had assured him he would not dine until he had found out.

(b) In the meanwhile the Father called

This is the brother of whom I said earlier[122] that he was tempted while out begging for alms.

(c) the bad things he himself had done

79 Our Father used this method with others to great advantage. He himself told me that in order to draw a very distinguished person away from a sin of which he was accused, he gave him an account of things that had happened to himself in the world,[123] and in this way Our Lord converted him.

(d) in this way he confessed to him the reason

80 The reason or occasion of this brother's temptation was that he had been told and promised by the relative he met when he was going begging for alms, that if he left the Society this person would give him a benefice he was keeping for this purpose. However, once he did leave, he discovered that it had all been a lie.

81 4. Permission should be given to *Lancillotto,* *(e)* who wants to make a general confession and the Exercises, which he is asking for insistently while in his First Probation; but he should also do the lesson.

(e) Lancillotto

He was the eldest of the three brothers of Petronio.[124] He hated

---

[122] See §43.

[123] "Until the age of twenty-six he was a man given up to the vanities of the world, and his chief delight used to be in the exercise of arms, with a great and vain desire to gain honour" (*Autobiography* §1): these opening words of the autobiographical account dictated by Ignatius to da Câmara in 1553 seem to skate over these events; indeed, da Câmara himself in his own Preface to that account says that Ignatius was more explicit: "Father called me and began to tell me his whole life, including his mischiefs as a lad (*travesuras de mancebo*), clearly and distinctly, with all their surrounding details" (see *Autobiography*, Introduction, p. 6, and also the full text appended by da Câmara below, §111). At some stage someone must have decided to omit part of what was dictated.

[124] See §§29, 76.

giving the Latin lesson, which those in the so-called First Probation[125] have to do if they know Latin, because apart from knowing very little Latin, he had a very shy temperament. Our Father did not want to dispense him from this.

82 5. Although he is master of novices, *Kornelius, who hears confessions,* [a] should not order any penance while he teaches them doctrine or in the grammar class; in order to remedy this there is to be a *syndic* appointed by the minister, who will impose them, etc.

[a] Kornelius, who hears confessions

83 Fr. Kornelius[126] was a Fleming by birth, and considered a great servant of God even before joining the Society. He was already a priest in Louvain when he joined. There he had a great reputation for sanctity: witness to his reputation was the high praise he won from Fr. Pierre Favre.[127] Our Father appointed him master of novices, and at the same time their confessor, in the residence at Rome, and he carried out these duties perfectly.

I recall that one day when we were together, he told me that novices should be led to mortification in the way one makes hens enter a small hole: to ensure that the hens go in it is necessary to shoo them ahead of you; when they go to one side, one has to go over there, and when they go to the other side, just the same, until at last they go where one wants them to go. In exactly the same way, in order for the novice to learn the way of mortification, it is important not to let him slip sideways, but to keep him away from those things to which his bad inclinations lead him, until he himself gently finds the way and follows it by himself. And apropos of the order that our Father had given him about novices' penances,

---

[125] See Glossary; the *Constitutions* and *Examen* lay down that novices should be tested for their former academic training, in particular by giving classes or lectures in different subjects (cf. *Examen*, 5, 6 [§109]; also *Constitutions* I, 4, 5 [§198]).

[126] Kornelius Wischaven (1509-59) had entered the Society in 1543, the first Jesuit from Flanders, and spent some years in Messina before being called to Rome, 1553, to be master of novices, spiritual father at the Roman College, and confessor at the German College.

[127] His remarks have been published in Latin in MHSI *Monumenta Fabri*, e.g. pp. 461, 465; however, Favre also warned Wischaven not to be too credulous about his feats of exorcism and urged him to give priority to confessions over liturgical singing: see Pierre Favre, *Spiritual Writings* [Bibliography], pp. 45, 354-361.

he told me that between the two of us we would make a good salad, if he poured the oil and I, being the minister, the vinegar.

84 7.[128] Concerning the novices of the First Probation, the Father says that it is necessary that *they be kept apart*[a] in the house, but taking into consideration their health and the weather; when it is very cold, there should be a fire. The purpose of this separation is to allow them to reflect better on what they have come for. When someone cannot bear the separation, the Father sometimes orders that others should go and talk to him and entertain him for part of the day; *or, as for those from the College*[b] who have come to the Society, he gives permission to go anywhere in the residence, but without speaking to anyone; still, ordinarily our Father likes the rule in this matter to be followed rigorously.

[a] *they be kept apart*

85 This separation is the so-called First Probation for those who join the Society.

[b] *or, as for those from the College*

Our Father agreed that the Germans of the German College who joined the Society could go along the corridors during the First Probation, as they were already trained in and accustomed to obedience and submission to the Fathers. But he would not give them permission to speak to the brothers. And this despite the fact that they were young men who for some time previous were already considered as if they were members of the Society in the German College. As far as I can recall the first were Paul Hoffäus,[129] who is now Provincial of Upper Germany, Heinrich from Bonn,[130] and Hermann,[131] three exceptional men.

---

[128] A paragraph numbered 6 seems to have been crossed out in the master copy, though traces of it are to be found in the manuscripts.

[129] Paul Hoffäus (1525-1608), one of the first students at the German College, entered the Society in 1554, and on completing his studies was eventually appointed rector of various German colleges, provincial, and later Assistant in Rome; an outstanding organizer, he also translated the Catechism of Trent into German.

[130] Heinrich Blyssem (1526-86) entered the Society in 1555 and succeeded Hoffäus as rector in Prague, later becoming provincial of the Austrian province.

[131] Hermann Thyraeus (died 1591), another important Jesuit administrator (he had joined in 1556) who also became provincial of one of the German provinces.

86 [n.d.] There is *much to reflect on*[a] in the way our Father uses completely opposite means for apparently identical purposes. One he treats with great rigour, another with great gentleness, and after the event one always saw that such was the remedy, although beforehand one had not understood. But he always inclines more towards love, *imo* [indeed] *to such a point*[b] that everything appears as love. And because of this he is so beloved by all; there is no one in the Society who does not love him greatly, and does not himself think that the Father loves him very dearly.

[a] *much to reflect on*

87 This was very common in our Father. I believe some examples of this will be found in this notebook.

[b] *imo* [indeed] *to such a point*

A sign of this great love is the great joy and pleasure he experiences in talking about, and listening to, news of the doings of the brethren. He ordered the "edifying letters"[132] and news from the colleges to be read two or even three times. Once in 1555, when I was at our villa, he called for me and talked to me with the greatest pleasure about this. He asked me to give him a reckoning of the numbers there were in the whole Society at that time, and I remember we reckoned nine hundred.

When I arrived there [Rome] from here [Portugal], our Father talked to me many times about the Portuguese brethren and about India. He took great pleasure in this, wanting to learn details of how they ate, slept, what they wore and many other such small and trivial details, so much so that one day while he was questioning me about India he said, "Indeed I would love to know, if it were possible, how many fleas bite them every night."

88 There are many things that keep alive this love of his subjects: first, the *great affability*[c] of the Father; second, *the great care*[d] which he takes of everyone's bodily health—this is so great that one can hardly praise it enough; third, the Father has such a way of proceeding *that whatever things might*[e] hurt a subject, he never passes them on unless by means of

---

[132] Precise instructions concerning the writing of these letters are given in the *Constitutions*, VIII, 1, 9 [673-75] and led to the production of the now-famous French series of *Lettres édifiantes*.

another person, without the subordinate thinking that the Father has been involved in it: on the other hand when there are things which should please the subject, the Father makes himself their author.[133]

(c) *great affability*

89 This affability was evident when he met one of the brethren in the house. Our Father would greet him smilingly, and give him such a welcome that he appeared to take him to his heart.[134] He dined with all those who had just arrived, or were about to leave on a journey, on the first or the last night, saying farewell to each with great affection. Nevertheless he maintained a due gravity towards all. Only with the indispensable consultors and immediate superiors did he discuss matters essential to the good government of the Society. Thus we can say that he was affable towards all, familiar with none.

(d) *the great care*

I have already said above what could be said about this point.[135]

(e) *that whatever things might*

90 An example of this is what he said to me, that is, that he wanted those who were imperfect and little mortified to be sent to live in the poor colleges, where they would suffer physical need. So I made them go, without their being able to guess that the order came from our Father, to such colleges as Padua and Venice, where at that time there was such a great lack of basic necessities that it often happened that when there were seven persons to supper, there were only six eggs. The more observant were kept by our Father in Rome or sent to other places where they were better provided for. He used an identical method in dealing with those whom he expelled from the Society, always giving them the order to leave through a third person and in his absence. In this way he never felt himself obliged to accept back anyone who, at the moment of dismissal, shed tears, made promises, and gave signs of

---

[133] See §§42, 199; and §§295-6, the case of Fr. Loarte.
[134] Literally, "in his soul (*n'alma*)."
[135] See §31.

repentance or amendment, even if he did receive back some who later had given sufficient satisfaction in their conduct.

91 [n.d.] Our Father always *speaks well of everyone*[a] and even with those who know about some faults, he does not talk about them except when it is *omnino* [absolutely] necessary in order to find a remedy for them. As for grumbling of any kind, he acts with such perfection that people are amazed.

[a] *speaks well of everyone*

The following marginal note is by Fr. Ribadeneira, who dictated it to the Brother who copied this notebook.

92 [*marginal note*] It would give me pleasure, brother, to include for you here some examples, but they are long affairs. One admirable thing is how he keeps the rule of the Exercises which says that each person should interpret the statement of another in the best possible sense,[136] so much so that among those who have dealings with him the interpretations of the Father *excusing the faults of others*[b]— both of those outside the Society and of those who are members—have become proverbial.

[b] *excusing the faults of others*

93 To do this he looked for what would be worthy of praise in those with whom he did not have good relations or who were the object of criticism, so that he could relate such things when he was told something bad about those people. Everyone is informed about how little regard Pope Paul IV had for the Society and for Fr. Ignatius both before and after he was created cardinal.[137] By chance then, on 23 May 1555, the Feast of the Ascension, I was in the same room with the Father. He was sitting in the window seat and I on a chair when we heard a bell chiming to announce the election of the new pope. Within a few minutes the news arrived

---

[136] This is the "Presupposition" that precedes the First Week (*Exercises*, §22).

[137] The Neapolitan Gian Pietro Carafa, Bishop of Chieti and co-founder of the Theatines, was made a cardinal in December 1536; already at that date Ignatius seems to have fallen into disfavour with him (see *Select Letters* No. 7 [MHSI *Epist.* I, 114-8]); there will be several references to him in the *Memoriale*, e.g. §§ 17, 182, 325-6, 346b.

that it was the Theatine cardinal himself who had been elected, and he had taken the name of Paul IV. On hearing this news the Father experienced a great shock and his face changed, and as I also learned later (though I do not remember whether it was from himself or from one of the older fathers to whom he had told it) all the bones of his body felt twisted.[138] He got up without saying a word and went to pray in the chapel. A little later he came out as happy and content as if the election had gone very much as he had wanted. Since the Pope was badly received and there were criticisms in Rome about him, because he was considered there as excessively rigorous, Father immediately began to look for and discover his good qualities and actions, since good works could be observed in him, and afterwards he pointed them out to those who talked about him.

This same Pontiff became a great friend of the Society and favoured it in the last years of his life,[139] saying there was nothing he more admired, and he tried to assist it financially with the revenues from abbeys, which he himself sought in order to transfer them to our colleges. Therefore even he demonstrated the often repeated saying of our Father, that there would never be a pope who was not a great friend of the Society.

94 To avoid this same vice of grumbling and detraction, he also used another method, especially when it was a question of the person or actions of the sovereign pontiffs; this was that not only did he not speak of what the pope might have done or ordered, but he did not even remotely insinuate or say what he might or ought to do in future for the good government and administration of the Church.

The only exception I recall was when Marcellus II, a great friend of the Society,[140] was elected [April 1555], and the whole of Rome had great hopes that he would reform the Church. When

---

[138] In the original Portuguese, *revolverão*, which is even stronger than in the modern Spanish translation *se le estremecieron*, "shuddered."

[139] The MHSI editors point out that this statement is somewhat dubious: certainly Paul IV began with open disapproval of the Society's colleges in Rome, but later he does seem to have made some donation to the Roman College; he also respected the wishes of Ignatius while he was alive, but as soon as he [Ignatius] was dead Paul IV imposed sung office and a limited General's term of office on the Society (both papal rulings becoming void at his death).

[140] See §330.

we fathers were discussing this subject in his presence, he replied that for any pope to reform the world he thought three things were necessary and sufficient: the reform of himself, the reform of his household, and the reform of the Papal Court and City of Rome.[141]

95 In the same way that our Father was very careful to say nothing that could in any way suggest a shadow of a fault in the person of the supreme pontiff, so he also ardently desired that all members of the Society should take the greatest pains to do the same. While preaching in Rome Fr. Gerolamo Otello[142] happened to say from the pulpit that there were such and such things the Pope should do. Our Father called for him and asked him how many popes there were in Rome. And when he replied that there was only one, the Father said to him, "And is it usual to talk about particular persons in sermons? Go away, then, and consider carefully the penance you deserve, and then come and tell me." At these words Fr. Otello went away and was so distressed that he felt he could not make satisfaction for so great a fault, and he proposed to our Father a number of penances so that his Reverence could choose the one that he thought most suitable: for instance, to make a pilgrimage on foot to Jerusalem (even barefoot, I believe), or to fast for so many years on bread and water, or to discipline himself through the streets of Rome for a long time, and others that I do not remember. But since our Father saw in him what he most desired, he only allowed him one or several disciplines in the refectory. Our Father sent this Fr. Gerolamo Otello to Sicily as preacher, when he ordered Benedetto Palmio[143] to come here to follow a course of lectures. And since he was a man of great virtue and much loved in Rome, people were very sad to see him go, so much so that once when our Father was saying Mass in the church on a feast day, shortly after the departure of Fr. Gerolamo, when he came to the Confiteor and said, *mea culpa, mea culpa* ["through my fault, through my fault"[144]] an old lady called out from the back at the top of her voice, "You're quite right to tell your fault, because you've sent Fr. Gerolamo Otello away from here!"

---

[141] See §343 with note.
[142] See §74.
[143] See §49; this transfer took place in 1553.
[144] The *Confiteor* ["I confess"] can still be said at the beginning of the liturgy.

96 Tonight our Father happened to make the following observation to me, "God always gives much strength and consolation in those things that the devil has worked to cause ruin in a soul and has not succeeded."

97 He also said that at Manresa he had seen *the little Gerson*[a],145 for the first time, and that since then he had never wished to read any other devotional book. He recommended it to all he had dealings with, and each day read a chapter one after the other; after dinner and at other times he would open it at random, and he always came across something that was close to his heart at that time and which he needed.

[a] *the little Gerson*

98 Our Father was so familiar with this book that when I knew him in Rome I thought I saw and recognized written into his conversation everything I had read in it; his words, movements and all the rest of his works were for him a continuous putting it into practice, and for those who had contact with him, a living lesson from Gerson. I can bear good witness to this because at that time I was very attached to the book and kept a special remembrance of it.

I recall equally well that I was greatly impressed there in Rome when I read the *Constitutions* for the first time, shortly before returning to Portugal,[146] for as I read them I seemed to see in them then a portrait of our Father.

He himself also told me that when he was studying in Alcalá many people, including even his own confessor (at that time Fr. Miona,[147] from Portugal, born in the Algarve, who afterwards joined and died in the Society and was already considered at that time a man of great virtue) advised him to read the *Enchiridion*

---

[145] This was the title commonly given at this time to *The Imitation of Christ*, now usually attributed to Thomas à Kempis (c. 1380-1471) and not to Jean le Charlier de Gerson (1363-1429), Chancellor of the University of Paris and influential churchman.

[146] Although officially published only in 1558, the *Constitutions* were written between 1544 and 1550 and Nadal began promulgating them in 1552 (in Sicily); so da Câmara could easily have had access to them before his departure from Rome in October, 1555.

[147] Manuel Miona, probably referred to, though not named, in the *Autobiography* (§60 with note) at the time of the second trial in Alcalá of 1527; Ignatius wrote to him from Venice in November 1536 explaining the importance of the *Spiritual Exercises* (*Select Letters* No. 6 [MHSI, *Epist.*, nn. 10, 1, 111-12]); he joined the Society in 1545, and later worked in Sicily before returning to Rome, where he died in 1567.

militis christiani[148] of Erasmus, but he did not wish to do so because he had already heard that author criticised by some preachers and those in authority. To those who recommended the book he replied that there would be no lack of other books whose authors had not been criticised by anyone, and it was those he preferred to read.[149]

99 [n.d.] I must recall the way in which our Father deals with affairs: (i) how he never uses emotions to persuade, but facts; (ii) how he does not adorn facts with words, but rather with the facts themselves, relating so many and so decisive circumstances that they convince, by their own force as it were; (iii) how his account is simple, clear and distinct. And he has such a good memory for events, and *even for important words,*[a] that he will narrate a past occurrence ten, fifteen, or more times *omnino* [entirely] as it occurred, so that he places it before your eyes; as for a long conversation on an important matter, he can repeat it word for word.

[a] *and even for important words*

100 When he was dealing with important matters, our Father would have them read to him, or have the details related, three or four times, so that they became so engraved in his memory that I remember having heard him tell and repeat them on widely separate occasions in the same order and with exactly the same words that he had said or heard them the first time. Other older Fathers have made the same observation over much longer intervals of time, because they had dealings with him before me.

---

[148] The famous *Manual of a Christian Soldier*, a devout work by Erasmus that became very popular; a Spanish translation was published in Alcalá by friends of Ignatius while he was studying there (1526-27), see §245. Some have questioned the accuracy of da Câmara's testimony at this point, as other contemporaries (notably Ribadeneira and Polanco) state that it was in Barcelona, in 1524-25, when beginning to learn Latin, that Ignatius was urged to read the text (partly as a school exercise) and even then disliked the work. The whole question is entangled by the ecclesiastical condemnations levelled at the *Enchiridion* (especially by the Dominicans, who were also fiercely critical of the *Spiritual Exercises*) in the intervening years. Thus, while there seems little doubt that the differences between the two men, despite their common respect for spirituality, were very far-reaching (cf. Terence O'Reilly, (1974) [Bibliography]); on the other hand, the similarities between them are very striking (cf. Mark Rotsaert [1982] [Bibliography]).

[149] The same remark is reported later, §245, and for the same reason Ignatius objected to the works of Savonarola (§244).

FEBRUARY

3 February

101 1. Father was asked if it would be good to encourage among these boys a little emulation and *competition*[a] in the fight for virtue. He said that it would, because as they were boys, one could play with them like kittens.

[a] *competition*

This was nothing more than inciting someone to virtue with the example of another telling him about or praising the other's deeds. The boys were Job, who joined when he was fourteen, and Cincinnato, who was about fifteen.[1]

102 Our Father often leads his subjects along this road, that is to say, praising them for their good qualities and flattering them. It is surprising with what *circumspection*[b] he treats any person whomsoever, unless it happens to be *a Nadal or a Polanco;*[c] these he treats without any respect but rather *duriter* [harshly] and with rigorous *capelos* [admonitions].[2]

---

[1] On these brothers see §§29,75; the use of (playful) emulation as a pedagogical means of helping Jesuit scholastics and other students is also found in the *Constitutions*, IV, 6L [§383], 13, 2-3 [§§454-56] and came to be incorporated in the influential *Ratio Studiorum* of 1599 (cf. *Constitutions* and *Examen*, p. 216, note 4); however, Ignatius clearly thought of it as a valid principle also in the promotion of spiritual development (cf. *Constitutions* III, 1, 19 [§276]).

[2] The word comes from the Italian *cappello, cappelli* (literally "hat[s]") which became a slang word in ecclesiastical circles for a reprimand usually with a penance. The French translator points out that the "circumspection" used by Ignatius is not simply clever psychology and prudent diplomacy, but is part of the spiritual discernment expected of a good Superior General (cf. *Constitutions*, IX, 2, 6 [§729]).

(b) *circumspection*

103 He was circumspect in his dealings with everyone, so that even if they had some weakness, they were not left hurt by his words or his style of conversation. He adapted himself to the state of soul and the character of his subjects; this happened even in very small matters, as for example when he ordered someone to tell Fr. Benedetto,[3] at that time a brother, that he had gained a listener for him, because once, when he left the house, he told an old lady that she should go to our church to listen to the sermon that Fr. Benedetto was going to preach; or when talking to Fr. Polanco he greatly praised Fr. Olave, or Fr. Polanco when he talked to Fr. Olave, because he knew they were great friends of one another.[4]

(c) *a Nadal or a Polanco*

104 He treated all the early fathers in the same way. Just as there was no one more affectionate and affable than he, so when our Father was angry, no one was feared as much. Fr. Ribadeneira told me that once when the Father was discussing an important affair with Fr. Laínez who was over-insisting on a certain point, the words our Father said to him were, "Very well, you take over the Society and govern it!", in a way that cut Fr. Laínez short, incapable of uttering another word. All this took place in the presence of Fr. Ribadeneira.

105 [n.d.] Our Father once said—a few days ago—that if anyone measured his affection by the way he showed it externally, that person would be greatly deceived, and the same of his lack of love or in his harsh treatment. *Vere* [truly] we may say of the Father that *suscipit infirmos in spiritu lenitatis, etc.* ["he gives help to the weak . . . in a spirit of gentleness" and so on][5] and that he gave *those already robust*[d] dry bread and food for

---

[3] This is Fr. Benedetto Palmio, mentioned above in §95; there is another version of the story, given by a Lithuanian Jesuit, Nicholas Lenczyski ("Lancicius" in Latin) who later in the century collected memories of Ignatius: he narrates that Fr. Palmio himself invited an old lady to come and hear him preach, and when Ignatius found out he offered to invite other old ladies to go and listen to him (MHSI *Scripta,* I, 495).

[4] They may have met in Paris as early as 1533 when Polanco was a sixteen-year-old student there and Olave a young lecturer.

[5] A combination of two Pauline passages: 1 Thessalonians 5:14 ("help the weak") and Galatians 6:1 ("if a man is overtaken in any trespass . . . restore him in a spirit of gentleness").

grown men.[6]

(d) those already robust

106 In the world Giovanni Battista[7] was a man who had considerable possessions. He was a dealer in spices; others who sold food that can be kept, such as honey, oils, cheeses, and similar products, thought much of him. He knew a lot about accounts, and a little Latin. He was a devout man even before joining the Society, especially in devotion to Our Lady. As a Brother he has been the cook in the house in Rome until now, and given great edification. He was much loved by our Father and therefore treated in accordance with this love, following his rule and custom. He trained him in every kind of mortification and penance; many times he ordered him to eat nothing except soup, if it happened that he put more or less salt than was required into the food, and similar mistakes, such as in the nature of his duties often happened.

He brought with him from the world a crucifix with a figure of Our Lady at its foot; it was an image of great value and devotion, and he was very attached to it. At first the Father allowed him to use it, but after some time he took it away to his oratory, and he told me that since Battista had planted and sculpted Christ crucified in his soul, he supported more easily having the image taken away from him. He would allow a whole year to pass without seeing him or speaking to him; he did not permit any fault of his to pass without reprimand, and he never praised him in his presence for the good things he was doing, though, in his absence he spoke of him with indications of great love and satisfaction as a perfect man, and particularly praised his humility, obedience and other virtues.

To sum up, I do not recall having seen him praise so much, or treat so badly, anyone else in the house, although he also greatly

---

[6] A reminiscence of 1 Peter 2:2. where the "milk" is for the "newborn babes."

[7] Giovanni Battista di Anzola seems to have entered the Society as a Brother coadjutor in 1553 and is mentioned in catalogues of 1571 and later; one of the miracles attributed to Ignatius in the process of canonization involves the cure of one of this Brother's badly burnt hands (MHSI *Scripta*, II, pp. 475-79).

praised Maestro Lorenzo,[8] the bricklayer; he said of him that the
bricks he laid in the walls each day were more than the words he
spoke, and in other ways he treated him very lovingly.

107 [n.d.] I must recall the details of this, how he treats each one of
those who are very virtuous and whom he greatly trusts, taking care not
to hurt them, if he does not know from experience that they are the sort
of men to accept one kind of treatment as happily as another. In this way
the Father when he begins conversing with someone, at first grants him
everything, and speaks to him in such a way that even though he might
be very imperfect, he could not take scandal. Afterwards, as he grows to
know him, and the man gains spiritual strength, the Father begins to
remove things from him little by little, so that without him sensing any
violence, he changes the whole game: e.g. a learned doctor joins the
Society, *as it might be*[a] Father Olave: our Father first calls him "Señor
Dr.," and "Your honour," but later drops one of these, and later still
leaves him only as "Dr.," and then plainly just with his name—*ut sic
diceret* [so to speak] at first "Dr. Olave, Sir, would your honour kindly do
so-and-so. . ."; later, "Dr. Olave, please do so-and-so. . ."; them simply,
"Olave. . . ," and so treats him accordingly in everything else.
Nevertheless in matters of health he always takes very special care.

[a] *as it might be*

108 I knew that this happened almost exactly as has been said.

As a further example of the same I will relate here how our
Father received me in Rome, and how he behaved towards me for
the first months after my arrival. When Fr. Dr. Miguel de Torres
came as Visitor to this province of Portugal in 1552, as has been
said,[9] he found many things that needed to be reported in detail to
Fr. Ignatius. Since he thought I had some knowledge of them, he
then ordered me to write down a minute account of them to send
to our Father. When I had drafted a long letter on the subject
(which, in order to relate the matter more freely, I pretended I was
writing to Fr. Master Melchior Nunes,[10] provincial of India) the

[8] Lorenzo Tristano became a Brother coadjutor in the Society in 1552 and worked
partly in his trade, partly as door-keeper until his death, 1586.

[9] Preface, §7; see also below, §269 with note.

[10] Melchior Nunes Barreto (1519/227-1571), a Jesuit since 1543, was sent to India in
1551 as Provincial; his brother, João, was Patriarch of Ethiopia (see §§52, 120), but died

father Visitor changed his opinion, and thought it would be better if I went to Rome to inform our Father about these matters by word of mouth, in order to give him full information on all these matters, as he wished and as was necessary. For this purpose he sent me to Rome, as I have already said.[11]

109 The day I arrived our Father spoke to me, even though he rarely did so with those arriving from abroad, and I think that I had supper with him that same evening. He received me standing up and welcomed me with great consideration and joy, but without the kind of celebration and warmth that we here [in Portugal] are used to show towards our guests. The following day, which was Wednesday, an Ember Day [24 May], we fasted; when Thursday arrived, partly from the exhaustion of the journey and partly from fasting, I had an attack of dizziness while saying Mass. Our Father heard of this and asked me in a tone of affectionate reproof (as he always began) why I had not told him the previous day how I felt and the harm fasting might do me. I remember that he was very pleased that I gave this reply, "I did not tell you, Father, because I am not so mortified."

Our Father used to order all the members of the Society who arrived in Rome for the first time to take some exercise in the fresh air of Rome every morning before sunrise, so that the local climate, which is harmful to foreigners, should not harm them. Accordingly I was told as soon as I arrived that I also should take the same exercise. I did so for two or three days, and as I thought that it was not an order imposed by obedience or a rule to be observed by all those arriving from abroad, but only a permission given to me, I neglected to do so one of the days of the first week. Our Father heard of this and sent for me; he asked me why I had not gone to take exercise, and when he had heard my excuse he imposed as a penance on me that next Sunday I should eat at the "little table" and that Antonio Rion[12] should reprimand me. But in order to lighten the penance for me, and to keep to the custom which I mentioned he observed with those he dealt with for the first time, he gave me as fellow penitents both Fr. Polanco and Fr.

in Goa in 1561; Melchior (whose name is regularly spelled "Belchior" by da Câmara) was the first Jesuit to enter China (1555), while visiting his subjects in Japan, 1554-57.

[11] Preface (above), §7.

[12] Brother Antonio Rion, an Italian Brother coadjutor, a specialist in dressing people down; see §§140, 324, and cf. Glossary.

Olave. From then on I followed exactly the rule of the house.

110 Although our Father knew perfectly well why I had been sent to Rome, nevertheless he kept me waiting several months without asking me anything about the affairs of the [Portuguese] province, as if I had not come for this reason (a style of silent mortification that he frequently employed, very prudently and forcefully). And, truly, I felt that I greatly benefited from being left forgotten like this. And therefore I resolved to reflect on myself and to read the Scriptures. During the whole of that summer I had no duties other than to say Mass, recite my office, and read the Scriptures with the aid of a commentary that a Brother Novice read to me.[13] I always ate, however, at our Father's table.

But during all this time I did not speak a single word to him about myself, until one Friday morning, 4 August, the eve of the feast of Our Lady of the Snows, when I talked to him in the garden with great comfort to my soul, as may be seen by the text that I wrote in Rome as a Preface to that which I wrote about the life of our Father, which he himself related to me. And even if it is not perfect, I have decided it would be good to put it here so that it will not be completely lost, since it contains some memories of our Father.

111 "In the year [15]53, one Friday in the morning, 4 August, the vigil of Our Lady of the Snows, as the Father was in the garden near the house or apartment which is called 'The Duke's',[14] I began to give him an account of some characteristic features of my soul, and among others I told him about vainglory. The remedy the Father gave me was that I should often make an act of attributing everything in me to God, working to offer him all the good I

---

[13] The Spanish translator notices that this may be a further indication of da Câmara's problems of sight.

[14] "Francis Borgia, Duke of Gandía, had spent three months in Rome in 1550-51, and he and his entourage had stayed in a wing of the Jesuit house. His membership in the Society was still secret at that point" (P. Endean, *Autobiography*, [Introduction], p. 11, note 6).

might find in myself, acknowledging it as his and giving
him thanks for it. On this he spoke to me in such a way that
it greatly consoled me, in such a way that I could not hold
back the tears. And so it was that the Father told me how
he had been troubled by this vice for two years, to such an
extent that, when he was getting on the boat in Barcelona
for Jerusalem, he did not dare tell anyone he was going to
Jerusalem, and likewise with other similar details. And he
added further how much peace in this regard he had later
felt in his soul.

"An hour or two later we went in to eat. While Master
Polanco and I were eating with him,[15] our Father said that
Master Nadal and others of the Society had many times
asked him to do something, and that he had never made up
his mind about it, but that, having recollected himself in his
room after having spoken with me, he had such great devotion and such a great inclination to do it, and (speaking in
such a way as to show that God had given him great clarity on his duty to do it) he had made his mind up completely. And the thing was to give an account of all that had
passed through his soul up to that time. And he had also
decided that it was to be myself to whom he would reveal
these things.

"The Father was then very ill, and never accustomed to
promising himself a day of life. On the contrary, when
someone says, 'I'll do this in two weeks' time or a week's
time,' the Father always says, as if astounded, 'Really? And
you expect to live that long?' Nevertheless, this time he said
that he expected to live three or four months in order to fin-
ish this thing.

"The next day I spoke to him asking when he wanted us to
begin. And he answered me that I should remind him about
it each day (I cannot remember how many days) until he
was in a position to do it. Then, not being in such a position, partly given his occupations, he later decided that I
should remind him about it every Sunday. Then the following September (I cannot remember what day in it),[16] the

---

[15] As he mentions later (§374) these two were regular guests at Ignatius's table.

[16] There is a discrepancy here with the statement in the *Autobiography* (§10) that
Ignatius was dictating the early part of it in August 1553; of course the Preface

*Father called me and began to tell me his whole life, even
his mischiefs as a lad, clearly and distinctly, with all their
surrounding details. Afterwards he called me three or four
times in the same month and arrived with the story at the
part when he was in Manresa for some days.*"[17]

112 [n.d.] One thing astounds me at times about our Father: it seems
from his manner of speaking that he holds a good opinion of everyone,
as though he presumes that they are perfect or have serious intentions of
becoming perfect. Still, when it comes to finding employment for them,
he places each in what suits him best. But this does not mean that he
always gives confidential tasks to those who have been well tested; rather
in Rome he sometimes gives people tasks to test them, whereas outside
Rome he very rarely allots confidential tasks to anyone about whom he
is not certain.

113 [n.d.] Our Father has great skill in dealing with souls. He uses so
many means that it seems almost impossible that anyone should fail to
profit, if that person really wants to gain some advantage. The ordinary
methods are: to recommend the making of examination [of conscience]
and the practise of prayer, to have *syndics*, to urge *the giving an account*[(a)]
to someone every day as to how much one is benefiting from these methods.

   [(a)] *the giving an account*

     This was a method so much in use in our Father's time, that
     from its continual practice I drew this general conclusion, without
     noting particular cases.

114 [n.d.] Our Father is accustomed to cooperate very closely with natural inclinations, *velut* [as it were] concurring with them, i.e., as far as
possible he never deals violently with anyone. On the contrary, even
things not usually undertaken voluntarily, such as public disciplines and
other penances for faults, these are set by our Father in such a way that
they are chosen and wanted. *Imo* [even more], he diminishes what a person has chosen, so that he who does the penance remains always full of

was not written until some time later, probably just before da Câmara departed for
Portugal and he admits that his memory of these dates is somewhat hazy.

   [17] *Autobiography*, Introduction, pp. 5-6; the translation is that by Philip Endean with
a few minor adjustments.

love, with the knowledge that he deserved more and without bitterness. In order to achieve this effect Father uses many means, *etiam* [even] including human respect, for example so that one may be held more esteemed etc.

> *Marginal note: Hoc est* [that is] by telling the subject that others would have a low opinion of him, if he did not give satisfaction and do penance.

115 All that is said in this passage about how our Father took into account the inclinations of his subjects, was on the understanding (which he also put into practice) that they were truly his sons, and sons of the Society. I mean to say that they were those who were perfectly obedient and entirely resigned to the opinion and will of the superior. For, in the case of those who did not have this indifference and self-abnegation, he did not rest until he had seen them completely dead in their self-judgment and self-will, or finally he expelled them from the Society. The superior of one of the provinces ordered one of his priests to go to Rome; the priest was a doctor of theology and generally reckoned a man of outstanding virtue, eminently learned and talented, and he was sent to Rome because he was so exceptional. Our Father talked to him, but finding he was a man of such fixed judgment that it was difficult to dissuade him from what he wanted, once he was convinced how difficult it would be for him to allow himself to be mortified and overcome, he expelled him from the Society.

Another priest, who was a learned man and had been in a position of authority, was also sent to Rome on important business by his provincial, who, like the rest of his province, had a high opinion of him. Despite the fact that Fr. Ignatius had received a good account of him, nevertheless simply because he noted he was little inclined to subject his own judgment and opinions, he decided and made clear that he felt obliged to keep the man with him until he had removed the man's confidence in his own judgment. In order to do this he strove hard to keep him in Rome; but it seems he did not succeed, because of the faults of the priest himself, since years later, after he had returned to his own province, he left the Society, not without some scandal.

116   To sum up, our Father enjoyed guiding according to their inclinations those men whom he saw equipped with those dispositions which he himself dictated word by word to Giovanni Filippo[18] who at that time helped Fr. Polanco in the secretariat, acting as his Assistant Secretary, dispositions which I have decided to insert here. Our Father dictated these points when Francisco Marín was expelled from the Society; Marín was an unwilling and disobedient subject, as has been said.[19]

Marginal Note: Here should be placed those points that will come from Rome.

[INSTRUCTIONS ON OBEDIENCE[20]]

(1) On entering the religious life or having already entered it, I must be resigned in all things, and for all things before God Our Lord and before my superior.

(2) I must desire to be governed and guided by that superior who looks after the abnegation of one's own judgment and understanding.

(3) I must, in all things where there is no sin, do his will and not my own.

(4) There are three ways to obey: first, when it is by virtue of obedience that I am ordered and this is good; second, when I am just given an order to do this or that, and this is better; third, when I do this or that aware of some sign from my superior even though he has not ordered or commanded me, and this is much more perfect.

(5) I ought not to take account of whether my superior is the highest, or the intermediate, or the lowest, but all my devotion in obedience must be because he is in the place of God our Lord, because if one makes distinctions the force of obedience is lost.

(6) When I hold an opinion or judge that the superior orders me to do something which is against my conscience, or a sin, and it seems the contrary to the superior, I must

---

[18] Giovanni Filippo Vito was ordained priest in this same year (1555), but died in Rome in 1558.

[19] See §48.

[20] The French translator notes that one scholar has questioned da Câmara's account here and suggested that Cristóbal de Madrid (see §27) may have had a hand in drawing up these instructions: cf. J.-F. Gilmont, *Les écrits spirituels des premiers jésuites*, Rome (IHSI), 1961, p. 257, n. 3.

believe him, unless there is some proof; and if I cannot stop my thoughts, at least putting to one side my judgement and way of seeing the matter, I ought to leave the judgement and decision to one, two, or three others. If I do not reach this stage, I am very far from perfection and the qualities required in a true religious.

(7) Finally, I must not belong to myself but rather to Him who created me and to him who is in his place, and I should allow myself to be governed and led, just as a pellet of wax allows itself to be drawn along with a thread,[21] whether it be about writing or receiving letters, or about speaking with people, these or those, putting all my devotion into what I have been ordered to do.

(8) I should consider my self to be (i) like a dead corpse, which has no will or understanding; (ii) second, like a small crucifix that allows itself to be moved about from one place to another without any difficulty; (iii) third, I should pretend to be and act like a stick in the hand of an old man, so that he can put me wherever he wishes and where I may help him most; that is how I should be prepared so that the religious order may be helped and served by me in everything that I may be ordered to do.

(9) I should not ask, beg, or entreat the superior to send me to a particular place or to a particular duty, but explain my thoughts and wishes; and once they have been made clear, cast them out, leaving the superior to judge and decide, and consider that best which he may judge and order.

(10) Tamen [nevertheless] in matters that are good but of slight importance one may ask permission, such as, for instance, to do the Stations of the Churches, or ask for concessions, or similar things, with the soul prepared to accept that whatever is granted or not, will be for the best.

(11) Similarly, as far as poverty is concerned, one should not consider or value anything as one's own possession, but recognize that everything that one has is only for one's use: so one is dressed and decorated like a statue, which does not resist in any way when, and for whatever reason, its covers are removed.

---

[21] The words "with a thread" are missing in some of the manuscripts, and Ribadeneira in his Latin version of this text suggests that the image may be of a pellet of wax being kneaded by the fingers.

117 [n.d.] Our Father once said these words, "I very much want every-one to have an overall indifference, etc., but even so, provided there is obedience and abnegation on the part of the subject, I have found it a great advantage to follow his inclinations." And the Father acts according to this principle, i.e., when he wants to send a man to study, or somewhere outside Rome, or to give him a particular task, he examines him to see where his inclinations lie (presupposing indifference). The way of examining the person is this: to make him pray or say Mass, and to ask him to give him three points in writing: first, if he is ready to go under obedience; second, if he is inclined to go; third, if it were left to him, which would he choose. He also uses another method of examining people, that is asking someone else to talk to the person and draw out his inclination. The Father uses the first of these methods in more important matters, such as missions, etc.; here he obliges everyone to write down their replies, as he did *for Prester John*[a] and *for Loreto.*[b] He uses the second method, in nearly all or in all cases when he is not certain of the inclination. The inclination counts for so much with our Father that when the consult deliberates who shall go to such-and-such a place, or who shall undertake such-and-such a task (once presupposed the aptitude), one of the reasons that weighs most with the Father is that the man is inclined or not inclined to it, and this is how things are normally done.

It is also true that while the Father approves these inclinations, in accordance with obedience, he nevertheless greatly praises those who never show any inclination to anything, except to obey. Such was the case with Fr. Nadal, the other day, when going to Loreto was under discussion; he indicated in writing that he had no inclination to anything, unless it was to not being inclined. *Such was the case with Olivier**,[c] the new Rector of the college at Loreto, from whom our Father could never elicit whether he would prefer to go to Venice or stay in Gubbio (because of this the Father praised him greatly). Such was also *the case with Ferrão***,[d] Father made him spend long periods of prayer for many days in the chapel, but he was never able to draw from him whether he was inclined to study or not to study, even though Father used various methods and *quasi* [almost] force to make him say.

*Marginal Note: This is the present provincial of France.[22]
**Marginal Note: Portuguese nobleman from Castello Branco.[23]

[22] See §125.
[23] See §126.

(a) *for Prester John*

118 Because of the many demands and requests of Prester John, the Emperor of Ethiopia,[24] King João III[25] decided to send a patriarch to those kingdoms, to convert them and instruct them in the customs and obedience of the Roman Church. In 1546 he sent to Fr. Ignatius a request to appoint Fr. Pierre Favre;[26] the king had already known him and appreciated his sanctity in the kingdom of Portugal, and he gave him letters of recommendation when he left here for Castile with Fr. Araoz.[27] When the king's message reached Rome, our Lord had called Fr. Pierre Favre to Himself, and Fr. Ignatius proposed Fr. Paschase Broët[28] in his place, but as the King knew nothing about him, he did not accept him. The matter, therefore, remained unsettled. It was, however, of such interest to our Father, and so close to his heart, that he set himself most diligently to compose an Instruction, in which he showed with many arguments how important it was, not only because of the fruit of the conversion and the good of the Church, but also for the service and temporal well-being of the King, that the matter should go forward. He sent this Instruction to me in this Province [Portugal] with letters for the King, and he wrote to me, if I remember correctly, in his own hand, in very definite terms, that it should be negotiated with all possible vigour and diligence.[29]

And I recall that after making much of the matter in the letters to the King, he offered him the whole Society from which to choose those men he considered most suitable for the task, saying

---

[24] Legends of a Christian kingdom in the East governed by a priest-king, "Prester John," seemed confirmed when an ambassador arrived in Portugal from a ruler, known later in the West as King Claudius; this was Galâwdêwos of Abyssinia/Ethiopia (1540-59): for a full account (in English), cf. Philip Caraman, *The Lost Empire: The Story of the Jesuits in Ethiopia, 1555-1634*, London, 1985; brief information in *Inigo: Letters*, No. 63 [pp. 239-49], where a translation of the long instruction drawn up by Ignatius to assist the new Patriarch is available; for the original text cf. MHSI *Epist.* VIII, pp. 680-90.

[25] João III, King of Portugal (1521-57).

[26] See §8.

[27] March, 1545.

[28] Paschase (or Pasquier) Broët (1500-62) was already a priest in 1534 when he came to Paris and joined the first companions (after Ignatius had left); he was one of the founding group in 1540, and was sent with Salmerón on the abortive Irish mission (1542); subsequently he did pastoral and administrative work (as provincial) in Italy until 1552, and then in France.

[29] Probably the letter published in MHSI *Epist.* II, pp. 304-09.

that if His Majesty judged it necessary he would himself leave everything to go in person to Prester John just for that purpose.[30]

119 But, in the end, nothing could be achieved at that time, until in 1554, after my arrival in Rome, the King asked again for three members of the Society, one of whom would at once be appointed Patriarch of Ethiopia, and the other two would be made bishops, with right of succession to the same patriarchate. He said that, if it were possible, he would be pleased if they were Portuguese, or, if not, of any other nation.

Our Father was very happy with this news and arranged for all the Fathers in Rome to reply in writing on the three points of which I speak here, and I believe, though I do not recall exactly, that at the same time he asked for the opinions and votes of everyone to elect those who should go. But since the Portuguese Ambassador deferred the execution of this matter for three whole months, Father sent me, every other day, to his residence, which was a long way from ours,[31] to remind him to execute the matter. This went on so long we called it "the Ambassador's tertian ague."

120 While the King was dealing with this for the second time, Fr. João Nunes[32] arrived in this kingdom [Portugal] from Tetuán to deal with the business of the redemption of captives, a work with which, under obedience, he was occupied in Africa. While he was at court dealing with this subject, he so pleased the King, that he recommended him expressly to Fr. Ignatius for the dignity of Patriarch. When Fr. João Nunes heard of this he wrote to our Father on the matter, telling him how deeply the weight of that dignity would weigh upon him and how he thought himself unsuitable and weak to bear such an honour. At the same time he showed much religious indifference[33] and great willingness to take

[30] A copy exists of a hand-written letter from Ignatius to João III, not dated but probably October, 1546, in which he offers to take on the Ethiopian mission if no one else is available, and if he is not forbidden by his companions (MHSI *Epist.* I, p. 429, Letter 140).

[31] The Embassy was in the suburb of Montecitorio.

[32] His life story is recounted by da Câmara; a few dates may be added: 1544 entry into the Society, 1548-54, work in North Africa, 1555 consecration as Patriarch, 1556-62 resident in India, 1562 death in Goa.

[33] "Indifference" is a key word in the *Spiritual Exercises* (e.g. §23), and has the technical sense of "an attitude of equipoise . . . neutralizing . . . the effects of disordered affections" (Ivens, *Understanding the Spiritual Exercises*, p. 31).

up whatever cross or work obedience might impose on him, especially in the conversion of infidels in those regions, and all the others of India. Thus it was clearly seen from this that while he completely disclaimed the honour of the office, he sought and desired the work it would entail.

Fr. Ignatius was so pleased with this letter that simply because of it and with the information gathered from those of us who knew him, he chose him. He did not then know about the supernatural vocation by which Our Lord has brought Fr. Nunes into the Society. I will tell the story briefly here because it touches on a person placed in such outstanding dignity within the Church of God, and of such exemplary virtue, and because I owe him so much for his having been for a long time my confessor, and we were companions on the mission in Africa.[34]

121 Fr. João Nunes was a native of the city of Oporto, born of very good and rich parents; he was so recollected and exemplary in his conduct that the students at Salamanca where he studied called him the "holy abbot." Since he thought he had already learned enough to fulfil his obligations, he went to live in a church that belonged to him in the Archbishopric of Braga, and stayed there for some time, each day making six hours of mental prayer, to which he was particularly attached.

At this time Fr. Melchior Nunes,[35] a brother of his by blood, joined the Society. He was the first student to be admitted to the Society from the University of Coimbra; he was sent on a pilgrimage to Santiago de Compostela in Galicia, and passing the church where his brother the priest was, he begged him and tried to persuade him then and there to join the Society. His brother was, however, so much given to the repose and peace of contemplation that he excused himself, saying that he did not see in himself the talents required for the practices of the active life which the Society also professes, even though all these practices seemed very good to him. Fr. Master Melchior departed after receiving this reply, and his brother stayed on in his retreat.

122 Not much later, while he was asleep one night, he dreamed that he saw a priest saying Mass: he was assisting him, and when

---

[34] In 1548 da Câmara had accompanied João Nunes to Ceuta, but had to return because of ill health.
[35] See §108.

he went to offer him the kiss of peace on the right-hand side, as is customary, the priest would not accept it, and indicated that he should give it on the left side. During this dispute about whether to give the sign of peace on the side contrary to that wanted by the priest, he became fully awake, and immediately interpreted the dream as meaning that he could not receive the greeting on the right side (which signified the contemplative life), which is where he had been seeking it, but rather on the left side (which signified the active life), where he had believed it could not be found. This made such an impression on him and he gave it so much importance that the following day he left for Coimbra to arrange his entry into the Society. When he saw Fr. Favre, who had just arrived from Flanders,[36] he recognized him as the priest whom he had seen saying Mass in his dream. He told him about all his affairs, and Fr. Favre immediately received him into the Society.

He lived in the Society for [eighteen][37] years, and all that time he was occupied in active works with exemplary edification. He died in Goa [eight] years after he had been nominated Patriarch, while he was hoping that the Viceroy of India would make arrangements for him to travel to the court of Prester John.

123 The two bishops whom Fr. Ignatius gave him as companions were Fr. Master Andrés de Oviedo,[38] a native of Illescas near Toledo, and Master Melchior Carneiro,[39] a Portuguese, a native of Coimbra. Both were in Rome when they were elected, and both resisted accepting the dignity and honour of the episcopate for which our Father had chosen them; so much so that they alleged

[36] December 1544, which is when Fr. João Nunes was received into the Society.

[37] Both this number and the "eight" two lines later are missing in the manuscript and have been supplied by the MHSI editors.

[38] Andrés de Oviedo (c.1517-1577) entered the Society in 1541 and had the rare distinction of being elected rector by his community in Gandia at a time (1547) when Ignatius was still searching for appropriate structures of government in the nascent Society (cf. *Select Letters*, No. 17); a man of deep spirituality, who helped attract Francis Borgia into the Society, he was also involved in a radical crisis (1549) which threatened the development of the Society (*ibid.*, No. 23); however, Ignatius recognized his value and appointed him rector in Naples (1551) before selecting him for the difficult Ethiopian mission (1555); he succeeded the first Patriarch and was able to enter Ethiopia, even though a change of Negus made the final years of his life very painful.

[39] Melchior Carneiro (1518-83) entered the Society in 1543; before leaving for India he had been the first rector of the new college in Evora; although he was never able to enter Ethiopia, he reached China, dying in Macao.

the Society could not oblige them to accept and Father Ignatius had to call a meeting of experts to decide what could and should be done, until finally they were chosen and nominated on the authority of the Pope, as the bulls of their consecration show.[40]

(b) for Loreto

124 In order to choose those who should go to found the College in Loreto, our Father used at home the same method he had employed for the mission to Prester John.[41] As this College was beginning, there was already anxiety about the difficulties, which later came because of the canons residing in Our Lady's House. They had hitherto heard the confessions of all the pilgrims, a ministry which the Society in large part took away from them, thereby taking also the alms and income they had formerly received.

(c) Such was the case with Olivier

125 The indifference[42] of Fr. Olivier[43] pleased Fr. Ignatius so much, as well as everything else he knew about him, that he sent him as rector to found the College in Loreto, of which there is mention here, in spite of the fact that he was so young and had been in the Society for so short a time. This Father was a Fleming by birth, whose language was French. He became later Provincial in France, and is now an Assistant and admonitor to the present Fr. General.

(d) the case with Ferrão

126 Bartolomeo Ferrão[44] was a native of Castello Branco in the

---

[40] This point is mentioned again below, §168.

[41] See §117.

[42] On the notion of religious indifference, see §120 note.

[43] Olivier Manare (1523-1614), born near Douai, had studied in Louvain; he entered the Society as a priest in 1550 and already in 1553 found himself appointed rector of the Roman College and then rector in Loreto (1554); he later became provincial of the French province, Assistant for Germany, and Vicar General on the death of Fr. Mercurian (1580); by the time he died (aged over 90) his numerous foundations in the Low Countries had won him the title (from Fr. Aquaviva) *of Pater Provinciae Belgicae.*

[44] Bartolomeo Ferrão had joined the first companions in Rome in 1538; he spent five years studying in Paris (1540-45) and succeeded Francis Xavier as secretary to Ignatius for a couple of years (1545-47), but died very young.

diocese of Guarda [Portugal]. He came from a noble family. When
I arrived in Rome in 1553, he had already been dead for some
years, but I found the odour of his sanctity was still fresh.
Everything I say here about him I learned from a very reliable
source. I am not sure even, if it was not from our Father himself,
who used to call him "inaccessible to temptation": he served the
Father as secretary, and was succeeded at his death by Fr.
Polanco.[45]

Marginal Note: Missing here are thirteen days,
because I spent them outside Rome on pilgrimage.

16 February

127 1. *Micer* Andreas,[46] a Fleming staying in this house for four or five
months, has been always all but decided to go back home to his country;
neither the Exercises nor other remedies have helped him very much. The
question is raised, what should be done for him?

Reply: the Father leaves the matter to the consult and to the Master
of Novices,[47] without himself taking part in the discussion.

Consult

128 Its advice is that he should be sent away; he should take money from
here on the surety of his own property, since he is a rich man: he should
leave immediately so that he can be accompanied by Nicolao.[48]

After the Father had given his earlier decision, he went to pray in the
chapel, recollecting himself, and when he had finished he gave orders

---

[45] A slight inaccuracy, as Polanco took over from Ferrão a few months before his death
[46] A young priest from Antwerp. Polanco, commenting on this unfortunate case, notes
that it brought out the need for a novitiate nearer home (MHSI, *Polanci Chronicon*, V, p.
297).
[47] This was Fr. Wischaven (see §83).
[48] This Nicolao is otherwise unknown, and Polanco, who also records the case of
Andreas, does not mention him (note of the MHSI editors).

that before the consult replied to *Micer* Andreas, they should inform him [the Father] of their decision; when he heard the decision, he said they should exhort Andreas to go alone, and make *Nicolao*[a] leave first without his knowing about Andreas; they should not take money from Andreas, nor give him anything more than he had brought with him, except for two or three *julios*[49] by way of alms. They should encourage him to go to Loreto, and tell him that if he first wishes *to be released from his vows*[b] here, that can be done. However, they should advise him to go and present himself to Our Lady, and decide before her whether he wishes to stay in this religious order or not. If he decides not, then his vows can be regarded as dispensed from that moment. And he should stay here for another week resting, either after he has received news of this decision, or for further reflection.

The Father added two further points: one, that we should give him everything that we can licitly give him, i.e. signs of affection, consolation, and love, i.e. everything he can ask of us; but not money, something he cannot licitly ask for, nor may we offer him the means to have it: it is much better for him to feel hardship and work. The second: that he should decide for himself at Loreto, because God usually helps more in a place where He is venerated than in another. Then the members of the consult told the Father about his temperament and temptation; this is not simply something from the devil, but seemed to be a fault in his temperament, because he was unable to explain himself and always went about as if bemused. To this the Father replied that even if this characteristic was due to his temperament, it might be all the more from the devil, who makes a man appear deprived of sense when the temptation is violent.

129 We were surprised when our Father, after having put everything into the hands of the consult, later changed his mind, contrary to his custom, asking that they should report to him what had been decided, so that he

---

[49] A small coin worth the tenth of a ducat.

could change it, as in effect he did.[50]

(a) *Nicolao*

Nicolao was a member of the Society who was sent to Flanders, but the Father did not wish the conversation of the Flemish priest to do him harm.

(b) *to be released from his vows*

The vows were those of the Society, but made solely out of devotion and before the fixed time had passed.

17 February
When the Father Went to the Villa[51]

130   1.   Concerning *the business of Paris*(a) the Father orders that our brethren there should send the authentic copies of the decree and of the privilege *permitting them the right to naturalisation.*(b)

(a) *the business of Paris*

This matter was the opposition to, and the decree which the Theology Faculty of Paris published against, the Society.

(b) *permitting them the right to naturalisation*

Ours[52] in France already had permission from the King to reside there as if they were naturalised citizens of that country.[53]

---

[50] See §220 for the further outcome of this case.

[51] In the early sources this is often called the viña (literally "the vineyard") and some-times the *granja* (or "farm"), but although it originally contained grape vines, when Ignatius arranged for its purchase (1554 or early in 1555), it was intended to be the site for a rest-house, or "villa" (in Portugese da Câmara calls it the "*quinta*") for the use of the Roman Jesuits, especially the students; and the term "villa House" became common in the Society for such establishments. It was situated on the Aventine, not far from Santa Balbina and overlooking the Baths of Caracalla: see §§134-35.

[52] Cf. Glossary.

[53] Henri II gave this permission, first by word of mouth (1550) and then by written decree (1551); but the *Parlement* refused to register this and appealed to the Theology Faculty, which issued a condemnation of the Society (1554); this subject will recur in the *Memoriale* (cf. Index, s.v. Paris).

2. He does not wish to do anything about this business at present until the bulls *about the donation*[a] of the College are sealed.

[a] *about the donation*

> Pope Julius III wanted to found and endow our Roman College, but this did not happen because of his death [23 March 1555]. The same occurred on the death of Marcellus II [1 May 1555], who also wished to found the College. And as correspondence came to Rome about the negotiations in Paris while our Father was occupied with the Bulls of this foundation, he delayed until he had settled the matter in hand, because he did not usually deal with two matters of importance at the same time, so as to be able to devote himself completely to each one of them.

131 3. This matter will never cause him any loss of sleep, because this is not the time to be as worried about these matters as at the beginning, when he was spending the whole day anxious about them; and even if he were sick he always found sufficient strength for such tasks. Because of [this] a common saying was coined in the house, which is still used, "When there's work to be done, Father's well." This is what happened with all the problems at the beginning: both about the bishopric for Jay,[54] and now, lately, this problem of Canisius.[55]

4. A letter should be written to Ours of the whole Society, beginning immediately today, telling them to send recommendations from rulers, governors, universities; and each college [should do this] on its own account, and each province.

132 5. The letter should be written in such a way, that all the critics can see it; *tamen* [however], in a confidential annex[56] our members can

---

[54] Claude Jay (c. 1500-52), one of the first companions in Paris and a close friend of his countryman, Pierre Favre; he worked in Italy and Germany, and also took part in the first session of the Council of Trent. In 1546 Ferdinand I, the King of the Romans, tried to get him appointed Bishop of Trieste but both Jay and Ignatius refused: see Sup. 2.

[55] Peter Canisius (1521-1597), born in Nijmegen, a Jesuit from 1543, and outstanding both as a theologian and as an administrator; in 1553, Ferdinand I, a great admirer, wanted him to be appointed Bishop of Verona, but once again could not convince either his candidate or Ignatius.

[56] The unusual term used is *hijuela* (literally, "little daughter"); but the Spanish

be informed about those matters which most support our cause and weaken the case of our adversaries, warning them not to disclose these things unless they judge it to be very necessary, *servatis servandis* [observing the rules that need to be observed].

These points in the annex did not seem to interest the Father much, but he agreed almost as a concession; later he said that they should not send them without first showing them to him.

6. He showed some inclination to write to the Emperor [Charles V] and to correspond with the princes; others he does not mention, although later at table it seems he was inclined to do so.

133   7. One should not forget to mention in the letter *the favour of the Pope*, [a] who has now made some donations and assigned very important missions.

[a] *the favour of the Pope*

This is Pope Julius III, who, as was said above, wanted to found the College.[57]

134   8. *In the villa* [b] there is a small mound. There have been discussions about levelling it, as it might breed poisonous things and is so placed as to create many other problems. Or, should a wall be built? This would level the ground a little and make more convenient space, supposing that the cost will be the same. The Father has gone there today taking with him the *syndic* of the house, the Minister, and our master mason, Lorenzo, and another member of the community; and he held a meeting with them after Maestro Lorenzo[58] had measured the site and estimated that the wall would cost 15 *escudos*. The points to consider—that is for each according to his conscience—were if the building of that wall would be something that would give bad example to those coming later, or even for people today. The wall that was envisaged however would be neither

editor claims that the Dictionary of the Spanish Royal Academy accepts a similar use of the word, "something added and subordinate to the principal one"; a little later (§146) da Câmara will use another unusual word, this time Portugese, *alminhas* (literally, "little souls") to refer to these extra, secret pages. This latter usage may rule out the more obvious interpretation that *hijuela* is simply a mistake for *hojuela* (the diminutive of *hoja*, "page").

[57] See §130.

[58] Mentioned above, §106, end.

whitewashed nor *emplastered*[b] and measure two palms in width. All four, after considering the matter, said that in conscience it seemed it should be done: but still he made them consider edification and good example, and they decided the same.

[a] *In the villa*

135 The *viña* ["villa"] is a small country estate which our Father arranged to have bought at a time when we were in great need simply because it seemed necessary to him for the sake of the brethren's health. There were many brothers of different nationalities, and Rome is very unhealthy, especially for foreigners; he was afraid that they would suffer from frequent and serious sickness. With this in mind, before the estate was bought, he arranged for Master Alessandro (Petronio)[59] to inspect the site. He, as the principal doctor in Rome, would judge if it was healthy. Because he thought it very good, our Father acquired it, even though afterwards experience showed the contrary.

[c] *emplastered (encolado)*

"Emplastered" is the same as "covered" (coated).[60] At that time I was the minister, and what I recorded in this passage were the doubts and scruples our Father had over a wall involving such small expense, though he was determined and generous in expenditure that was clearly beneficial for the brethren's health.

136 9. I must recall the stratagem that Father told me he had used leading someone—a person suffering from depression—to understand, etc., that he himself did not understand, etc.

10. I asked Father the reason why he had decided that the members of the Society should not wear a religious habit.

Reply: At the beginning I did many penances and I wore a different habit: the judges[61] ordered me to wear ordinary clothes that were in common use. From that time I had this devotion: since I was ordered to do so, I wish to do so, because a religious habit is not important.

---

[59] See §35 with note.

[60] Da Câmara has used a slightly unusual Spanish word and feels a Portuguese term would be clearer in his commentary.

[61] In Alcalá (1526-27), appointed by the Inquisition. Cf. *Autobiography*, §§58-59.

The reply to this question, and those which follow on as far as
No. 14, are the exact words of our Father.

137 11. What was the reason for not singing office?

Reply: I thought that, if we did not sing office, everyone would think
that we were lazy men when they did not see us doing anything to help
souls, and so this would spur us on to seek their greater good. And for the
same reason we wished to live in poverty in order to be able to help souls
more, without the trouble of handling rents, and having this also as an
incentive.

12. I asked him the reason for pilgrimages.

Reply: Because I had myself experienced how advantageous they
were, and I had found how well they suited me. Later, seeing how pilgrims became ill, etc., we moderated such practices and left it to the discretion of superiors. And for all these things there will be an answer with
some experience that I underwent[a] at Manresa.

   [a] *some experience that I underwent*

   [a] This experience [literally *negocio,* "negotiation"] was a great
   illumination of the understanding in which our Lord at Manresa
   showed to our Father these and many other things later established
   in the Society, and he only alluded to it for me here because he had
   already promised to relate at length the whole course of his life.[62]

138 13. Who first thought of the colleges?

Reply: Laínez was the first to raise this subject.[63] We were encounter-
ing many difficulties because of poverty, and so some found one solution,
others found another.

14. Who was the first in the Society after Favre?

   [62] An account of the revelations given on the banks of the Cardoner, and of the training he received, was indeed dictated shortly after by Ignatius to da Câmara; cf.
Autobiography, §30. This remark fixes an important date for a stage in the dictation of the
Autobiography.
   [63] These discussions must have taken place by (if not in) 1539, when the first draft of
the nature and aims of the new religious order was being prepared for the Pope; even at
this stage it was clear that the formation of young Jesuits would raise problems. See also
§17, where the case of the German College is mentioned.

Reply: Laínez and Salmerón made the Exercises at the same time, before Francis Xavier, because he was lecturing[64] in the Arts Faculty, but Francis Xavier was already very much better acquainted with the Society. And the Father told me the same thing, perhaps two years later.

139 15. Afterwards at table, discussing the affair at Paris, they were saying that Master Paschase[65] had not done well in *showing the Bulls*[a] and other privileges; our Father said: "I hold myself that it is better to have shown them than not to have shown them, because our Lord usually helps most where the devil makes most effort."

[a] *showing the Bulls*

The Theology Faculty of the University of Paris, when they issued the decree I mentioned, wanted to see and inspect the Bulls and privileges of the Society. It was Fr. Paschase Broët, the French Provincial, one of the first companions of our Father, who showed them. And since he was not obliged to do this, because they were neither superiors nor judges in our affairs, some of our Fathers in Rome thought he had not been right in allowing them to be seen.

140 16.[66] The Father saw two [of Ours] going out in the street, and he called me and reprimanded me severely, because I had sent them out together without knowing them well, and he protested at the slight modesty[67] they showed while walking along. And so he ordered them as a penance to go without meat and to be admonished by Br. Rion,[68] and further, that they should now walk together up and down the refectory modestly throughout supper, and *the one who went ahead*[b] should go behind. I was observing this when they told me that I should perform the same penance with the two of them at the "little table";[69] and Andrés

---

[64] Xavier had already completed his philosophical course and was teaching at the College of Beauvais while living at Sainte-Barbe, but he had not yet made the Spiritual Exercises when he joined the others in making the initial promises at Montmarte. For an exhaustive account of Xavier's academic career, cf. Georg Schurhammer, *Francis Xavier*, vol. 1, pp. 77-273, and in particular on his teaching, pp. 148-53.

[65] Paschase Broët; see §118.

[66] The MHSI editors point out that this number is doubtful as it is missing in one of the manuscripts.

[67] Cf. Glossary.

[68] See §109.

[69] Cf. Glossary.

de Orvieto[70] should publicly announce the fault of all of us.

There was one member of the community *who was spiritually weak*[c] and a novice, and he was sorely tempted, and so yesterday he was on the point of leaving. He could not bear seeing such serious admonitions given by a man who knew nothing more than the *Our Father*, and if he were so admonished he would not be able to restrain himself from replying, and perhaps saying even more. Even so I spoke to him and God has willed that he is now quieter. May the Lord console him.

[b] *the one who went ahead*

141 Because one of the features of the lack of modesty had been that they went one ahead of the other in the street, and not both together.

[c] *one. . . who was spiritually weak*

This man was a priest, a recent novice, the first one received into the Society in the College at Genoa, sent to Rome: he was weak and disturbed. And because I, in order to help him, had showed him affection, he was greatly affected by the penance and reprimand I had been given. He did not persevere in the Society.

18 February

142 1. The Father did not think we should be called "Fathers" or "Brothers" since, just as he thought we should not wear different habits, so we should be treated in speech. He ordered that there should be a consult to find suitable means of speaking properly, both in the residence and in the college, and it should report results to Father. And his Reverence proposed that one could use the expressions "one of Ours," "one of the Society," "a priest," "a layman," and refer to the rest *by their names.*[a]

[a] *by their names*

The custom of calling one another simply by their own names is

---

[70] His arrival in Rome in November, 1554, is mentioned; he was expelled in the following June.

very old in the Society. Br. Iñigo of Ochandiano, of whom I have spoken earlier,[71] told me that he had heard from Fr. Araoz how, before joining the Society, he was in Rome one day to visit our Father Ignatius, who was his uncle. He arrived at the door and the porter, who at that time was Fr. Francis [Xavier] of India, announced him in these words: "Iñigo! Araoz is here and wants to speak to you."

Fr. Pierre Favre used to speak to our Father Ignatius in the same way, as can be seen from many of his letters still in circulation among us.

On this subject Fr. Araoz told me in Valencia[72] in 1545 that one day Fr. Favre sent the porter of the College there to call someone from the residence, who was already going out into the street. And because when he called him he used the word "Brother," Fr. Favre reprimanded him, saying that he should address him by his own name. And the same Fr. Favre used to say (according to what I was told by Fr. *Micer*[73] Juan the Aragonese, his companion for a long time, who died and is buried in this college of St. Antony) that when they asked a member of the Society who he was, he should reply that he was a man who had no name.

143 2. The Father had already given an order that in the whole Society no doctor should prescribe directly or discuss with a sick man a change of air; and now he adds that I should tell our doctor that he should see the sick in the infirmary, and he alone should decide what is required, and afterwards tell the infirmarian outside the infirmary. However, I, or the sub-minister, should always be present to judge whether such a remedy could be given or not, always supposing, *tamen* [however], that he must be given all that is still possible. And consequently Father ordered *that I should speak to the doctor*[a] freely about his way of providing the cure, to help him, but that I should first say by way of preface how much esteem I have for him, etc.

---

[71] Cf. §40.

[72] As mentioned above, da Câmara had been sent to Valencia for his novitiate.

[73] The Spanish priest in question probably came from Aragón (it is unlikely that this is a family name as he was also known as "Aragonés"); he had been chaplain to the daughters of Emperor Charles V, entered the Society through the influence of Pierre Favre, and worked in Portugal from 1544 until his death in 1553.

(a) *that I should speak to the doctor*

This was the doctor who had made a mistake in healing our Father. And because while I was minister two of the brethren died because of his lack of expertise, I proposed to Father that we must find another doctor, and according to his order I dismissed him quite frankly, first assuring him of the goodwill we bore him.

144   3. The two novices in their First Probation[74] fell ill, Guillaume[75] the Frenchman, and Alonso[76] the Spaniard. The residence is already weighed down with more than seventy persons, it has been such a difficult year, and these [two] are without university training; some thought it would be better for them to go to a hospital for attention, since they had not yet joined our resident community, and we should arrange how they could be received and properly cared for.

Reply: "Not that, not that! Do nothing further along those lines, but rather let doctors and remedies be multiplied. It is not right that those who have left the world for the love of God, should be abandoned by us when they are in need."

The Spaniard had just spent time in a hospital; the Frenchman had wanted to enter as his servant, but they had not wanted to receive him because of the famine; and the Father knew this, and that neither of them had received any university education.

4. Italian Grammar should be studied every day, and not just every other day, as they had started to do.

5. The Germans, Stephan and Jeremia, should stay in the house without going to college, even though everyone was quite satisfied with them, until they knew the language better and were more familiar with the customs of the house.

145   6. Our Father, concerning the manner of writing,[77] decided yesterday when he was talking about it, that such a letter should be written

[74] See Glossary.

[75] See §77.

[76] This may be the Alonso sent to Sicily in June of this year and mentioned in a letter to the rector as a person who should be kindly but firmly asked to leave as unsuitable for the Society; he may be the novice referred to as "the philosopher." (§77).

[77] He is referring to the particular letter concerning the problem in Paris (§§130-32).

neither as a confidential extra sheet, nor in any other way, but rather so that it could be read out at the University of Paris with edification and satisfaction for all. And so, *having seen the letters,*[a] he ordered others to be written in this fashion. And our Father said very clearly, how satisfied he was in his soul with this, and how much he valued the bodily strength which enabled him to read those letters, and to prevent them from being dispatched as they were. Today Father has seen them and made considerable alterations. He had them read and re-read so many times, that it took more than two and a half hours, nearly three. Father gave them admirably close attention, for even though in everything he does he gives such attention, still in this matter he displayed even more. He made many changes and additions, as has been said, above all in the confidential annex, causing it to be almost completely erased. In addition to the other matters, he added the whole of the last three or four lines. These letters can be read in the register of important letters of the Society,[78] and I should remember to recover those letters which the Father made me amend with my own hand as he was dictating the corrections to me, in order to remember the reasons for each particular alteration.

[a] *having seen the letters*

146 These are the public and confidential letters which I mentioned above;[79] our Father ordered copies of these to be sent to all of ours. I think it will be appropriate to add copies of these here, and they are the following.

Marginal Note: Here are to be copied the résumés of the public and confidential letters that will come from Rome, and whatever Fr. [da Câmara] remembers about the corrections.[80]

Although as I said above,[81] this Paris affair did not cause our Father to lose much sleep, nevertheless in the great care he took in

[78] Probably the *Regesta* still preserved in the Jesuit Roman Archives, from which two letters dealing with the Paris question have been published in MHSI, *Epist.* VIII, 453-56 and 484-85; but see Supplement 3.

[79] Cf. §132: the Portuguese word used here for "confidential letters" is *alminhas*, a term used to refer to stone tablets showing the souls in Purgatory and presumably suggesting hidden, inner messages.

[80] This note is placed opposite an empty gap in the manuscript, and the particular letters mentioned have not been found.

[81] Cf. §131.

amending and revising these letters one can see clearly the exactitude he showed in all important matters. He showed the same care
in the year [. . .][82] trying to keep the peace between King João of
Portugal and Pope Paul III, as can be seen from the letter on this
subject which he wrote to Fr. Master Simão.

> *Marginal Note:* Here should be placed [a copy of] this let-
> ter, which is to be found in the book in Evora.[83]

147 I have kept for this place an account of what our Father did
with reference to the bishopric of Claude Jay, about which I spoke
above,[84] so that from it can be better understood the exactitude and
diligence he put into important matters. And since everything that
occurred in this matter is referred to at length in a letter Fr.
Bartolomeo Ferrão wrote from Rome to Dr. Miguel de Torres it is
enough to transcribe it here.

> *Marginal Note:* Here should be placed [a copy of] this let-
> ter, which is to be found in the same book in Evora.[85]

148 Here I shall add an example of a small matter from which one
may gather the great exactitude of our Father in more important
matters. After the two bishops of Prester John had been elected, as
has been said, given that they had to get ready to leave for this
Kingdom [Portugal], Father Ignatius took the trouble to equip
them with all the things and information they needed for the journey, both for their personal use, and for the mounts they had to
take. And when the evening before the day they hoped to depart
arrived, he asked them to show him all their belongings—blankets,
hats, the spurs on their feet, the horses saddled, and all the rest.
When this was done he asked them if there was anything missing;
they said, "No," and the Father said to them: "Well, now that you
are perfectly well provided for and without any worries that you
will be lacking something on the journey, we would like to spend
this evening and all day tomorrow in bidding you a perfect
farewell." And so he kept them that evening and the whole of the
following day simply for this purpose.

[82] The exact year is missing, perhaps because the affair da Câmara has in mind
dragged on from 1541 to 1545.
[83] Cf. Supplement 1.
[84] Cf. §131.
[85] Cf. Supplement 2.

149 7. *Pacem meam do vobis, pacem relinquo vobis.*[86] Our Father cited this passage when some people told him it would be good to write against that decree of Paris, and we were so sure of it that we were already discussing about who would write, etc. But our Father began to give us an exhortation on how bad these hatreds and passions appeared to him which were being spread by books, and it seemed to him that the Society should not write or defend itself in such a way, nor was it proper to nourish a perpetual hatred against a University. When someone said to him that it would be good that at least somebody write a gentle letter, etc., or a member of the Society who was also a son of the University and well known in it, might perhaps write it, neither did that seem good to the Father.

The further process of this business of the opposition from Paris was that four of the outstanding professors[87] of the University of Paris came to Rome to deal with other important matters. When our Father learned of this he asked a French cardinal[88] to arrange a meeting so that they might kindly set out the reasons why the Faculty of Paris would not receive them, but rather rejected the Society; so that, if we were to see our faults and mistakes, we might correct them, as was reasonable, or rather if, after carefully examining the matter, they found there was nothing to criticize in our Institute, they might withdraw the decree they had issued against us.

The four professors agreed to this easily, and drew up some articles in which they made clear more explicitly the reasons for their decree. On the orders of our Father, Fathers Laínez, Polanco, des Freux, and Dr. Olave replied to these with such exactitude that both the cardinal and the four professors were satisfied. The responses were in the name of Fr. Laínez. It was Fr. Olave who wrote to me about all this from Rome, because it happened after my arrival in this province [of Portugal].

Marginal Note: [. . .] Supplement 3[89]

---

[86] See John 14:27.

[87] Claude d'Espence, Jérôme de Souchière (Cistercian), Crispin de Brichanteau (Benedictine), Jean Benoît (Dominican).

[88] Charles de Guise, Cardinal of Lorraine, who had come to Rome for political matters and happened to be accompanied by the four professors in question.

[89] Most of this marginal note has been lost: cf. Supplement 3.

19 February

150 1. Today N.[a], [90] threw himself onto his knees in front of our Father
and never wanted to get up, however much Father ordered him to do so,
until he had finished his explanation. And so with his eyes full of tears
and his joined hands raised up, he said: "I make a vow of obedience,
poverty, chastity, etc., and so to act in all things and for all things, etc.,
and thus I judge and think that your Reverence will never order me to do
anything which may be against my conscience." When he had done this,
he came to me and told me of it with great joy, telling me he now felt so
relieved and so content. He had been overwhelmed by the Father's
virtue. And indeed, soon after he had ceased a little to think *about certain
things,*[b] had felt such great love for the Father. It is quite clear, *inquit* [he
said], that since there are such branches, there must be such a trunk,
meaning that from the achievements of the Society, it might be judged
how the Father is like the trunk from which everything springs. And that
in the last resort there is nothing comparable to each one looking after his
own soul and not concerning himself with anything else.

When N. made this gesture, our Father replied to him very calmly, *ut
solet* [as was his custom], that he should give many thanks to God for the
gift that He had given him, and that he would think about it and *would
speak to him the next day.*[c]

[a] *N.*

151 This brother was the son of a very illustrious gentleman; after
he had joined the Society and had been in his province for four or
five years, he became very disturbed and restless. His superiors
thought it would be better if he went to Rome, and he himself
requested this, in order that contact with our Father and the
change from his own country might help him. He had already
been in Rome for some months with few signs of becoming calmer
when our Lord granted him this emotion and fervour. What

[90] The initial "N" stands for the name Teotonio de Bragança, a Portuguese Jesuit since
1549, despite the opposition of his aristocratic parents. In 1552, being much attached to
the maverick Fr. Simão Rodrigues, whom he thought had been unjustly treated, he began
to give trouble and in 1554 was sent to Rome. Despite the conversion experience recorded
here he could not settle down in the Society, and in 1555 left both Rome and the Society.
Later in life, he was appointed Bishop of Evora and became a friend of the Jesuits.

happened to him afterwards we shall mention later.

(b) *certain things*

These things were that our Father had punished a Father for whom this brother had great respect, and to whom he was completely devoted, something that caused him to distance himself from our Father and to think ill of him.

(c) *would speak to him the next day*

Our Father postponed until the following day the acceptance of that fervour and the renewal of his vows.

152   2. Today[91] Master Nadal[92] departed. N.[93] and I went to accompany him. He was going with a German, Jonas.[94] While we were travelling I asked him about spiritual matters[95] and about my defects. He told me *that defects preserve virtue.*[d] For remedies, *unctio docebit* ["his anointing will teach you"[96]]. He said to me in second place: whoever is well initiated into things in Rome is well established in the Society. Thirdly, that I should not tire our Father much, except when he himself wished it and therefore I should ask him on which matters in general, concerning the house, he would like to be kept informed, and inform him of those. The thing we must all try to achieve is that our Father be left in peace: this must be obtained either through the villa or in whatever way, because his peace of mind (as he is so intimate with and united to God) sustains and carries the weight of the whole Society. I begged him to tell me my faults in that business. He told me that in me he found no fault, but in

[91] 19 February 1555.

[92] Pope Julius III had appointed Frs. Nadal and Laínez consultant theologians to Cardinal Morone, Pontifical Legate to Ferdinand I. The Cardinal had left Rome on 18 February, and Nadal followed him the next day. They were to meet up with Laínez in Florence.

[93] Teotonio de Bragança.

[94] Br. Jonas Adler; he subsequently left the Society in 1561.

[95] Literally, "about my soul (*mi alma*)."

[96] 1 John 2:27: "But the anointing which you received from him [the Son] abides in you, and you have no need that anyone should teach you, as his anointing teaches you about everything, and is true, and is no lie; just as it has taught you, abide in him."

N[97] he did: this had been partly a fault in him, and partly something mysterious. When I insisted on his indicating to me the excesses I had committed, he told me that the right thing for soldiers is to be spirited and go a little further ahead than their officers ordered; that this is good, and that as long as it exists in the Society, i.e. such zeal, etc., things would always go well; as for example now in the business of Paris, it is good for us to show zeal, and for our Father to moderate this zeal.

153 As a Diet of German princes and bishops was being summoned in Augsburg, Pope Julius III [1550-55] sent Cardinal Morone[98] as his legate, so that if they dealt with matters concerning religion, as he presumed they would, he could defend the side of the Catholics against many heretical gentlemen, who would of necessity have to be present there. For this purpose he asked Father Ignatius to provide two theologians from the Society, with whom the cardinal might discuss the matters of his legation, and from whom he might obtain help in the difficulties and controversies that might arise. Our Father gave him Fathers Laínez and Nadal. The latter went ahead accompanied only by this German brother.

I remember two things that our Father advised him very earnestly shortly before they left. Firstly that they should work together as far as possible to reinforce each other's authority, and that they would achieve this if, whenever a difficult matter was raised with Fr. Laínez, he would reply that they consult Fr. Nadal, who would better be able to say what should be done in this, and that if they communicated first with Father Nadal, he should pass on the matter in the same way to Fr. Laínez. Secondly, that when they were to dine at the Legate's table, they should never discuss important negotiations, but only agreeable, easy matters requiring little concentration.

(d) *that defects preserve virtue*

Fr. Nadal did not wish to say anything else except that from our natural defects, which we overcome with difficulty, we can draw humility and self-knowledge, which safeguard solid virtue. His

---

[97] This "N." stands for Simão Rodrigues and the "business" in question is the crisis in he Portuguese province which led to his removal as provincial; see §7.
[98] The cardinal behind the founding of the Roman College; see §§16-17.

opinion on this was not contrary to the practice, which our Father Ignatius used, to work at the mortification of the natural and exterior defects of each one: for it is clear that someone who tries diligently to attack natural defects, which rarely involve any guilt, must be well clear of those defects which by their nature are blameworthy.

154 3. I must recall what I had asked Jonas, viz. to find out from Fathers Laínez and Nadal their idea of obedience of judgement and to write to me, with everything else that he might learn from them, and he promised to do this.

The following, as far as the line [§156], is the reply that our Father gave to Master Polanco in my presence.

155 4. A Slovenian youth came here today, the 19th, and says he wishes to bring two brothers, good people, to the Society. One has already seen the minister. He also wishes to join: there has been some doubt about him because of the habit with cowl he has worn for four months, not the habit of any particular order, but just a vague gesture. Your Reverence has however given some guidelines on this in accepting similar applicants, such as Miguel, later dismissed, and another Spaniard, also already dismissed this year.

Reply: The Father says that the reasons he had in recognising this as an impediment,[99] as far as he recalls, were two: one, because such candidates are accustomed to different rites and ceremonies, which would be difficult later to reconcile with our own practices; the other, because of their inconstancy. The same reasons apply to hermits who have their own way to perfection. But he did not remember the other reasons Master Polanco touched on when he made this an impediment, which are these: the man who takes up that kind of life seemed to be a bit light-headed, or eccentric, and fit for little, etc.

As far as this particular case is concerned, as this person had brought two brothers, our Father would let himself be played with;[100] but if he had not done so, he would not let him be considered. *I must remember*[a] the points raised in the consultation on this case.

---

[99] *Constitutions, Examen* II 3, 6 (§§27, 30), and Part I, 3, 5E (§§171-72).

[100] The phrase used here, *se dexara jugar,* is not clear but seems to mean that Ignatius was willing to give the benefit of the doubt, even if he was being tricked.

(a) *I must remember*

I cannot recall the nature of this case; I can only remember that
the Slovenes were not admitted.

156   5. As far as perpetrators of homicide were concerned, the Father was
thinking in the first place of hired murderers, etc., not someone acting on
impulse without deliberation or intention. As far as the man about whom
the question was raised there is no difficulty.

I learned this from our Father himself, but I neither questioned
him about it, nor did he tell me this with the intention of explaining in this way the passage of the Constitutions where this impediment is mentioned;[101] nor have I written it here with such an intention.

157   6. *To my room-mate*[a] I must speak clearly, putting before him the
four colleges where he did not persevere. The Father says, moreover, that
he wants no one in the Society who is not able *to be of use in some
way,* [b] and in this case one of two courses must be followed: either dismiss him from the Society or spur him on.

(a) *To my room-mate*

I call him my "room-mate" because he wrote several things for
me in my own room. He was a brother born in Naples,[102] as far as
my memory goes: he joined the Society as an ordained deacon,
and although he was (generally speaking) a good man, nevertheless, since he did not strive hard enough to perfect himself in mortification and virtue, which our Father desired to find in all, he did
much to help him, and for this reason he ordered him to be moved
four times to different colleges in Italy: but seeing that he did not
give satisfaction in any of them, when he came at last to the house
in Rome, the Father ordered me to put all this to him and to disa-
buse him, and to advise him that unless he was determined to continue with greater perfection, he would dismiss him from the
Society. And our Lord willed that this advice should affect him in
such a way that he soon changed and afterwards lived peacefully
and died in the Society in an edifying and exemplary manner.

---

[101] *Constitutions, Examen* II, 2 (§25), and Part I, 3, 4C (§§168-69).
[102] Probably a certain Pietro, mentioned in a letter (18 April 1555) to Fr. Mercurian
(No. 5348, MHSI, *Epist.* IX, 17-18).

(b) *to be of use in some way*

158   I recall that our Father told me very often that he did not want anyone in the Society who came simply for his own salvation, but he said that everyone should be prepared in addition to help the salvation of others. And if, when it was a question of keeping or dismissing someone in the Society, the reason given him was that at least such a man would be saved if he joined or remained in the Society, he attached no importance to this argument, but rather rejected it.

He did not want to say either, that only well-educated and gifted men should join the Society, and those gifted enough to persuade their neighbours, but rather only that those should be admitted who, beyond the need of their own perfection, helped by good example others both in the house and outside. For this reason he greatly enjoyed the company of the coadjutor Brothers, when he saw that they were devout men and lovers of obedience and holy simplicity. He often said that obedience made up for the lack of prudence; but by contrast none of the other virtues satisfied him, when the virtuous resignation of one's own judgement and will were lacking, as has already been said.

159   7. As to the question whether the *syndic*[103] of Ethiopia[a] should correct others, the Father said no; because the syndic's task is simply to observe and to notify the superior.

(a) *syndic of Ethiopia*

Our Father had decided that the professed[104] of the Society should take a vow that if they were to become bishops, they would follow completely the General's counsels, if they judged them better than their own opinion;[105] to carry out such a vow in practice with the patriarch[106] sent to Prester John, and with his two

---

[103] Cf. Glossary.
[104] Cf. Glossary
[105] *Constitutions,* Part X, 6 [§817].
[106] The mission to Ethiopia, led by the Portuguese Jesuit, João Nunes Barreto, newly appointed Patriarch to Ethiopia, set out in 1555; cf. §118.

companions, who were the first to be raised to episcopal dignity, he ordered that there should be a *syndic* among them, so that from Ethiopia he could inform the General Superior of the Society on matters for which he thought the General should give advice.

20 February

160 1. N. [a], [107] confirmed today early in the morning all that he had said yesterday, and our Father told him that he himself would think about his affairs as if they were his own: and so in the afternoon N. came with his confessor to put all this straight; and in front of him the Father told the confessor that he wished to know nothing of what they had been talking about, that the confessor should not impose any hard penances, but only some prayers as a reminder, and if he had to make amends for anything, he reminded him that the person should not be humiliated.

[a] N.

This was the brother about whom I have said before that he renewed his vows on his knees before our Father: the latter was leading him by the way of love.

161 2. I must recall the reason why the Father changed the declaration on future bishops in the new *Constitutions*,[108] and how the Father weighed each word.

3. The business of the infirmary [b] was remitted by the Father to Fr. Polanco and he gave me the means to convince him: I should show the need from the evidence of others without any preference of mine, and suggesting other places, but not that which was envisaged.

[b] *infirmary*

While I was minister, we had an urgent need for an infirmary in our residence in Rome because there were many who were sick and the place where they were nursed was most inconvenient:

---

[107] Teotonio de Bragança; cf. §150.
[108] The first draft of the *Constitutions* had been finished by 1550, but the new text was added to Part Ten, paragr. 6 with Note A [§§817-18].

part of it was in the rooms kept for the so-called First Probation[109] and part in some rooms near the porter's lodge. I put the need to our Father and suggested to him how an infirmary might be planned and built at small cost. This seemed a very good idea to him.

But since Fr. Polanco was in charge of overseeing the expenses of the house and it was he who must find the money for this work, he did not want to decide immediately, but was hoping that Father Polanco himself would realize the need and would decide to effect it on his own account. And for this reason he wanted me to propose it to him in this way: I told him only the opinion of the other Fathers and the reasons they gave why an infirmary should be made, but I did not express my own preference with regard to doing it. And as he raised difficulties about where to put it, I took him around the whole house and showed him a number of areas little suited to the project and which would require great expense. Finally, arriving at the place which I had marked out with our Father, he himself chose it: and as if it had been his own discovery, in a short time he made it into a good infirmary.

21 February
and about My Going Away[110]

162 1. The Father says that he never dares to do anything of importance, even though he might have all the reasons for doing it, *without turning to God*;[b] he said this apropos of *his confessor, Don Diego.*[a]

[a] *his confessor, Don Diego*

Father Don Diego de Eguía[111] was a native of Navarre, an exemplary man of great virtue. Father Pierre Favre called him "Don Diego the Saint." The case related here is the following:

---

[109] See §144 with note.

[110] The elliptical phrase "*yendo fuera*" seems to refer to the account (added later) of da Câmara's departure from Rome in October; this addition was intended to illustrate Ignatius's use of the phrase, "I'll sleep on it!"

[111] As early as 1527, while still a student at Alcalá (cf. *Autobiography* §57), Ignatius had been befriended by the priest Don Diego, brother of an important printer; already advanced in years, he joined the Society in its foundation year, 1540, and died a few weeks before Ignatius on 16 June 1556.

Our Father had had him as his confessor for a long time: and as he was a man of great simplicity and candour, he used to say some things in praise of our Father, giving them such importance that they could scandalize someone who was not aware of his innocence and holy zeal. So, for example, he said that Father Ignatius was not simply Father Ignatius, but a saint and more than a saint. At other times he said, "Father Ignatius is pope and more than a pope! Father Ignatius is Christ and more than Christ! Father Ignatius is God and more than God!"[112]

For this reason the Father, after having prayed about it, stopped going to confession to him, in spite of the fact that he was opposed to changing confessors, and this is the situation about which I am speaking here.

[b] *without turning to God*

163 Our Father used to keep to this way of acting very exactly. I remember that in the case of Tarquinio, which I have described above,[113] he took advice on his coming to Spain; when two of his consultors[114] said this was not necessary, because they had experience of his fortitude, the Father replied, "We'll sleep on it." This expression was one he used frequently when he wanted to say he would pray about some matter.

In October 1555 we had to leave Rome,[115] Fr. Nadal for Castile with five brothers of whom he was the Superior, and I for Portugal with the thirteen or fourteen I brought with me.[116] Father Ignatius wanted us all to travel together as far as Spain. At this time the King of France [Henry II] and the Emperor [Charles V] were at

---

[112] The fear of scandal was well founded: for the effect of such unbalanced praise on a Dominican visitor, cf. Terence O'Reilly, "Melchor Cano's *Censura y parecer contra el Instituto de los Padres Jesuitas*. A translation of the British Library manuscript," *From Ignatius of Loyola to John of the Cross: Spirituality and literature in sixteenth-century Spain,* Variorum, 1995, ch. V.

[113] §68.

[114] For the system of "consultors" and the holding of consultations with the "consult," see the Glossary and the Index ("consult").

[115] The date in question is mentioned above, §9, viz. 23 October 1555.

[116] This is written in 1573 or 1574; when he left Rome da Câmara requested leave to take back with him to Portugal about a dozen scholastics, of different nationalities, in the hope that they would strengthen the international character of and cooperation in the Society.

war, a factor which made our journey difficult, as much by sea as by land: by land, our passage would be impeded in France, since some of us were Spaniards and we were going to Spain; and by sea there was the French fleet from Marseilles, which we must needs encounter, and which was robbing and taking prisoner the Spaniards who sailed that way.

One day after supper, a little before our departing, our Father put the matter to the consult, and although Fr. Nadal and I were in favour of making the journey by land, nevertheless we listened to the other Fathers' opinion without showing our own preference. Votes were divided and the Father closed the meeting with his habitual expression, "It's necessary to sleep on it."

At five o'clock[117] the following morning, that is to say the hour at which he finished his prayers, he called Brother Martín,[118] who helped him in his room, and said to him, "Go and tell Master Nadal and Luís Gonçalves to go from Genoa to Spain by sea with a great blessing." (I do not remember having heard him use this expression at any other time.)

164   We travelled by land as far as Lerice, where we were to embark for Genoa; and when we arrived the brothers, who had journeyed there from Rome before us, had already left the evening before. But the storms were so strong, and the weather so contrary, that though we put to sea twice we made no headway and had to return ashore. From Lerice we could only make our way as far as Portovenere, a distance of three miles. Embarking again at Sestri (which we were obliged to reach by a land journey of nine leagues) we disembarked on a beach because we could not go further. In the end we decided, even though it should be at the cost of great labour, much difficulty and a rough road, as well as in bad weather, to travel the remaining thirty miles to Genoa by land, so that over the sixty miles from Lerice to Genoa we spent [ten][119] days.

At Genoa we found a Genoese ship getting ready to sail for Alicante. But since the storms and winds already experienced did

[117] Da Câmara gives the Roman reckoning: "at 9 hours" of the nightly division (which began in winter at 8:00 p.m.).

[118] Mentioned in §§327, 352.

[119] A gap in the manuscript can be filled thanks to the account of the journey in the *Chronicon* of Polanco.

not abate, we had to wait a month and a half for them to stop. During that time we were occupied in very fruitful tasks of service to God. Although we had been informed that they had been advised at Marseilles of the departure of our ship and that the French were waiting for it, and we were fearful that they would board the ship and take prisoners, since it was carrying many Spaniards with their belongings, nevertheless as the weather improved we set sail from the port on the morning of 2 <1>[120] December 1555, and though it was in midwinter and there had been severe storms we sailed with a light wind in clear weather and a calm sea, and had no more difficulties except for two or three days without wind, during which the ship was becalmed and could not move.

165 I do not recall any of us being sea-sick, although both Fr. Nadal and I were prone to this; and this had been the chief reason why we had wanted to travel by land. The sailors said they had sailed that Gulf forty times, and were not able to remember any time, whether in summer or winter, when they had had such fine weather.

We had only a slight fear and alarm of a French attack as we sailed almost in sight of Marseilles, but nothing happened. Finally we arrived at Alicante[121] after only nine days' voyage. By landing at this port we had saved more than seventy leagues of travel by land, since it is that distance below Barcelona, and thus we had avoided the perils of Catalan brigands.

166 2. He never told his confessor about anything *except his sins,*[a] not mentioning any special grace that God might have given him.

[a] *except his sins*

The Father said this apropos of Don Diego,[122] indicating that those praises which he had mentioned, did not arise from any of his confessions.

167 3. He always had a fixed confessor without changing.[123]

[120] The error in the date may be due to the copyist.
[121] On 30 December 1555.
[122] See §162.
[123] Da Câmara is referring to the period when Ignatius had settled in Rome.

168 4. The *vivae vocis* [verbally expressed] directions should be authenticated—in which the Pope [Julius III] orders a member of the Society to visit the Patriarch, and which obliges them under pain of sin to accept the bishoprics—so that they will remain *ad perpetuam rei memoriam* [for perpetual memory of the fact]. And since up to this day the Father had not thought about it, he said these words: "*How many oversights*[a] are due to us!"[124]

(a) How many oversights

169 The care and attention with which our Father treated important matters surprised those who had dealings with him. It was he who brought matters to the attention of those directly concerned—those by whom things were to be done, or with whom they were to be raised. I cannot recall that in matters of this kind he ever said to anyone that they should remind him.

The way in which he took advice and dealt with matters was this: every day, having finished a meal, whether lunch or supper, the Brother who cleared the table placed on it an hour glass timed for one hour, and if a subject had to be followed up which had already been raised, he also placed an orange there as well as a sign. All the Fathers who were consultors brought their papers, where they noted what our Father's wishes were on a particular subject. He then asked each one in order, never dealing with more than one matter. And so he listened and replied to each one until the sand in the glass had run out. When the hour had passed, he rose and closed the meeting.

170 5. *The letter*[b], [125] of João Nunes, in which he asks that somebody be appointed for him as commissioner [on behalf of the General], so that he may be under the obedience of the Society, should be authenticated, and recognised to this effect.

(b) The letter

After Fr. João Nunes had been nominated by our Father as Patriarch, and before he knew that they were discussing in Rome if bishops in the Society would keep that sort of submission to

---

[124] The Spanish phrase "*Quantos descuidos pasan por nosotros*" is ambiguous, and the French translator takes it to mean, "How many oversights we have to put up with!"
[125] More than one such letter has been preserved; cf. MHSI, *Epist.*, VIII, 710-12, 717, 718-19.

the General mentioned earlier, he wrote to our Father asking him to assign someone to him as his [the Father's] commissioner in India, whom he would obey as his substitute. This greatly pleased Fr. Ignatius, and he made me read it many times, praising it and considering it a good example for everyone else.

171 6. The Father said he wanted to place a statue on the mound[126] in the villa so that all visitors to the villa might pray. When I suggested that such prayers should be said kneeling, he preferred *to leave it to the devotion*[a] of each individual.

> [a] *to leave it to the devotion*
>
> Fr. Ignatius earnestly desired that in spiritual matters concerning God's service we should all be moved and inclined by devotion and internal impulse, and that there should be as little recourse as possible to external principles. My reflection, when I noted this, was that he proceeded in this way so that our works should be more voluntary, and also to test and display the dispositions of his subjects when he left them free.

172 7. The Father thought it necessary for the College to have a country house. *He used to say that these things,*[b] arranged in good order now, would not give a bad example to succeeding generations, but would, rather, help them, provided that they were used in moderation, and with adequate rules from the beginning.

> [b] *He used to say that these things*
>
> At the time that Fr. Ignatius ordered the purchase of this country estate, and built some good houses in it for the colleges in Rome, there were some difficulties raised by the Fathers, such as the very severe lack of funds, about which I have spoken already,[127] and the example and edification that would be given to members of the Society later. When I was talking to our Father about this at the estate itself, he replied that because he foresaw that those who would come to the Society later (and to their good example he attached more importance than to all the other considerations) would need to look for some recreation to relieve the stress and

[126] See §134.
[127] See §135.

mental labour arising from their ordinary work, and perhaps would be more self-indulgent in this matter than was really necessary, for this reason he wanted criteria to be laid down now about what should be done in this regard, and that the first should provide a rule and example for those coming after them.

173 In order to do this he himself indicated and arranged those games that the brethren might play at the country house, which were only the tablet game and the quoit or target game. The first was in imitation of the College of the Sorbonne, which is the most important in Paris and has the most learned and dedicated members. There the teachers are accustomed to play a game after dinner with the keys of their rooms: whoever gets nearest to the edge of the table wins. And instead of the keys, our Father ordered the tablets, which we still use now. For the second game he had some thin iron round disks made, about a palm's width wide, with a large hole in the middle for the fingers to fit in easily. With his own hand he made a model out of red wax of the size he wanted.

174 No other game of any kind was allowed at the country house. He imposed a serious penance on Father Doctor Olave, superintendent of the College, and on Father Ribadeneira and others for playing games with oranges, throwing them to one another continually, with the one who dropped the orange having to say a *Hail Mary* on his knees. He gave two others a good penance for playing at *castro*[128] in the villa. To sum up, he seemed to be continually alert to stop all the gaps through which dissipation might slip into the villa. And for this purpose he drew up the following rules which we called the rules of the villa.

Scribe's Marginal Note: Here are to be added "The Villa Rules," which will come from Rome.

---

[128] This game used to be popular among Spanish children and was played with pebbles along lines that resembled military emplacements: hence the name, which means a "camp" (cf. *Diccionario Enciclopédico Hispano-Americano*, Montaner y Simón, Barcelona, 1888, t. IV, p. 941).

+

IHS

Rules Which Ought to Be Observed
by Those Who Go to Villa[129]

1. No one shall go to the Villa without the rector's permission or that of his substitute.

2. No one shall eat or pick grapes or other fruit, unless he has permission.

3. No one shall eat grapes or fruit except when he has been allowed to under obedience, lest anyone should fall sick because of the disorder.

4. No one shall leave clothes around the villa, except in the place designated for them.

5. No one shall go into the kitchen without permission from the cook or whoever is in charge of it.

6. No game except the quoit game is to be played at the villa; singing is also permitted.

7. Neither the players nor anyone else must lean on the fences, or damage them or put anything on them, or climb them.

8. No one shall pull branches from the vines or trees, or make marks on them.

9. No one shall play the quoit game on the paths which cross the villa breadthwise.

10. The rector should appoint somebody to be responsible for the quoits whenever there is a visit to the villa. When the game is over he must count them and put them back in the frail which is to be kept there for that purpose.

11. Each must take care to return the quoit he has played with, to the front door, and hand it to the one in charge.

12. Each must stop playing or singing when the person in charge calls him back to the house, either because it is too hot, or too windy in the winter, or for whatever reason he shall judge convenient.

13. No one shall draw lines or other marks on the walls of the house or the rooms, either indoors or outside.

14. No one shall throw anything into the well.

---

[129] This version of the Villa Rules is to be found not in the manuscript of the *Memoriale* but in a separate copy in Italian which dates from the time of Ignatius.

15. No one shall bring any outsiders to the villa with-out Father Master Ignatius's permission.

16. Persons in charge must be appointed to make sure these rules are kept and to keep order among the students at the villa; and when they go to the villa, there should always be someone who is a superior, or his substitute until such time as they return to the house, whom everyone must obey, etc.

22 February

175 1. The Father was praying during *the whole journey,* [a], [130] as could be gathered clearly by the changes in his facial expression. And *the ease he has*[b] to attain union with God is something especially to be noted.

I must recall *how often I found him*[c] shut in his chapel in such devotion, that it seemed this could be seen in his features; *still, it constantly appears*[d] that this devotion can be seen in him.

[a] *the whole journey*

176 One of the things that the Father observed carefully, and which he wanted those of the Society to observe, was interior rec-ollection with God and exterior modesty whenever one was out-side the house and among people of the world. He gave orders that in Rome on all the Sundays and holy days on which there was preaching in the house, all the students from the Colleges, both those of the German College and ours at the Roman College, should attend the sermon. It was well worth seeing how this was carried out. When the sign was given to leave the Colleges, each one went at once to the porter's lodge with his cloak. Before leav-ing they were drawn up in pairs, each with his companion, accord-ing to their physical height, and once in order they went out as it were in procession, two by two, the youngest at the head; and the nearer they came to the tail, the older they were and the greater their authority; and the last who came along were the superior and his companion.

---

[130] On the way back from the villa house.

They all behaved with such modesty and in such an orderly way that all of Rome used to turn out to see them walk along the streets, as if it were an object of great devotion and astonishment. However when they went to the country villa, our Father ordered them to walk with the same modesty, but without so much order and split up by different routes.

(b) the ease he has

177 Something that greatly raised him up in prayer was music and the singing of the divine services, such as Vespers, Masses, and the like; so much so that he admitted to me, that if he happened to go into a church while sung offices were being celebrated, he immediately felt completely carried out of himself.

178 This not only helped his soul, but also the health of his body. And for this reason, when he was ill, or experiencing some great disappointment, nothing helped him so much as to listen to a brother singing a holy song. And it quite astonished me that even though the people with whom he was living knew this, no one ever looked for a brother or student from the German College, where there were many and excellent singers, who could have provided him with this consolation. The nearest thing to this I saw, in all the time I was in Rome, was once, when he was sick in bed, Fr. des Freux was called to play the clavichord for him, without singing, since even this helped him. And also a very simple and virtuous lay Brother, who used to sing a number of devout ballads imitating the tone and voice of the blind singers, so that it seemed he himself must have been a blind man's guide as a boy. And all this took place so very rarely, that in the nearly two and a half years I was in Rome, it happened no more than five or six times.

(c) how often I found him

179 At this time, our Father, on medical orders and because of his continuous illnesses, rose a little later than the brethren. He immediately recited the Hail Marys, which had been set for him as a substitute for the Divine Office. When he had finished he went to a chapel, next door to his room, to hear Mass on those days when he himself did not celebrate. After Mass he remained in mental prayer for two hours, and in order not to be disturbed he ordered that all the messages for him at the porter's lodge should be passed

on to me, as minister, in his place. Some of these messages, being important and from people to whom it was proper that he should himself reply at once, I took to the chapel.

I remember that whenever I entered the chapel, and this happened frequently, I found him with his features so resplendent that although my mind was concentrating completely on delivering the message, I was astonished and overcome with emotion; for what I was seeing was unlike anything I had seen when I had visited devout persons at prayer, but clearly seemed to be something from heaven and most out of the ordinary.

(d) *still, it constantly appears*

180 The internal devotion of our Father shone through and could be seen constantly in the great peace, tranquillity, and composure of his outward appearance. Whatever news one gave him, whatever event, sad or joyful, spiritual or temporal, he showed not the least sign of agitation or inner disturbance. When he wanted to welcome someone warmly, he showed such joy that he seemed to take the guest into his soul.

His eyes seemed naturally so full of joy, that, according to a story told me by Fr. Laínez, when a man who had suffered from demonic possession at Padua spoke great praises of him, and wanted to identify him by his appearance, he gave this description, "A tiny little Spaniard, a bit lame, with joyful eyes." Even so, ordinarily he kept them so cast down that they seemed to be those of a dead man. And one of the things that he most reproved in the brethren was lifting one's gaze. It was only permitted to the superior to look his subject in the face when he spoke to him; our Father wanted all the others, when speaking to the superior or with one another, not to raise their gaze above the level of the other person's chest.

181 One day I was walking with him along the covered way from the garden to the church, and we met a brother called Giovanni Domenico. He had been a novice for only a few months, a Roman by birth, whose eyes were always very lively and alert. Our Father wanted to admonish him and to help him alter his manner, but bearing in mind that he was still weak, he said to him, very gently, "Giovanni Domenico, why don't you show outwardly in your eyes the modesty that our Lord has impressed upon you in your soul?"

182 [n.d.] Once when the doctor had told him he should avoid any bout of melancholy, because that would harm him, the Father said afterwards, "I have considered what might cause me melancholy, and I have not found anything, except if the Pope were completely to undo the Society: and even this, I think, *if I were to recollect myself in prayer for a quarter of an hour,* [a] I would be as happy as before, and even more so."

Our Father told me this soon after my arrival in Rome.

[a] *if I were to recollect myself in prayer for a quarter of an hour*

A good proof of this is what I related above at the election of Paul IV.[131]

183 [n.d.] The Father was used to weeping[132] so continuously that unless during Mass he had wept three times, he felt he was without consolation. The doctor ordered him not to weep, and he accepted this through obedience. And so having accepted it through obedience, he finds, as often occurs in these matters, that now he receives much more consolation without weeping than he had previously. The Father admitted this to Fr. Polanco, according to what Fr. Olave told me.

[n.d.] Anything to do with God that the Father undertakes, he performs with an admirable recollection and promptness: and it appears clearly that he not only imagines God in front of him, but sees Him with his eyes. This might be seen *even when saying grace at table* [b] And for this same reason, so it is thought, comes the serious harm his body suffers *when he hears or says Mass,* [c] if he is not in good health; and even when he is, we have often seen him become sick on the day he has said Mass.

[b] *when saying grace at table*

184 He used to say grace before meals standing, preparing and recollecting himself briefly first, as he did in all the things of God. During the grace, he behaved with such devotion and special reverence that very often we were astonished, and those of us present turned our eyes to him. He said grace after meals in the same way, but I do not remember whether he was standing or sitting.

---

[131] See §93.
[132] The best witness to this frequency of tears is to be found in the *Spiritual Diary*, the second part of which consists mainly of a record of their daily occurrence.

He used this form of words for the grace before meals.

Marginal Note: Here is to be added the grace before meals that will come from Rome.

Benedicite.
Deus.
Nos et ea, quae sumpturi sumus
benedicat Deus trinus et unus,
Pater et Filius et Spiritus Sanctus, Amen.[133]

And for the grace after meals he used this form.

Marginal Note: Here will be added the grace after meals that I have requested from Rome, since I have forgotten the original.

Laus Deo, pax vivis, requies defunctis.
Pater Noster . . . et ne nos inducas in tentationem.
Sed libera nos a malo. Amen.
Christus Jesus det nobis suam sanctam pacem, benedic-tionem, et post mortem vitam aeternam. Amen.
Beata viscera Mariae Virginis, quae portaverunt aeterni Patris Filium. Amen.[134]

And now, as the mention of grace before and after meals provides a good opportunity, I will note here what I remember of our Father Ignatius at table.

185 Father Ignatius used to take his meals in a room[135] next to the

---

[133] The short grace, which is well authenticated as the one commonly used by Ignatius, has a mnemonic jingle, even if not strictly in verse form:
"Give the blessing!
Oh, God!
May the God who is One and Three
Bless our food and you and me,
Father, Son, and Holy Spirit,
the One and the Three."
[134] "Praise to God, peace to the living, and rest to those who have died!
Our Father . . . and lead us not into temptation, but deliver us from evil. Amen.
May Christ Jesus give us his holy peace, blessing, and after death eternal life. Amen.
Blessed the womb of the Virgin Mary, which bore the Son of the Eternal Father. Amen."
[135] The early Constitutions gave superiors leave to follow this custom of not eating in the normal refectory; however, subsequent General Congregations began by restricting the

room where he slept: the Fathers whom he consulted for advice on
the Society's business dined with him. Those were, at the time that
I was in Rome, Fathers Laínez, Salmerón, and Bobadilla, when
they were staying in Rome; and Fathers Nadal, Polanco, Madrid,
and myself, when we were living in the house; Frs. Olave and des
Freux often came from the College to the house, and Fr.
Ribadeneira, whom our Father sometimes called for from the college where he was. Besides these, when some Fathers or Brothers
departed from Rome or returned again there, they would eat with
him on one of the last days as a sign of charity and warm feeling.
At other times there were persons from outside the Society, those
having authority and virtue, and devoted to the Society. To these
our Father used to say when inviting them, "Sir, please stay with
us, if you would like to do some penance."[136]

186 The food we ate at table was the following: in winter, mutton,
and in summer, *comparicha*,[137] that is to say, veal, which costs the
same as mutton in Rome; no other kind of meat, such as goat or
fowl, was ever served at table even though there were guests. No
one was served separately at table, but the meat dish was placed in
the middle of the table, and each one served himself on his own
plate. I do not remember if there was an *antipasto* at the midday
meal; at supper in winter some cooked vegetables were served as a
starter, or small dishes of carrots, and in summer some herb salads
or some local fruit. The dessert was usually cheese or some fruit as
I have mentioned, and that ended the meal. However, when the
Father was sick, he was given chicken if we were eating meat, but
for lack of a cook who knew how to prepare it properly, it was usually insipid and badly cooked.

187 I remember I once spoke very badly about a chicken he was
eating, but the Father made no reply and finished eating it impas-
sively. However, after the meal he reprimanded me because of
what I had said, remarking that it showed a lack of discretion to
disparage to a sick person what he was eating, because this could

---

privilege to the General in Rome, and then abolished it.
    [136] The MSHI editors point out that this phrase has a place in the Dictionary of the
Spanish Academy of 1734 (with quotations from Cervantes), and was probably a set
expression of polite invitation.
    [137] Perhaps a slang word in Italian or Portugese.

do him no good, but only hindered him from eating something which he needed.

188 Our Father ate very sparingly, and accordingly the portions of meat or fish that were served to his table-companions were small. Apropos of this I remember that one day we were served dogfish (a fish which in Rome is more unwholesome than in Portugal); one of us told Fr. Bobadilla that he should not eat it because it was bad for him, to which he replied, pressing on regardless, "*Modicum veneni non nocet.*"[138]

189 Returning to our Father Ignatius: everyone who dealt with him was astonished at the great mortification he displayed in his eating habits. For far from making any comment or showing any satisfaction about what he ate, either during the meal or afterwards, he did not even show the slightest sign of liking anything, however exquisite it might be; simply, having risen from the table, if his companion referred to the meal, he used to repeat the simple expression: "It suited me." Similarly, if the dish served at table was not well cooked, was too salted or insipid, and even if it might have damaged his health, he still did not criticise it or complain with the slightest gesture or remark while at table, but later after the meal he would give Giovanni Battista, the cook, a penance to train his virtue, as I have already said.[139]

And since his stomach could not take any form of acidic food, he was given a little sweet wine on the doctor's orders, and even if frequently, because it had been kept badly, the wine was very sour, the Father drank it without saying anything or giving any indication of his feelings. After the meal he would call the Brother in charge of this, and inform him, saying, "The wine today was a little acidic." This characteristic was so marked that he really seemed to have lost his sense of taste in this area. And so, in all the time that I was in Rome I do not remember him ever ordering anything special to eat, or giving any hint as to how he would like his meals to be cooked. The treat that we used to give him sometimes was four roasted chestnuts: as these had been products of his native country and he had been brought up on them as a child, they seemed to make him happy.

---

[138] "A pinch of poison does no harm." Bobadilla may have been quoting the Latin tag or may have invented it.

[139] See §106.

He had another custom: while at table he never said to his companions that they should eat up, nor did he offer them any dish.

190 Although, as I have said, he ate little, he still never finished his meal before his companions: and so he used to take a small piece of bread, and crumble it and then eat it slowly in such tiny fragments (at the same time making the most of the conversation), so that in the final reckoning he finished eating at the same time as the others, giving the impression that all along he had been eating with them. Such was this habit that sometimes, when already at the end of a meal, if someone arrived from outside, one of those he used to invite "to do penance," the Father would sit him down, and in this way, with his little bits of bread, keep company with the one who had only just started eating, not leaving off until he had finished.

191 Just as he was himself very polite in his demeanour while eating, so he wanted no member of the Society to arouse adverse comment in this matter. There used to eat at his table one of the earliest Fathers whose manner when drinking was somewhat unedifying. I remember that once our Father said to me: "I have just had a visit from Ponzio[140] and he told me that N. has the habit of drinking in this way. I noticed it a long time ago, but as I thought others would not pay attention, I did not mention it to him, but now that other people have noticed, I will speak to him." And so he did.

192 At table our Father listened more to the conversation of others rather than spoke himself. Those conversations were not on subjects of great importance, or that required much reflection. Instead the Fathers told him about current affairs, as much in Italy as elsewhere, which might have some bearing on the good government of the Society, and also some entertaining and pious stories, some of which are included in this folder.[141] In these familiar discussions our Father showed himself not at all a spoil-sport or a bore, but he had a religious cheerfulness and ease of manner, balanced with his gifts of gravity and prudence. And so not lacking

---

[140] Fr. Ponzio Cogordan, who held the post of procurator in the house; he is mentioned below, §§193, 216.

[141] The words used by da Câmara here, *neste cartapacio*, seem to refer to a folder containing the papers and notes connected with the *Memoriale*.

these virtues, he applauded with humour what others said and did.

The table itself, although, as I said, poor, was always very clean in every respect.

On one occasion I and several Fathers of the community were eating without our Father being present. On that occasion we were given only two or three eggs apiece, and afterwards the Brother serving at table presented us, on a plate, with some toothpicks, dipped in wine and covered with sage leaves. One of us said to him. "Now you bring us toothpicks to clean our teeth, but we still haven't had anything to make them dirty!" Our Father enjoyed that sally when he was told about it later.

193 The Captain of La Goleta[142] asked our Father for a preacher for that garrison. There was hardly anyone available for this in the house, but Fr. Polanco thought that Fr. Mendoza, at that time in Rome, would be able to go. He suggested this to our Father, but he did not want him to go without our first hearing him preach at home, so that we could judge for ourselves how he seemed. Therefore he told him to preach in the refectory. At that time I was still new to Rome, and although I would usually have been eating with our Father, Fr. Polanco took me to the refectory to hear the sermon. We were together listening, and Fr. Polanco, who wanted to know if I was satisfied with the sermon, kept nudging me with his elbow and asking, "What does your Reverence think of the sermon? Is he up to going to La Goleta? Is he up to going to La Goleta?" I did not want to discourage him by saying how I felt, so I kept quiet for as long as I could, but he so persisted with his question that I replied, "Father, he's up to going if he can find a good ship for the passage." Fr. Polanco told this little story afterwards to our Father, who was very amused to hear it.

Once when Fr. Ponzio, at that time procurator of the house, was dining with our Father, he happened to say humorously that a cardinal with whom he went to eat, had served lampreys. He was temperamentally rather mean and our Father wanted to mortify the cause of that particular tendency and perfect him in charity towards his brothers. For this reason he replied thus: "Do you

[142] See §15, where the name Cristóbal de Mendoza is mentioned.

think it is all right for you to eat lampreys, while the brethren have only sardines? Now go and look for some lampreys so that all the brethren may enjoy them." He began to shilly-shally and to worry about the lack of money, but our Father did not take back what he had said until some days later, during which he kept him in a state of anxiety and mortification, but since it was only this that he was after and not that we should actually eat lampreys, he finally decided they should not be bought.

(c) *when he hears or says Mass*

194 By this time for reasons of health our Father could not say Mass except on Sundays and holy days. Because he suffered so much from stomach pains, even when changing into a fresh shirt its chill caused him such great discomfort that he could not say Mass the following day; so he took the habit of changing on Saturday morning, or on Friday evening. The evening before he had to say Mass he sent for the missal, and read it several times in his room, studying all the details; then afterwards he said Mass in the Roman style, in which the priest speaks out so loud that he can be heard all over the church. And so the Father, although he was celebrating in the chapel, intoned out loud as if he were in the church.

195 [n.d.] When the Father speaks about prayer, it always appears that he takes for granted that the passions have all been fully mastered and mortified, and *it is this that he most respects.*[a] I remember that once when I was speaking of a good religious[b], [143] whom he knew and I said that he was a man of much prayer, the Father altered my remark and said, "He is a man of much mortification." And indeed one seems to see all this quite clearly in the Father's way of proceeding.

{a} *it is this that he most respects*

196 The first time that Fr. Nadal came as "Visitor"[144] to Spain, which was in 1555, members of the Society in some places spoke to him about the Society's manner of prayer; they complained

---

[143] Identified in §198 as Fray Luis de Montoya (1497-1569); the General Chapter mentioned there took place in Bologna, but he visited Rome in 1551 and then came to know Ignatius.

[144] See Glossary. Ignatius began the custom of appointing official "Visitors" to different provinces of the Society, their duties varying from those of trouble-shooters (as happened in Portugal), to those of heralds for the newly written *Constitutions*.

of the little amount of time we gave to such a holy exercise, saying that we could not sustain ourselves unless it were increased, and that it was shameful to reply to those who asked us, that we allowed no more than one hour of prayer the whole day. Because of these arguments Fr. Nadal was rather inclined to take the same view when he returned to Rome.[145] Then on the feast of St. Cecilia, 22 November 1554, as he reported to our Father on affairs in Spain, he put the complaint to him, somewhat favouring that he should, at least in that province, concede to it. Our Father was in bed and only I was present with the two of them. He replied to the argument with an expression and words of such aversion and displeasure that truly I was amazed; and he reprimanded Fr. Nadal and imposed such a heavy penance that I admired Fr. Nadal's patience, even though I was very aware of his great virtue. Finally he said, "For someone who is truly mortified a quarter of an hour of prayer is enough to unite him to God." And I do not know if it was then that he added on the same theme something which we heard him say many times: that of a hundred people given to prayer, ninety were subject to illusions. And I can remember this quite clearly, though I am not sure if he used to say ninety or ninety-nine.

197 Apropos of illusions, I will relate something here on the subject that surprised many people. In the year of '44 [1544] there became known in Italy a woman,[146] born in Bologna, famous for her spirituality and sanctity. After she had spent a long time in contemplation and had undergone extraordinary experiences, she withdrew to the mountains near Bologna to apply herself exclusively to perfection, very remote from people. In those mountains she attracted and converted many brigands, murderers and outcasts who live there; she led them to penance, confession and the other sacraments, which were administered to them by respectable priests who for this purpose dwelt there with her. What caused the greatest astonishment in Italy was that she had an open wound in her side, like that of St. Francis, from which blood truly flowed. This marvel became so famous that people came from everywhere to see it. Even two of the Fathers of this province of Portugal,

---

[145] 18 October 1554.

[146] Identified in §344 as "Jacome"; the MHSI editors note that there was a certain Giacoba Bartolini, about whom very similar accounts are given in a 17th-century work, but without any indication that she suffered from illusions.

while returning from Rome, went a little out of their way, so that both, or one of them, could see her. When they arrived here in 1551, they showed such satisfaction in telling me this, that even I, critical as I am in giving credit to the spiritual experiences of women, had a good impression of the occurrences. Since I felt it was a matter of great importance I told the Queen about it, so that she very much wanted to receive more news about the events.

When later I went to Rome for the first time,[147] I fell into conversation one day with Fr. Ribadeneira on this subject. He told me that at the time that this woman was most esteemed, there was in Rome a certain friar,[148] who was an elderly, highly virtuous, and very prayerful man; he had been her confessor in Bologna for a long time. As he was a great friend of Fr. Ignatius and of the Society, the Father invited him to eat at our house. While he was at table he talked the whole time of the marvellous sanctity and virtues of that woman, and especially of the wound, which he asserted he had seen and had confirmed that the blood was really flowing, as was said. But our Father made no reply except vague words of approval of what he had been saying. After the friar had left, Fr. Ribadeneira asked our Father what his Reverence thought of that wound and the other matters he had talked about. The Father made no reply except with the same generalities, saying, for example, "Everything is good, everything is a grace of God," and other similar remarks. He pressed him strongly to give his opinion more precisely, until our Father closed the discussion by saying: "Our Lord can, and is accustomed to, grant graces and mercies from the inside and from deep within; the devil can do nothing except from the outside, and sometimes God allows him to do this sort of thing."

And it happened exactly like this, because already at the time when Fr. Ribadeneira told me this, both the wound and the other extraordinary phenomena had been converted into just wind and nothing.

(b) a good religious

198 This was the priest, Friar Luís de Montoya, a reformer and provincial of the Augustinians in this Kingdom [Portugal]. He

---

[147] In 1553.
[148] Fr. Reginald Nerli, O.P., according to Ribadeneira, who dates the following conversation between Ignatius and Fr. Nerli to 23 May 1553; MHSI, *Scripta*, I, 341-42.

went to Rome for a meeting of his general chapter, and had several conversations with our Father, to whom he made his general confession.

199 [n.d.] The Father has subtle tricks for getting to know the feelings and inclinations of each individual, for example by touching on general themes and waiting till the person spoken to opens up what is on his mind. When chatting with someone he is such a master both of himself and of the person to whom he is speaking that, although it may be a Polanco, the Father seems to take the upper hand like a prudent adult with a child. I must recall details of this, because certainly it is well worth dwelling on how the Father may look someone in the face, though rarely, how he sometimes stays silent, and how, finally, he employs such great prudence and divinely inspired stratagems, so that the first time he converses with someone, *he immediately knows him*[a] inside out.

[n.d.] Usually he works in this way: everything he wants to know about someone and can easily learn, he finds out from a third person. Similarly, if he wants to reprimand someone he does so by means of a third person, in such a way that he runs no risk that the person reprimanded will lose the affection such a person feels for him.[149]

[a] *he immediately knows him*

Good examples of this (in addition to many others that I do not remember) were the two Fathers of whom I spoke earlier,[150] whom Fr. Ignatius immediately recognised as unsuitable for the Society, even though in their own province they held great authority and were highly esteemed. Not only did he know those he was talking to through and through, but they themselves clearly appreciated that he knew them and penetrated them entirely.

200 *At one time*[b] the Father was accustomed to spend seven hours in prayer every day.

[b] *At one time*

Our Father himself told me this when he was narrating his life to me.[151]

---

[149] See §88.
[150] §115.
[151] Cf. *Autobiography,* §§23, 26; the narration took place in 1553 and 1555.

23 February

201 1. On the occasions when there are as many people at second table, there should be reading in the refectory for them, the same reading as that at first table. *But firstly,* [a] before starting this, let everyone be told that this is being done only for some time, while there are so many people.

[a] *But firstly*

He did not want to give the impression afterwards that this custom had been introduced without consideration, or abandoned through inconstancy.

202 2. When I changed a subject of conversation without warning or asking permission to do so, the Father stayed a long time without speaking to me. This is a characteristic of his that is continually observed: he never changes a subject of conversation without preamble, nor do those who are in conversation with him *without asking his permission.* [b] His conversation is so orderly, that he says nothing by chance, without first having thoroughly reflected on it. For this reason all his remarks are like rules, and all are in agreement one with another, even when they have been uttered at different times and with regard to different subjects of discussion.

[n.d.] It is also remarkable *how patiently he listens to so many* [useless] *topics* [c] from visitors, and even to long accounts from those of the community that could well be made shorter, and later how he will make a reference in such a way that one can see that he had kept his mind separate from the topic, and was applying the conversation to some spiritual matter to which it seems he was trying to adapt it. So, for example, if an outside visitor speaks of wars, he will apply it to spiritual conflicts, etc.

[b] *without asking his permission*

203 Thus, for example, when we might be talking about affairs in Italy, and someone wanted to ask about Spain, we had first to ask, "If your Reverence will allow me" or "Will your Reverence allow

me to raise the subject of a matter in Spain which has occurred to me?", or "I am afraid I may forget," or similar words.

(c) *how patiently he listens to so many topics*

204 However, there was one thing in conversation he could not abide, and that not only among ourselves, but even among outsiders: this was to speak pompously and authoritatively, as though laying down the law, as for example if someone says, "It is necessary that we do so and so; there is no other possible way than this; the truth of the matter is so and so," and other similar modes of expression. Our Father used to call those who employed such expressions "decretists,"[152] and as I say, he reproved them; and he considered such manners so bad that he criticized them even in a most important ambassador, a friend and supporter of the Society in Rome. He came to the residence a few times and expressed himself in this way: "The Pope ought to do this or that. . . ; Such and such a cardinal must do the other. . . ; You need such and such a thing in that garden-plot. . . ; It is essential to have an order given for it to be made," etc. Our Father therefore replied to him in the same way, advising him and reminding him of his duties and he said to us afterwards: "Since he is a decretist, he will put up with being given decrees!"

205 3. Our Father says of our neighbour who wants to go to law over the construction of the *solana*[153] that he will never agree to do this; rather, we should give him whatever he wants. Because if we lose something for the love of God, God will compensate us some other way.

I remember the Father having said to me several times that he had never gone to law over a temporal matter: and so it was that for so many years *Mutio kept the cortil [courtyard]*[a] of our house, which was so necessary to let light into the refectory; and later, when he sold the house last year, he took away the doors and windows, even the iron gates and stones, etc.

(a) *Mutio kept the cortil*

206 Mutio was a Roman gentleman, our neighbour, an individual

[152] A medieval term for students of law.
[153] The term *solana* is used for a room or gallery that catches the sun; it may have functioned as part of the infirmary mentioned above, §161.

of violent temper.[154] He used a courtyard, called the *cortil*, which being on our site undoubtedly belonged to our houses. He, however, seeking to have us buy all the houses from him, on this account not only kept the use of it for himself, but prevented us from opening some small windows in the wall of the refectory, which was next to the *cortil*, without which we could not have sufficient light in the refectory. Not satisfied with this he let loose some peacocks in that patio—I do not know if this was just to create a bad neighbourhood for us—who with their incessant squawks disturbed us and made our heads ache, since some of us had rooms with large windows onto this courtyard. And despite being very anxious to sell us the house, he went round Rome complaining about us, saying that there were none worse than these Theatines,[155] who wanted to take his property by force, and what he would do to us, and what would happen to us, and similar silly remarks. Finally we bought them for much more than they were worth. . .[156] and when he left he took with him the doors, windows, iron grills, and even some of the carved stones.

Our Father preferred to suffer all this with consummate patience, to avoid lawsuits with him. Nevertheless, at the same time, and with his approval and permission, we were dealing with the lawsuits that people were bringing against us over the properties of many colleges.[157]

24 February

207 I must remember what Fr. des Freux told me about our Father: (i) grace seemed to be connatural to him; (ii) he had so accustomed his natural passions to virtue that even they of their own account served him, it

---

[154] This gentleman, Mutio Muti, is known from other sources for the difficulties he caused.

[155] The Theatines were something of a rival religious congregation, recently set up by the saintly Cajetan of Thiene and the formidable Cardinal Carafa (the future Pope Paul IV so dreaded by Ignatius, cf. §93); the Jesuits would not have been amused to find themselves confused with them, as Mutio probably realized.

[156] The manuscript here is worn away, and some words have been lost.

[157] It is a little surprising that da Câmara does not refer to the different legal status of the colleges (entitled to accept and protect capital given by their founders) and the professed houses (residences), which deliberately renounced the right to possess fixed income.

appeared, for nothing else but good.

And certainly in this there is good reason to give great praise to God for the complete dominion over his soul God has given him.

208   2.   The Father has ordered the examination of three candidates: although he was more inclined to examine all three together, nevertheless he left it rather to their preference.

This examination, as far as I remember, was that customary in the so-called First Probation for those entering the Society.

25 February

209   During the pilgrimage to the Seven Churches[158] of Rome Fr. Ribadeneira has told us about the solemn profession and the election of our Father along with the others.[159] It was made at the altar of the Blessed Sacrament at St. Paul's. Our Father wrote *an account of this*[a] in his own hand, and Fr. Polanco has to give it to me.

[a] *an account of this:* This account, which I will ask from Fr. Polanco,[160] will be included here.

210   I must remember how the Father went without eating for three days, praying that one member of the Society would not fail to make his profession.[161]

---

[158] It was customary in Lent to make the round of seven designated churches (the major basilicas: St. Peter's, St. John Lateran, St. Mary Major, St. Paul outside the Walls, Santa Croce, St. Lawrence and St. Sebastian—both outside the Walls) in order to gain a plenary indulgence.

[159] Following the Papal approval of the new religious order (September 1540) it was possible, early in April 1541, for six members of the original group still in Rome (viz. Ignatius, Broët, Codure, Jay, Laínez, Salmerón), with the agreement of the other four (Favre, Xavier, Rodrigues, Bobadilla), to proceed with the election of the first General Superior. They chose Ignatius, who was thus authorised to receive the first solemn vows. This ceremony took place in St. Paul's Outside the Walls on Easter Friday, 22 April. Ribadeneira, then a lad of fourteen but already admitted as a novice, was present at the ceremony, which he was to describe later, and then went back with them to help cook the midday meal.

[160] Although not included in the *Memoriale* this account has been preserved and published elsewhere: MHSI, *Fontes Narrativae*, I, 16-22.

[161] This is taken to be a guarded reference to the mercurial Bobadilla, as Nadal mentions the difficulties he raised against the vows when he returned to Rome; if so, Ignatius's prayer was soon answered as Bobadilla made his solemn profession before Ignatius in the same chapel in October 1541.

211 Last Saturday[162] one of our community asked our Father's permission to invite a certain religious to dine in the house. He was a great friend, well known and used to visiting us. But when he [the host] said he had given a hint to the friar before asking permission, the Father ordered him to take a discipline for the length of a psalm, and gave him a public reprimand. Afterwards he called him and said he agreed to the religious's coming, provided he did not learn about the discipline.

26 February

212 1. Today[163] the Father asked the doctor together with others responsible to examine those who are to fast, *or to observe Lent*[a], and since he has been asking this for two days, he gave the order that neither Fr. Polanco nor the rest of us should eat today until we had given him a written account. It was brought to him before the meal, and after eating the Father spent two hours examining each one to see what he was able to do, those who were doubtful, and those not old enough, including both members of the residence and of the College, and he wishes to do the same at the German College.

The Father was always inclined towards kindness, and that was the way he said was good; even so, this was with regard to some for certain particular reasons; for some it appeared better to him to let them fast for the whole of Lent, for children, one day in the week, for those aged nineteen or twenty, three days, and for those doing manual work, such as builders, none at all.

The Father, even though the doctor orders that he should always eat meat, said nevertheless that he would look into it, given that last year he ate meat on only three days.

The Father ordered that a good reprimand [*capelo*] should be written to Sicily because they had allowed the boys to fast for the whole of Lent; he usually disapproved of making all the novices fast simply because they were novices.

[162] 23 February.
[163] Shrove Tuesday.

(a) *to observe Lent*

To "observe Lent" means to eat fish during Lent.

213 The Father said today, and I have heard him say so on other occasions, that for the German College it was more likely that it would have too much income rather than too little, and *therefore when*(b) the Cardinal of Augsburg[164] was discouraged, and did not wish to undertake responsibility for this enterprise, the Father told him that if he fell short, he himself alone would take it on.

(b) *therefore when*

Here again is an example of the great constancy of our Father, of which I wrote about apropos of the same German College.[165] And what he said about providing finance for the College turned out to be so correct, that at present, the expenses of thirty members of the Society living and working in the college are met from the income from the boarders.

214 2. The Father examined a man who was weak both physically and psychologically[166] with regard to his physical infirmities, and ordered him to put in writing everything that could cause him harm or was necessary for him, and he ordered this should be carried out accordingly.

215 [n.d.] The compassion that the Father shows to the sick is something to be admired; thus it is his custom, whenever he finds novices a little weak or looking pale, to order them to sleep longer, or to take some respite from their tasks; in everything, *videtur induisse viscera misericordiae* [he seems to have "put on bowels of compassion"].[167] As for having things put in writing, it is his custom to do this with every affair, and afterwards he himself will read it and reflect on it.

216 On the 8th of this month four members of the College visited the Seven Churches[168] and they took something to eat with them, since the

[164] Cardinal Otto Truchsess von Waldburg, Bishop of Augsburg from 1543 and a Cardinal from 1544.
[165] See §§16-17.
[166] The Latin tag *in utroque homine* is used to express "physically and psychologically" (body and soul).
[167] Cf. Col. 3:12.
[168] See §209 (with note) and §237.

visit took all day. On the same day three of the older men from the residence, who took nothing with them, also went, and later told the Father that they had met the four from the College. And to one of them, who was *micer* Ponzio (the one who told our Father), he replied with great praise for having spoken, so that he could remedy the situation. *And so our Father ordered*[a] penances to be given to all those who had gone from the College, and to the ministers who had allowed it; also it was to be made a rule for both the College and the house that no one visiting the Churches or making the stations should carry anything to eat or the means to buy it, or ask for alms on the way, but that they could make some visits before the meal, return to eat at the house, and then continue to visit the remaining churches.

The reason for making this an order is the scandal it causes to those who see them behaving otherwise. And so our Father wishes that those who are not strong enough to proceed in this way should not go at all.

The rector[169] of the College excused himself, saying that he was new, and had found that custom being followed, that is, that those who were visiting the Seven Churches should take something with them to eat. The Father did not accept this excuse, and said the duty of a rector, when there was a bad custom, was to inform the superior; because at the beginning one person does something small, then later another person adds to it; so that what may have been tolerable at the beginning later becomes intolerable. When the Society began in Rome the Father tolerated this; now it no longer seems tolerable, since the Society is well known.

[a] *And so our Father ordered*

217 The method he chose for the execution of these penances was the following. He sent me on my own expressly for this from the residence, where I was minister, to the College, with instructions about what was to be done written on a piece of paper. In accordance with these there went to the refectory to confess publicly their fault not only the four who had done the round of the "stations," viz. the superintendent,[170] the rector, the minister, and the

[169] Fr. Sebastiano Romei, successor to Olivier Manare and rector from 1554 to 1568; he died in 1574.

[170] At this period Ignatius had appointed for the Roman College, in addition to the rector (i.e. the normal superior), a "superintendent" who was his personal delegate (cf.

sub-minister, but also all those office-holders through whose hands had passed the food they had taken outside. Each one held in his hand a symbol that best displayed his fault: e.g. the baker, the bread; the pantry man, the fish; another, the nuts; the launderer, the table napkins; and the upper superiors other symbols of greater penance, that I do not recall well. After they had walked in order round the refectory, they all received a reprimand at the "little table."[171] This penance is an example of what the Father used to impose, each of which was, as far as it could be, correspondent to the fault.

218 I recall another, which, because it corresponded to the fault, greatly satisfied the Father. One of the fathers preached in the refectory, and in the course of his sermon laid down rules for the minister and sub-minister on the conduct of their offices. He was a man whose virtue and simplicity were well known, and at the same time he was so very fond of preaching that whenever he wrote a letter to his superior or to any other member of the Society, he always signed himself, "So-and-so, willing to preach." During the meal when he preached that sermon I was eating with our Father, but when the meal had finished, and I was going to the kitchen, they told me about the rules he had given and other things he had said. At once I sent him a message saying that I would like to profit from his sermon for my own office as minister, and since I had not heard him, I said that he should give the same sermon again at second table, which he did word for word. When he had completed it the second time, I asked him to repeat it a third time, and again a fourth, and then a fifth time, which he did in full, losing none of his fervour, and citing the same authorities, as if it were for the first time. And he did all this though there was only Fr. Don Diego (whom I shall mention soon) left in the refectory, who listened to him always very attentively. When Fr. Ignatius learned about the sermon, every time they went to tell him he was beginning once more he showed great pleasure and satisfaction.

219 3. Today, the 26th, Shrove Tuesday, the Father allowed many to take the discipline in the servery[172] as their devotion inclined them, and many

Constitutions, IV, 10, 3A [422]; VI, 2, 1A [558]). The practice continued under Laínez, who appointed Nadal to this position, but this multiplicity of "heads" inevitably led to friction and was later discontinued.

[171] See §140, with note.

[172] The Italian word used here (*tinelo*) may refer to a smaller refectory used by staff.

others wanted to do the same. In this the Father's custom was to be liberal.

220 Today *Micer* Andreas, a Fleming, departed, consoled and edified.

> This is the Flemish priest about whom I wrote above,[173] whom our Father wanted to make a pilgrimage as far as Loreto; he was dismissed, as explained in the account.

221 *Today a father has taken*[a] a discipline for the length of three psalms; three others were in the room next door, with the door open, and heard him, and he repeated after each psalm: "You must speak clearly and without equivocation in matters that can give scandal." He will perform the same penance on two more days. The Father had imposed it because he had spoken of him with such excessive praise that others, who did not appreciate his simplicity and praiseworthy zeal, were scandalized.[174]

> [a] *Today a father has taken*

> This father was Don Diego de Eguía about whom I wrote above.[175] Fr. Favre always called him "Saint Don Diego." In order that the prudence and candour of this good old man be more appreciated, I am going to relate here some of the things I still remember about him.

> He often used to repeat sayings of the kind: "The man who thinks he is good for something, is good for very little; he who thinks he is good for a great deal, is good for nothing." To explain how little confidence he had in his own merits for his salvation, and how much he placed it in the Society and order where he was, he would use this simile: "If you offer payment only with a damaged coin that has no value, no one wants to accept it. But when you pay a thousand *cruzados* to a merchant dealing in bulk, even though one of the coins lacks its correct value, it slips through. In the same way my only hope of getting through is thanks to the rest of the Society."

---

[173] Cf. §§127-28, where da Câmara explains the peculiar nature of the expulsion, which was more an invitation to reconsider and leave if he so desired.

[174] Perhaps the Dominican, Melchor Cano, is being referred to here; see §162 with note.

[175] Cf. §162.

He had a special gift from God for comforting and retaining those being tempted, even if it was to leave the Society, and he was so zealous in this matter that there was not a single person suffering temptation in the house, to whom he did not go to help, and he would not leave him till he saw he had a remedy. Indeed it was a sign that someone was troubled when Don Diego was seen to be looking for him and spending a long time talking to him. And to those who talked to him about their affairs, however misled they might be, he always replied, "That's going fine! That's going fine!" For example, if someone said to him, "Father, I really can't bear so much subjection and mortification of my own will!", he would reply with great efficacy and good judgement, "That's a good way to go! That's going fine!" And, "Father, today I have decided to ask for permission to leave this house: this sort of life is not for me," he would chime in at once, "That's going fine!" And it was the same in everything else; he always sought for victory over the temptation and for the great benefit that could come to them from that.

222 In this way he guided and retained many. In particular I remember a doctor, a very learned and distinguished man, who experienced great difficulties at the beginning of his religious life because he suffered many indispositions and because of the extraordinary physical treatment he had given himself in the world. It was only because of his long conversations with Father Don Diego that he stayed in the Society, persevered, and died in it, giving a most edifying example.

To outsiders, whether he met them at hostels or wherever else he might meet them, he talked only about God and spiritual things, without making any use of human preparation.

223 Father Araoz told me that once, when the two of them were going from Rome to Spain,[176] after he had converted a soldier he had met on the road, he told him he should go to Rome and make the Spiritual Exercises. The soldier replied that he did not have enough money for the journey, and Fr. Diego gave him I don't know how many *escudos*. I would be surprised if he did not do the same on other occasions, but I remember well enough that he sent and brought many to the Exercises.

[176] In 1542.

224 4. Our Father learned that a man on the point of death had asked at the residence for a confessor, but when the confessor arrived he found the man already dead, because he had had to delay a little. The Father felt this deeply and ordered a consultation of all the priests to prevent this happening again, so that as soon as someone arrived with a similar message, the confessor might go immediately. The Father said they should see whether perhaps it would be a good idea that as soon as the request arrived at the door, the porter should ring the bell in a special way so that all the confessors would know what it was, and would be obliged to go to the door so that one of them might go immediately.

225 [n.d.] Concerning our affairs in Paris, when during recent days the ques- tion was being dealt with, our Father was talking about how bad it seemed to him to use biting words in writing letters. He then said that many times people had written strong criticisms to him about himself, even after he was in his position [as General Superior], *and he never wanted*[a] to reply or return evil for evil, even though he could easily have done so, *etiam in opere* ["even in deeds"].

     [a] *and he never wanted*

     Everyone knows of many examples of this.

226 [n.d.] Speaking about the [Spiritual] Exercises, he said that of those he knew in the Society Fr. Favre took the first place in giving them, Salmerón the second, and then he put Francisco from Villanueva[177] and Jerónimo Domenech.[178] He also said that Estrada[179] gave those of the First Week well.

     [n.d.] I must recall one thing, namely, how many times I have remarked how the Father in his entire manner of proceeding observes all

---

[177] Francisco (1509-57), born in Villanueva, an uneducated layman sent to Rome by his parish priest; he joined the Society in 1541 and was much esteemed by Ignatius and by Salmerón, with whom he would give the Exercises. Later appointed rector in Alcalá de Henares, he was always known as "Brother Francisco" even when ordained to the priesthood.

[178] A native of Valencia, Domenech (1506-1593) was already a canon with an M.A. when he joined the Jesuits (1540); he was influential in persuading Nadal to enter, and was later appointed Provincial of Sicily.

[179] Francisco de Estrada (1518-1584) joined the companions in Venice as early as 1538 and was a Jesuit from the foundation of the order; he preached in the Netherlands and Spain, becoming Provincial of Aragon for four years (1554-58).

the rules of the Exercises exactly, in such a way that he seems to have planted them first in his soul, and that all the rules have been drawn from the reactions he felt.[180] The same can be said about Gerson[181] [*The Imitation of Christ*], to such a point that a conversation with the Father seems like a reading of Jean Gerson put into practice. And I must remember many particular cases from which this general conclusion can be drawn. The same can be said about the *Constitutions*, especially the chapter in which he portrays the General,[182] in which he seems to have painted a portrait of himself.

227 [n.d.] The Father's way of speaking is always factual, with very few words, and without any reflection about the facts, but simply telling them. In this way he leaves it to his listeners to make the reflection, and draw conclusions from the premises. And in this way he is astonishingly persuasive, showing no inclination to one side or the other, but simply narrating. Where his art comes in is that he touches on all the essential points that can persuade one, and leaves aside all the others which are beside the point, as seems necessary. As for his way of talking to others, he has received such gifts from God that they can hardly be written about.

228 [n.d.] For *the Polish business*[(a), 183] Cardinal dal Pozzo,[184] as protector of that kingdom, wanted two members of the Society, and was not content with Bobadilla alone. The Father went to talk to him, and gave him a *discourse*[(b)] about everything that Bobadilla had done until now in the service of the church, touching on those points from which you could see that he would be very appropriate for this task on his own; on the other hand he stressed all the needs of the Society. But Cardinal dal Pozzo, although he took the point to some extent, nevertheless spoke afterwards to the Pope (Julius III), telling him that he should order the

---

[180] The Spanish reads: *de los actos que tenía en ella [i.e. en su ánima],* which seems to refer to the various spiritual movements (of consolation and desolation) so carefully noted in the Exercises.

[181] See §§97-98.

[182] *Constitutions* IX, 2 (§§723-35).

[183] This was linked to the appointment by Julius III of Luigi Lippomano, Bishop of Verona, as Apostolic Nuncio to Sigismund (II), King of Poland; it was thought that somebody should go with him. Eventually, when Paul IV was elected, as Bobadilla was unwell, he was replaced by Salmerón (alone!), who left Rome with Lippomano at the end of July 1555, and returned at the end of November. For the problem of Fr. Salmerón's mule, see also §406.

[184] Da Câmara uses the Latin-based form *Púteo*, which translates the Italian *pozzo* of the Cardinal's name (meaning a "well"); Giacomo dal Pozzo (1497-1563) was Archbishop of Bari and Cardinal Protector of Poland.

assignment of two men. However, the Pope did not wish to decide anything, but referred the matter to our Father. The Father then decided *to
add on another one*[c] and so he added Fr. Battista Viola,[185] who is in
Genoa.

[a] *the Polish business*

229 I do not remember what the purpose of this embassy was, but
I certainly do recall that in the end it was not effective.

[b] *a discourse*

This is an example of the way our Father would describe things
when he wanted to persuade someone. Possibly the Cardinal
would have understood less of the situation if the Father, leaving
aside his simple narration, had extolled and exaggerated the qualities of Father Bobadilla.

[c] *to add on another one*

I think he added Fr. Battista as a companion because the Pope,
in referring the decision to him, showed some inclination in favour
of this decision; if he had shown no inclination at all, the Father
would have denied him to the Cardinal.

230 [n.d.] Last year our Father wrote to Spain that they should have letters *from the Prince*[a], [186] to the Pope [Julius III] and some cardinals in
support of the Roman College. The letters reached here in the summer,
but the Father kept the letter to the Pope until the news of the reconciliation of England[187] arrived, which was in December. That same day, the
Pope being very happy and full of good will to Prince Philip,[188] the Father

[185] Battista Viola (b. 1517), a priest from Parma, joined Ignatius in Rome in 1541, and
was involved with the troubles with the *Parlement* in Paris in the mid-1550s; he was the
recipient of an interesting letter where Ignatius first tackles the notion of "blind obedience" (*Select Letters*, No. 11).

[186] The future Philip II; his letter to the Pope in favour of the Roman College is dated
22 April 1554.

[187] According to Pastor (*History of the Popes*, XIII [English ed., R. F. Kerr, London,
1924], pp. 286-89) England returned to the Roman fold on 30 November 1554, at ceremonies presided over by Cardinal Pole; news of this reached Rome only on 14 December.
Incidentally, the word Ignatius uses for "reconciliation" is *reducción* (cf. §34).

[188] Prince Philip, as husband to Mary Tudor since July 1554, had been influential in
the reconciliation that brought this "good will" at the end of 1554.

had him given the letter by Montesa, who is acting as ambassador,[189] and giving the latter this message, that as soon as he had spoken he should have a written report sent to the Father about everything favourable that he had heard from the Pope. The Father *sent this report*[b] to all the cardinals, who had to speak on this subject to the Pope, so that they would not be afraid of speaking, seeing he was so well disposed, as indeed he was. And so after many days had been occupied with this, and after the Father had taken a great deal of trouble, on the 6th of this month of February the Pope decided in a consistory to give the College a financial reserve fund of 2000 ducats for income, and 50 more each month from his own income, starting straightaway.[190]

[a] *from the Prince*

231 The prince was Philip, now King of Castile, and at that time governing Spain because the Emperor [Charles V] his father was in Flanders. Letters were written to some of our Fathers who had influence with him here.[191]

[b] *sent this report*

I am not absolutely certain if our Father used on this occasion another precaution that I have seen him employ in many matters of this kind. It was that when he wanted to show a similar document to cardinals or other important people, he had as many copies taken along as were required for those who needed to read them, and beside this the original as well, which was shown them first, so that on reading it they could see what authority it had, and later a copy was made available, saying, "Here is a copy as an *aide-mémoire* and reminder for Your Lordship."

232 [n.d.] Later, on the 15th of the same month, as the cardinals were saying that it would be good to give the residence the 50 *escudos*

---

[189] Fernando de Montesa was standing in for the Imperial Ambassador (of Charles V), viz. Juan Manrique de Lara, who was occupied with military operations against Siena.

[190] This financial settlement was cancelled on the election of Paul IV only five months later.

[191] Two Jesuits had great influence in the Spanish court: Antonio Araoz (1516-1573), who was related to the family of Ignatius, and Francis Borgia (1510-72), a former Spanish grandee.

monthly because it was in dire straits, and that it should not be a permanent income, so that the residence could accept it,[192] the Pope [Julius III] said: "I would like the payments to be permanent once and for all. Moreover in order that the residence may benefit from them, a means can be found, viz. that the Bull should be addressed *to the Protector*[a] of the residence *pro tempore existente* [i.e. whoever happens to be the Protector at the time], and he can allocate them to the College or to the house, as he thinks preferable."

When he learnt this, our Father called a meeting of consultors in which he decided, for he was present, on two points: first, if the Pope were to give this as alms, in so far as it was his wish to do as the cardinals did, it would be better for the Society [to accept]; second, that as for the method proposed, in no way in the world was it suitable, and therefore the money should be assigned to the College *in perpetuum* and in no way be accepted by the residence.

[a] *to the Protector*

> Although the Protector we had at that time was Cardinal Carpi,[193] a man of great virtue and especially devoted and friendly to the Society, nevertheless our Father often repeated that the Society did not need, and should not have, any Protector other than the Pope himself.

27 February

233 1. As for the man from Modena, a companion of the one from Ferrara, who wishes to enter the Society: he has a good knowledge of Latin, and is a good scribe, but is deficient both in his hearing and voice. Our Father orders that the defects of his companion should be put to the one from Ferrara, and then by making him the needle in the balance, the matter should be put completely in his hands; if he decides that the

---

[192] The vow of poverty approved for the new Society excluded the possession of a fixed income for any residence or person; this prohibition did not apply to the colleges, which were considered financially autonomous with respect to the Society.

[193] Cardinal Rodolfo Pio da Carpi (1500-64) was the first and last "Protector" of the Society; on his death, Fr. Diego Laínez, the second General, asked that no successor should be appointed and the Pope, Pius IV, agreed, saying that he would fulfill that function.

Modena man should be accepted, then he can be told how he would not be suitable for the priesthood, nor for other services, because he is very frail, but that he could be suitable for the duties of a scribe. Thirdly, the Father wonders if it would be good that he himself should talk to him, but he will do [as others think best] in all this.

234 2 Even though money has to be sought through loans and societies,[194] the infirmary[195] for the residence and in the villa should both be started. The Father says to Polanco, "Let them throw us both into prison!" The reason for this haste is that the residence and the College have grown and are growing so much in such a short period of time that, because of the number of the sick, it is probable that there will be nowhere to put them. And the Father rounds off this speech by saying that God will help us, that we must trust in Him.

[n.d.] In his undertakings, the Father very often seems to lack human prudence, as was the case in making this College here without any income for it, and there are other similar cases; but it seems that everything he does is founded solely in trust in God. However, just as it looks that in undertaking these things he goes beyond human prudence, so in following them up and seeking means to carry them forward he employs every possible prudence, both divine and human.[196] It appears that in whatever he undertakes, he has first negotiated it with God, and since we ourselves do not see that he has negotiated with Him we are appalled at what he takes on. I must remember [to note] how *the College was founded,*[a] etc.

[a] *the College was founded*

This can be seen be seen in the way the foundation was made of the Roman College itself.[197]

235 3. As for *the priest*[b] from Milan, who has never been at peace, and as a last resort is making the Exercises (although the Father had said he would not gain anything from them), as there is no remedy, let him

---

[194] The predecessors of the banking firms that were developing at this time.
[195] See §161.
[196] A well-documented Ignatian characteristic; cf. J.P.M. Walsh, "Work as if everything depends on . . .who?", *The Way Supplement* 70, 1991, pp. 125-36.
[197] §§230-32.

be gone with God to Loreto.

This was the one who had come from the College in Genoa, and let himself be tempted to think ill of that corrector, when he reprimanded me, as I mentioned above.[198]

236 4. As for *John from Alba,* *(a)* who wanted to make the Stations[199] each day during Lent, the Father gave him reasons why he should not: because if everyone went, there would be no one to serve in the house; neither do members of other religious orders make them daily.

(a) *Juan from Alba*

He was a youngster from Alba, a temporal coadjutor, who at first behaved in an edifying way and to whom our Father showed signs of affection. I shall be relating in the proper place what happened to him later.[200]

236b It is our Father's custom if he refuses a request to anyone, to give the reasons for doing so, so that he himself should come to see that it is good to deny him his request. If he granted the request he showed him also the reasons against, so that he would recognize the favour conceded.

He was accustomed to employ this method with the weaker men; with them he used more circumspection, as has been related.[201]

237 5. With regard to the way of making *the Stations,* *(c)* the Father refers it to the consultors, mentioning that it would be good for a certain number to go every day, so that each week all would have made visits: this was decided. If anyone had never been *to the Seven Churches(d)* he could go at once, if devotion moved him.

(c) *the Stations*

During Lent in Rome there is every day a station at a

---

[198] See §§140-41.
[199] This practice is explained below, §237.
[200] There are several references to this Brother later in the *Memoriale*, cf. Index.
[201] See §§102ff.

particular church with a plenary indulgence, all the churches sharing this out for all the days; the people of the city go the rounds of them with great devotion. And so that members of the Society might make these visits conveniently, the Father gave the norm I mention here.

(d) to the Seven Churches

These Seven Churches[202] are not visited so frequently because there are about 15 *milhas* between them, three *milhas* making one of our [Portuguese] *legoas*.[203]

237b Our Father himself *would like to make more visits*[a] to the Station churches, but does not dare to for love of the others.

(a) would like to make more visits

Our Father used to go the rounds of the public Stations in Rome dressed in old clothes with the sleeves half out, tied with his belt, without a cloak on top. I accompanied him sometimes when he was dressed in this way.

238 6. The Father had forbidden in general[204] the students of the German College to speak to ours, because among our members were two or three Germans who were rather tender. As this reason no longer applies, and *instead they rather help one another,*[b] they can talk freely, and even go to the villa when ours are there.

(b) instead they rather help one another

Our Father very much wanted these Germans to join the Society, and for this reason he tried to arrange that they be helped in every way by the conversation of ours.

239 Eight[205] of the most suitable students of the German College have felt the wish to enter the Society, and because of the problems this would

---

[202] See §209 with note.

[203] "Miles" and "leagues" differed considerably from country to country.

[204] Da Câmara uses the Latin tag *in universum*.

[205] The names of eight German students accepted by Ignatius from the German College have been preserved and are noted by the editors of the MHSI edition.

cause, the matter has been discussed by the consultors for many days. The Fathers have proposed many solutions, but the Father would only reply, *"There's a difficulty. "[a]* And at this time it happened that the Pope [Julius III] was inclined to endow the College, and he mentioned that as the Society did not wish to accept bishoprics, it would be good *to set up a college[b]* next to ours, of young men directed by the Society, so that these men could have posts of spiritual responsibility. And because of this the Father decided not to accept the Germans all together, but one a month, so as not to arouse comment; with such a procedure neither the Pope nor the cardinals would know about it.

[a] *"There's a difficulty. "*

The difficulty our Father met was that it might seem to the Pope that the Society was frustrating his intention (given that his purpose was to create a college so that Germans would come from there, nurtured on the milk of the Society, who would be able to serve particular churches in Germany as priors, rectors, etc.), and that for our own interest we wanted to have a seedbed[206] for our own College, given that we were accepting so many all together.

[b] *to set up a college*

Our Lord gave such knowledge of the Society to Pope Julius III at the end of his life that, in addition to the German College, he wanted to set up another college for all nationalities, in which might live under obedience to members of the Society those persons who, with this education, might later serve the Church all over the world. However, with his death this was not carried out.

240   [n.d.] I must remember to find out in distinct detail the persecutions[207] which des Freux told me the Society had suffered: 1. from

---

[206] The word used, *seminario*, came to signify an ecclesiastical "seminary" (especially in the aftermath of Trent), but here probably keeps its original meaning.

[207] Da Câmara never fulfilled his resolution, and further details on the four persecutions mentioned have been pieced together by the industrious MHSI editors: (1) Mathias de San Cassiano, Post Master of the Papal court, attacked the Society both verbally and physically because his mistress had been persuaded to enter the House of St. Martha (for reformed women); St. Ignatius brought the matter to court but there was eventually a reconciliation; (2) this calumny came from the Giovanni de Torano, mentioned in fourth place; (3) Laínez had a case brought against him in Parma by a Carmelite, whose Pauline interpretations Laínez had refuted, but there was more general opposition to both

Mathias, the one in charge of the pontifical post; 2. when people were saying that we were breaking the seal of confession; 3. against Laínez in Parma; 4. from Giovanni of the Mercato Church against the Father.

241 On the twenty second of this month the Father gave an order for a rule to be added to those of the minister's office: viz. where there were two beds, there should always be a mat-screen placed between them, so that one should not be visible to the other. He made someone responsible for inspecting this, and if it was not completed within three days in the whole house he should give a penance to the minister.

Last Day of February (28th)

242 1. When the Father saw the household linen *put in a place*[a] which he had forbidden, he ordered the minister himself to remove it. As for the laundry-man in charge of the linen, he must reprimand the minister at the "little table," explaining the cause of the reprimand, that it was because the minister had not imposed a penance on him.

[a] *put in a place*

The household linen was hung to dry in a place where our Father had told me it should not be put. Because I had done no more than inform the laundry-man, without giving him a penance for it, when the Father saw it there he ordered that the laundry-man himself should give me this reprimand.

243 Two days ago,[208] and yesterday, Polanco, who stands in for our Father, and the minister, with other priests, received a reprimand at the

Laínez and Favre because of their encouragement of frequent communion; (4) Giovanni de Torano had been Rector of the church of San Giovanni del Mercato (Market), and was entrusted by Ignatius with the house set aside for the instruction of Jews (the so-called House of Catechumens); however the relation turned sour and in 1547 he presented Pope Paul III with a long list of accusations against the Jesuits. The case turned against him and he was first imprisoned and then banished from Rome.

[208] The MHSI editors have problems with the phrase *dos días de antes* and suggest that something has dropped out (perhaps the words "the Rector"); however, da Câmara uses the same expression *de antes* elsewhere (see §245b) to mean "before." Moreover, in the residence there was no rector, Ignatius holding the top post, or in his place, Polanco. What has surprised da Câmara is that even the highest person in the house after Ignatius could be required to do a penance like anyone else.

"little table," *on the orders of the cook*[a] because they had gone to eat with the College students without telling him.

[a] *on the orders of the cook*

> The cook gave this order because our Father had made him responsible for this reprimand to be given to us, and for telling the corrector how it should be observed and what he had to say.

244 2. The Father ordered that *the books of Savonarola*[b] that the novices had brought should be removed from the house, not because the author was bad, but because it is something that is considered doubtful, so Polanco told me.

[b] *the books of Savonarola*

> These were books on spiritual matters, composed by Friar Savonarola, which Paul IV later prohibited. I remember that we examined them in our residence [in Rome], and that I had a part in the task.[209]

245 When the Father, at the start, was at Alcalá, there were many who were persuading him, including his confessor, that he should read the *Enchiridion* of Erasmus,[210] but when he heard there were disagreements and doubts about the author, he never wished to read the book. He said there were more than enough good books about which there were no doubts.

3. The man from Dalmatia, who asks to be received, is to be received, and Joseph[211] is to be received on probation for one month.

245b To the rule that no one should make the Stations without asking permission the day before, is added that the same rule should apply to going out to take exercise.

---

[209] Da Câmara refers here to his later stay in Rome, 1558. Paul IV (1555-59) ordered the examination of the writings of Savonarola (1452-98) after the death of Ignatius; some of his works, but not all, were placed on the Index in 1559. Ignatius himself had prohibited their use as early as 1550, and in 1553 had ordered the burning of any copies to be found in the residence.

[210] See §98.

[211] Mentioned again below (§393), but otherwise unknown.

I must recall *the particular reason*[a] why the Father made this rule.

[a], 212 *[the particular reason*

The reason was that our Father did not want us to act lightly in anything, simply because it appeals to us. And thus, when someone asked permission one day before to go to the Stations, or to take physical exercise, it was clear he was doing so in a reasoned way or because of a need.]

---

212 The part in square brackets has been crossed out in the manuscript.

MARCH

First of March

246 1. The Father established a rule that no member of the residence should take a meal at any of the colleges without special permission, so that the rectors could with a more clear conscience take an oath that no member of the residence had taken advantage of any of the colleges.[1] When I asked the Father if things might be borrowed for a short time, he said they might be moved from one place to another, but this should not be put into the rule.

I must recall instances of how strict our Father was in not allowing the acceptance of any thing which was given to anyone personally: for example, with the marzipan cakes given to Mario,[2] which by no means were to be accepted, or the venison sent by the Cardinal de Montepulciano,[3] which was only accepted on behalf of the residence.

[n.d.] I must recall what strictness he shows in not allowing acceptance of presents, as for example he was with Don Cristóbal,[4] who was staying with us as our guest and it was his uncle, Cardinal de la Cueva, who gave it. Similarly, with the present that the *College of Palermo*[a] sent to our residence: the Father decided that this should be accepted by the College and not the residence.

---

[1] Professed members of the Society were prohibited by their vow of poverty from taking advantage of the incomes permitted to the colleges.

[2] Mario Beringucci: see §65.

[3] This Cardinal is mentioned below (§281); he had been appointed in 1551.

[4] Fr. Cristóbal de Mendoza, although a Jesuit, was not a regular member of the community. He is mentioned in §§15, 193.

(a) *the College of Palermo*

Our brethren of the College of Palermo sent a generous present of fruit and farm produce to our residence in Rome. The Father did not want it to be received or used except in the College; this was because he did not want the residences to profit in any way from the colleges, unless it were as a loan, as has been said.

247   2 The Father said today, "Now we will be able to tell Polanco that he can have greater hope than the day before yesterday."[5]

Today letters arrived for Fr. Polanco from Florence, saying that they were holding 250 *escudos* at his disposal from a source from which he had expected little until now. Indeed, with the great trust he placed in the words of the Father, he had been of the opinion that work should start straight away on the house for the sick at the villa, and on the infirmary here, as well as on the *solana*,[6] the church, the orchard,[7] and the villa, all of which are already under way, and this despite the fact that there are 160 members of the Society in Rome, and bread costs 7 or 8 *escudos per ruxo*,[8] and a *bota*[9] of wine 15 or 16 *escudos*. All the money we have in the residence at present amounts to 25 *escudos* to pay for all this, and there are many debts.

[n.d.] I must recall the many other occasions when, having been in similar straits and our Father maintaining great faith and joy, God has come to our help: like the time when a visitor gave our buyer a small handkerchief containing 100 *escudos,* and our Father told him to hold on to them for a few days as he was doubtful whether they were genuine. Similarly, when Fr. Polanco was on his way to borrow money on interest, he met someone in the street who offered him a large sum to look after, etc. In these situations Fr. Polanco is always slow to spend, because of the difficulties he can see to exist. And despite that, when the Father decides that something has to be done, he has as much confidence as if he already

---

[5] See §234.

[6] Mentioned in §205.

[7] The word used here, *huerto,* instead of the more usual *huerta,* suggests that there was an orchard or vegetable plot in the garden of the residence.

[8] In early Italian the *rùbbio* (also spelled *ruggio,* and by da Câmara as *ruxo)* was a cubic measure; the bread was bought not by weight, but by size, one *rùbbio* being the equivalent of 290 litres.

[9] Another Italian measure, this one equivalent to sixteen barrels of 60 litres each.

had before him the means to achieve it. So he usually says, "The Father has said it should be done: God will provide the wherewithal."

248 [n.d.] Last January, as one of the principal priests, who was procurator of the residence, said outside the house that a fever had made *one of our invalids*[a] say mad things, the Father imposed a big reprimand on him and made him take the discipline for the length of three psalms.

[a] *one of our invalids*

The invalid was someone well known, but a person of such a kind that a short while later the Father dismissed him from the Society.

249 [n.d.] To some extent[10] our Father's wish is that those who are under obedience should have no concern for themselves in any respect, but that they should leave everything to the superior. And the Father takes such great care of them, particularly in respect of their good name and reputation, that they themselves can amply disregard all care of themselves. As for their good name, the Father seeks to protect it not only with outsiders, but just as much with those at home. So he always has to speak well of everyone, and never reveals anyone's faults to anyone else, unless it is necessary to consult with another person. And if it is enough to consult one person, he will never tell two about it, and if two, never three.

One thing in this connection to be observed in the Father, is that even when consulting others, he simply states the fault baldly, without condemning or discussing the degree of culpability involved.

250 [n.d.] As for reprimands, one can clearly see that the Father *induit personam quam vult, aut ut iudex severam, aut ut pater benignam* [he takes on the role he wants, whether that of a severe judge or that of a benign father].[11]

I must recall several particular cases, when with Fr. Polanco and

[10] The Spanish here, *por una parte,* would normally mean "on the one hand," but there is no answering "on the other hand" in this sentence; so the sense seems to be that that was only part of Ignatius's teaching on obedience (he also expected an intelligent execution of orders).

[11] The ease with which da Câmara slips into Latin would not have been surprising at that time when it was a sort of lingua franca; he does not seem to be quoting at this point.

Fr. Nadal he played the severe role; with others, who were less strong, he acted a more gentle part. I want to note here especially how once he summoned *Micer André des Freux*[a] to give him a reprimand. Beforehand he had been talking in a cheerful and friendly fashion, but as soon as des Freux came in he assumed his full authority: to all appearances he displayed anger and annoyance for the fault (which was not to have reported to Licentiate Madrid[12] the good result of negotiations concerning the German College, although previously he had—at the Father's order—given him a report of the crisis in which it was). And so the blessed des Freux was standing there *with his biretta*[b] in his hand. Finally he went to look for the Licentiate, and finding him where the work was being done, laid himself on the ground and kissed his feet, since this was part of his penance (besides eating *in his own College*[c] at the "small table," and other acts I do not remember, etc.). At this the Licentiate, being new, was absolutely astonished, and said he could not prevent him from kissing his feet, there in the midst of all the objects of the work site.

[a] *Micer André des Freux*

251 Fr. des Freux[13] was rector of the German College. Our Father ordered that the Germans there should normally speak Italian, not their national language. This was so that they would adapt in everything to the customs and style of the Roman Church (to which he wished them to be greatly attached), and also so that their conversations could be understood by those in charge of them. They mutinied against this, all joining together into a body, and even went so far as to say that for this reason they wanted to leave the College. The rector came at once to report on the affair to our Father. When the post-prandial chat was over, our Father discussed the problem and means of solving it with other Fathers, and charged Fr. Madrid, who was there, with dealing with any further developments, and he appointed him, as far as this was concerned, [above][14] Fr. des Freux, though the latter was one of the earliest members and was held in great respect by our Father, whereas Fr. Madrid had only been a novice for a few days (though he had been familiar with the affairs of the house for years while still outside the Society, and was a sort of consultant for Fr.

---

[12] See §27; the academic title given to Fr. Madrid by da Câmara is *licenciado*.
[13] See §39.
[14] Something has dropped out in the manuscript: perhaps "superior to."

Ignatius on affairs of the Society). When after some days all that agitation quietened down, Fr. des Freux neglected to come and inform Madrid of the course of events and of the happy end of the affair. I was telling the Father about the case, and when he heard about it, he summoned Fr. des Freux immediately. While he was waiting for him to come he continued laughing with me and said, "Do you think, Father Minister, that I do not know how to give a reprimand? Well, now you will see." As soon as Fr. des Freux entered the room, the Father changed his expression to one of such severity to give the reprimand, that I have described here, that I was absolutely astonished.

(b) *with his biretta*

Our Father wished, and had given orders, that those who were speaking to him, once they had taken off their birettas at the beginning of the interview, should put them on again and remain covered until they left. As for himself, I do not remember well, but I do not think he used to take off his biretta when the fathers of the house, on visiting him, removed theirs. Nevertheless, with regard to all the other superiors, whether it be the rector, the minister or the sub-minister, he ordered that the subjects should show them such respect as not to put on their hats until they were told to do so. I recall that once when I was minister, I went with Fr. Loarte,[15] the sub-minister, to Fr. Laínez's room. Fr. Laínez rose and stood uncovered for some time without my noticing, until I asked him to put his hat back on, because Fr. Loarte had said to him, "Your Reverence might as well wilt away, because Father Minister will not tell you to put your hat on as he does not see it!"[16]

(c) *in his own College*

He ate at the "small table" in the same German College of which he was Rector, under the eyes of the students.

---

[15] Mentioned below, §294.

[16] The MHSI editors see in this remark a reference to da Câmara's short-sightedness (cf. §55) rather than to his absent-mindedness.

2 March

252 1. Lancillotto,[17] who is 17, and Jean the Frenchman, who is 19, are asking if they can fast for the whole of Lent; they are allowed to do so during the first week, on condition that they report how they feel; from then on, if they feel able to fast more than three days they must ask permission; and they should be told that our Father would like everyone to fast, if it were possible, but not beyond one's strength.[18]

The Father, up to a few years ago, used to fast for the whole of Lent even though he was very sick.

253 2. As for asking for alms, the Father thought it was good to do so as an "experiment,"[19] and also so as to learn from the start that we are poor, but not for the sake of begging. Rather, he thinks *that this means*[a] of sustaining oneself is not good for the Society. It has been introduced into Rome through weakness and through the importunity of the procurators.[20] The Father would like it stopped as soon as it could be and he wants to be reminded of this each month. In the meantime, while they still go, no one should go to beg who might *be in danger.*[b] The Father said this to me about a month ago.

[a] *that this means*

> The means being used was that customary among the Franciscans. We went out with a satchel on our backs through the streets of Rome, knocking at doors and calling out so loudly that we would be heard in a house of three or four floors, "Give me alms, for the love of God, for the Society of Jesus!" I remember that I went in this way several times. This style, which the Father thought appropriate for us,[21] is the same that is used today at São Roque and in the other houses of the Society.

[17] Lancillotto, brother of Petronio; cf. §§75, 81, 262. His French companion has not been identified.

[18] See §212.

[19] The term "experiment" is used for various experiences (like working in hospitals, pilgrimage, etc.) that form part of the novices' probation period.

[20] See Glossary: "procurator."

[21] See the short instruction drawn up by Ignatius: MHSI, *Epist.*, XII, 656-57, *Iñigo Letters,* No. 60 (p. 236).

[22] Mentioned above (§45). The Jesuit residence in Lisbon was dedicated to São Roque.

(b) *be in danger*

He made this remark because of the youngster from Siena who, as has been said, fell into temptation while begging for alms.[23]

254   3. The Exercises are better for someone who is not decided on a state[24] of life, because then there is a greater diversity of spirits; also, for the same reason, when someone has been tempted and is distressed. The custom of giving the Exercises at the beginning [of the novitiate], which is followed in Spain, is generally good.

[n.d.] I must recall what the Father said to me one day: he did not want anyone to go to the College[25] without having first made the Exercises, at least those of the first week, including the methods of prayer.[26] And I must remember also to ask the Father about giving the Exercises, what he definitely thinks about it.

255   Last January, when Fr. Nadal was talking to our Father about the taking of vows, the Father said that he had never liked to encourage novices to make them before two years had been completed.

On the 22nd of November last,[27] Father Nadal spoke to our Father about the hour and a half of prayer he had established in Spain. The Father said they would never change his opinion that one hour was enough for students, if one presupposed mortification and abnegation as well, which makes it possible for someone easily to pray more in one quarter of an hour, than a non-mortified person in two hours. But still, when someone felt very troubled and in greater need, more time for prayer might be granted to him.

The following day, speaking to me on the same subject, he said that he thought no greater error was possible in spiritual matters, than to seek to direct others according to one's own way; he spoke about the long hours of prayer he had made, and then he added that of a hundred who spent long hours in prayer and penances, most developed great problems,

---

[23] See §§43-45.

[24] Guidelines to help retreatants make the "election" of a state of life—marriage, priesthood, etc.—are provided in the *Exercises,* §§169-89.

[25] i.e., to move from the Jesuit novitiate to the first stage of studies.

[26] An outline of the "three ways of praying" is given among the additional material towards the end of the text of the *Exercises,* §§238-60.

[27] See §§195-96.

above all of stubbornness of understanding, and therefore the Father considered mortification and abnegation of the will to be the only foundation. And when he said to Fr. Nadal that one hour of prayer was enough for college students, the whole emphasis he put was on the presupposition of mortification and abnegation. And so one sees that the Father considers as fundamental the special characteristics of the Society, such as the indifference which is presupposed, the examination[28] after the tests through which members pass, and the witness which should be left behind by them, and not prayer, except for that which is born from those other things. And at the same time the Father greatly praises prayer, as I have noted many times, especially the prayer in which God is always brought before one's eyes.

256b *In the same conversation*[a] with Nadal, who was insisting that the novices should be moved to the *Torre Rosa* [= Rossi Tower],[29] as a house of probation, the Father said decidedly that he was not in favour for the time being; afterwards the Father told me that in time he thought a house of probation would be set up in Rome with the income contributed from the colleges in Italy and Sicily.

> This is the conversation that our Father had with Fr. Nadal, as I said above.[30] I did not refer to it in detail at the time because I was dictating these things to a Brother Novice, who wrote them down for me in a notebook, and he might have been scandalized if I had related the reprimand as it happened, the more so since at that time Fr. Nadal was the Vicar General of our Father.

[a] *In the same conversation*

> Fr. Nadal was suggesting to our Father that, if he thought it a good idea, the novices who were mixed with the older members of the Society in the residence should be moved to some more remote houses we had, to live there and form a separate novitiate; the

---

[28] Ignatius is referring here to the various "probations" mentioned in the *Constitutions* (e.g., *Examen*, ch. 1, 12, §16 [Ganss, pp. 83-84].

[29] A house next to the residence acquired (5 December 1553) to provide more rooms; Ignatius asked da Câmara to meet him there when he dictated part of his *Autobiography* (cf. *Autobiography*, p. 7). The name used for it by da Câmara *(Torre Rosa)* derives from the previous owner, but has been frequently misunderstood as an indication of its colour.

[30] See §196. That paragraph, like the present, belongs to the later stage of composition and reveals under what circumstances da Câmara was working.

Father responded with a further reprimand, similar to that which
I have referred to above.

257 I must recall how much the novices are tested here, so that each one
can show what he is *according to his own nature*[a] and also how Fr.
Polanco spoke to me many times on this subject.

[a] *according to his own nature*

> The novices allowed their own natural way of being to be seen,
> and were recognized and mortified accordingly, because at that
> time they lived in greater freedom—I mean without so many rules
> and external ceremonies, thanks to which now each one can cover
> up any spontaneous reactions.[31]

3 March

258 1. The Father orders that the box of figs be given to Job[32] so that he
can do what he wants with it, provided that he keeps enough for himself
and for the other boy, his little brother, so many per day for each day of
Lent.

Two months ago, before he joined the Society, Job had brought these
figs as a gift for the Father, and the Father had told him then that he was
going to keep them for the day when he joined. It is very remarkable how
the Father remembers what he has promised, and how he fulfils his promise. The reason for this is, apart from his great constancy, that he never
utters a word without having thought about it first and offered it to God.

259 2. One of the latticed galleries that have been remade can be used by
those of the novices *for whom rather more*[a] consideration is to be had.

[a] *for whom rather more*

> The novices were not forbidden from listening to the preaching
> in the common areas of the house, but at that time some latticed

---

[31] This sharp criticism of the developments introduced into the running of Jesuit
novitiates (mainly under Francis Borgia) is very likely to have motivated the later prohibition issued by Aquaviva against the wider dissemination of the *Memoriale*, despite
requests from the Jesuits of Castile (1584).

[32] One of the brothers of Petronius, he had joined at the end of January; see §29.

galleries were constructed (from which one could see and hear more conveniently), and, since there was little enough room for the older members (among whom some outside visitors were also invited), our Father ordered that since there was not enough room for all the novices, at least some of them should have places in the gallery, those for whom it was felt that more consideration should be had.

260 [n.d.] The Father's style of rule follows closely the natural order of things, for example *he shows slightly more*[a] respect towards those who were respected in the world; on the other hand, he does not think that such external matters have any importance.

[a] *he shows slightly more*

This he showed particularly to cultivated, rich and noble people at the start of their entry into the Society, as has been said;[33] such as these he treated so softly and gently that they themselves wanted to be on a par with the rest, and even lowered themselves in relation to the others, and desired and asked for contempt and humiliating treatment.

261 [n.d.] A member of the Society who was talking with an outsider, who nevertheless was very close to him, and he said something about his[34] academic knowledge which scandalized the other, so much that he men-tioned it to someone else, another outsider, a friend of the Society. Our Father felt no less regret than he about this fault committed by a member of the Society outside the house, and so our Father worked hard to remedy all this. As for our own man, he imposed the sort of penance usually given for an insult; the other person was thereby placated and the Father arranged for both to beg pardon from one another. This problem lasted for many days, during which the Father did not cease from dealing with it or from seeking a solution; finally it was resolved with much edification to all concerned.

261b [n.d.] Where there is some disagreement between two of the brethren, our Father usually relates to the one everything that he has heard from the other that may please him, and keeps quiet about

[33] See §107.

[34] The Spanish is ambiguous here: either the Jesuit is boasting about his own academic achievements, or (perhaps more likely) is disparaging the academic achievements of his friend.

anything to the contrary. He also often does something quite deliberately so that it will be known, and for the same reason our Father will very often say things intentionally so that they can be relayed to those he judges need to hear them.

4 March

262   1. Petronio and Lancillotto[35] can make the Exercises of the First Week, in order to make a general confession.

2. It will be good to encourage N.[36] to make a radically fresh start with his studies. The Father will not refer this matter to the consultors. It would be good for N. to receive private classes while he is here.

[n.d.] In the matter of studies our Father is very precise; he always wants to build on a firm foundation, and above all that students should know Latin and the humanities well, as he did in the cases of Neyra[37] and Benedetto.[38] These two had been preaching for many years and everyone thought they were ready to study theology, but the Father never wished it so, but rather that they should begin the course in humanities, while continuing to preach in Rome, the one regularly, the other on certain occasions.

5 March

263   The Father wishes an infirmary to be built promptly,[39] and that I should speak to Master Domenico,[40] and afterwards persuade Polanco, telling him to speak to the Master, and if this is not enough, that I should

---

[35] See §29; these are two of the five brothers.

[36] Probably the same individual (Teotonio de Bragança) designated in this way above, §150.

[37] This seems to be a nickname for Fr. Ribadeneira; if so, it is the only example of such familiarity, though mention has been made of the use of first names among the first companions: see §142.

[38] Fr. Benedetto Palmio; cf. §95.

[39] See §§161, 234, 247.

[40] The MHSI editors wonder if this could be Domenico de Verdino, a master builder sent from Rome to Sardinia in 1565, but note that the catalogue entry for him suggests that he was not a Jesuit as early as 1555.

ask his permission to speak to *S.R.*,[41] and that I should do so in the presence of Polanco.

[n.d.] Our Father is accustomed to do all that he can gently without obedience, viz., without recourse to obedience. On the contrary, when something can be done without knowing what is His Reverence's preference, but being self-motivated, this pleases him much more. And when someone undertakes an action because he has seen His Reverence's own preference, but has not been ordered to undertake it, he is more pleased than if he had been obliged to order it, and finally, for the same reason, when the action is taken under orders, but not by virtue of obedience.[42]

[n.d.] Our Father often says that he who lacks obedience of the understanding, even though he has that of the will, has only one foot in the religious life.

It is worth noting how our Father makes Fr. Polanco demonstrate his faith, and how Fr. Polanco in fact demonstrates it. Yesterday he wanted to know the extent of the residence's debts, and he found they amounted to about 3000 *escudos*, about as many as are owed to the residence, but there is little hope of recovering them very quickly. The day before yesterday we received two novices, and tomorrow we shall receive others. The Father was saying to me today that in these matters, i.e. in similar necessities, one must sail against the wind.

6 March

264 1. As for the departure of N.[43] for Genoa, he thinks it is a good idea, and the Father explained to me more at length how he had come to this decision: at first he had not felt so strongly in favor, he had even felt some aversion, but because Master Polanco and I were so decided, he allowed

---

[41] The initials used here, "S.R.", usually stand for *Su Reverencia* ("His Reverence"), viz. Ignatius; but here they probably refer to Fr. Domenico, who would be in charge of the building operation.

[42] If a superior orders a subordinate to do something "under virtue of holy obedience," the non-compliance of the subordinate ranks as a serious sin against the vow of obedience; but a superior may invoke this authority only in matters of importance.

[43] This time the reference is quite uncertain.

himself to be guided, especially when we had said to him that N. was not suitable for anything.

265 2. The boy Bartolomeo[44] must be told to learn something by heart each day, and to make a public penance if he fails to do so, giving the reason, so that if he is not suitable, it should be known in the residence that he is not, so that he can be sent home, *as he was sent on the 29th of this month.*[a]

> *(a) as he was sent on the 29th of this month*
>
> I wrote this on the same day, the 6th—the day on which our Father ordered it—in the little notebook I carried with me; but when I transferrred it to the other notebook it was already the 29th of the month, therefore I made this addition here.[45] The boy was not yet a member of the Society, and our Father only kept him in the house at the request of a cardinal, so that he could be trained in the customs and subordination of a religious house.

266 3. The Father no longer goes to confession to Don Diego[46] because of his extreme fervour and exaggeration in praising him, and he asked three of us to examine what he had said: he ordered us to put in writing the various expressions Don Diego had used, as well as the interpretations he gave. He ordered a penance to be given him, about which I have spoken on the 26th of last month.[47] And the Father said he had done this *so that he would have an answer*[b] if by chance any person outside should come to hear of it. As for Don Diego, his holy simplicity is well known. The Father has continued going to confession to him until now because he is opposed to changing confessors.

> *(b) so that he would have an answer*
>
> Our Father took especial care to foresee future evils and to prepare beforehand the means with which they might be averted. An example of this was the care he took, as I have related above, to

---

[44] He had been the servant of Petronio and his brothers when they came from Pesaro in November 1554. As da Câmara notes, he was sent home 29 March 1555; Fr. Mercurian, Rector in nearby Perugia, was informed.

[45] This note indicates that da Câmara was able to write short entries in his own hand, and did not dictate all the entries.

[46] See §§162, 221.

[47] See §221.

obtain a verdict of not guilty for those of the Society when they were accused in Rome.[48] Many other instances will be found in this notebook.

267 4. All those of us who took part in the consultation must do penance for the measures taken about meat for the sick this Lent, and the Father said that if the butcher is scandalized, they should not accept a morsel of meat from him, and go to other butchers, *but I must go and speak to him about it.*[a]

> *(a)* but I must go and speak to him about it

> I remember this affair very well: our Father gave all the consultors a penance, because the order to buy meat had not been given, so that the butcher would not be scandalized. Our Father placed such a value on edification, that he wanted the minister himself to go and explain to the butcher that it was the doctor who had ordered some of the sick members of the residence to eat meat that Lent. This was so that any scandal that might be caused by the order to buy meat would disappear completely.

268 5. With regard to the four brothers,[49] who say make their vows to God every day, the Father does not disapprove of their wanting to make them tomorrow, but *the three others must not do anything without the consent of the eldest.*[b]

> *(b)* the three others must not do anything without the consent of the eldest.

> 269 Our Father was a great friend to the idea that each should be given his due.[50] And as Petronio was a grown man with some sort of responsibility for his three brothers, lads young as they were,

---

[48] The MHSI editors take this to be a reference to the troubles of 1538 (cf. *Autobiography* §98), and point out that the *Memoriale* does not mention them; however, da Câmara probably has the later troubles in mind, of which he has written above, §240, and which he knew were mentioned later in his notes, viz. §314.

[49] Petronio, Cincinnato, Lancillotto, and Job; see §§29, 274.

[50] The long reflection that follows (§§269-272) is something of a *cri de coeur* by da Câmara, who by 1554 had seen successive generals (Laínez, Borgia, Mercurian) adopt different styles of government, some much more centralizing than others, and had also seen different provincials, some much less inclined to give free rein to rectors of colleges. His own preference is clearly indicated, although the hook on which he hangs his argument

he wished that even in this matter his orders should be followed.

In matters of greater importance he followed more meticulously this gentle style of government, which consisted in giving each man his due by reason of his person or his office. I remember that he used to summon a Father when he was sending him to conduct weighty business with grand people in Rome, and he would say to him, "Come here, I want you to arrange such and such a matter with such and such a cardinal, and I want you to have full power to do so. I would like to obtain this and this, and I have thought of such and such ways of getting it." And after giving him all the necessary information and instruction, he would add, "But when you are there I want you to use the means that the Lord will show you as most suitable, and I am leaving you in complete liberty so that you can do whatever you think best." Sometimes he spoke to me in the same way, and when I returned in the evening, the first thing he asked me was, "Are you happy with yourself?" He took it for granted that I had dealt with the matter freely and that everything achieved was my doing.

And although this trust he had in his subordinates was very general, he exercised it very particularly with subordinate superiors. In 1553 our Father sent as Visitor to this Province[51] Fr. Dr. Miguel de Torres,[52] who had entered the Society less than a year before, but so that he could undertake the visit he ordered him to make his profession. Although there were very difficult and important negotiations in hand, he still did not impose on him any rules or laws to deal with them, such as might have limited the authority or freedom which he wanted him to exercise in all these matters. Yes, he did give him long instructions about everything, and advice that occurred to him that he might need in such and such circumstances; but in no way did he oblige him to this or that particular

argument (Petronio's being given full authority over his "subordinates") may seem very minor, he is probably correct in claiming Ignatian support for his preference.

[51] Portugal, of course, where da Câmara is writing this part of the *Memoriale*. This famous visitation was organized to deal with the disastrous situation created by the Provincial, Simão Rodrigues (one of the first companions of Ignatius); the Visitor moved Rodrigues to Spain and expelled a large proportion of the Portuguese Jesuits. To heal the wounds da Câmara suggested to Ignatius from Portugal that he should write a letter to the whole province on the subject of obedience, and the result was a letter acknowledged to be one of the most important from Ignatius (cf. *Select Letters*, No. 31).

[52] See §7.

course of action. Previously he had given him a great number of blank sheets with his signature, so that he could write commands or letters as he judged fit to whom he wished and how he wished.

270 In the same way our Father wanted the provincials to have as much freedom as possible in the government of their provinces, and they, in their turn, should not diminish the authority of the rectors and other local superiors with respect to their own subordinates. This can be seen clearly in the following passage of a letter which he wrote to Father N.[53] when he was provincial.

"It is not the duty of a provincial, or a General Superior, to concern himself with the last detail of affairs: rather, though they may have all possible ability for such affairs, it is better to place others in charge of them, who can then refer what they have done to the provincial, and he can decide, after having heard their views, on what it falls on him to decide. And if it is something that can be referred to others, both in the conducting of the matter and in its resolution, especially in temporal affairs, but also in many spiritual matters, it will be much better to do so. For my part I keep to this method, and not only do I experience help and relief, but also more quiet and security in my soul. So then, as your office requires, hold on to love, and concern yourself with the common good of your province. As for orders that must be given in certain things, listen to those who are (in your opinion) best suited to understand the situation.

"Do not get involved in the execution of affairs or embark on them, but acting like a universal engine set in motion all the particular engines, and then you will achieve more and better things, more appropriate to your office, than in any other way. If they break down, it is less inconvenient than if you were to break down. It is better for you to mend the failings of your subordinates than for them to have to mend you when you break down, something that will often happen if you become involved in details more than is required.

"May our Lord Jesus Christ, our God and Saviour, always give grace to know His most holy will, and to fulfil it completely. From Rome, 17 December 1552."[54]

---

[53] Fr. Diego Mirón, who, although a Spaniard, became provincial of Portugal; for another letter to him from Ignatius, cf. *Select Letters,* No. 30.

[54] MHSI *Epist.* IV, 144: No. 3104.

271 In his day this was so practised to the letter that I remember when I was rector at Coimbra, and still a newcomer[55] in the Society, I wrote several times to Fr. Master Simão, who was provincial, asking him what I should do in certain matters, and he did not want to answer me, except by saying I should fulfil my office as it seemed right to me. He left matters so much in my hands that I set myself the task of looking through all the letters he had written to the rectors of colleges. I collected them together in a large bundle, and read and annotated them with underlining, so as to make a rule to help me in any other cases, such as those about which he had written. From this freedom which overall superiors granted to local superiors, there was born a great thirst to know their opinions, wishes, and preferences in everything, in order to tend towards them and follow them. Such was this desire that at the time when Fr. Dr. Torres came to visit this province,[56] there was a saying, common among the older Fathers, which Dr. Torres particularly liked, viz. that in the Society of Jesus there was only one person, the superior.

From the same root grew a great zeal and fervour in the execution of business, since men naturally perform with greater pleasure those deeds that they consider to be especially their own. And this was, I think, the feeling of our Father when he asked us, on our return from dealing with some affair that he had charged us with, if we were happy with ourselves, as has already been said.[57]

This way of proceeding of Fr. Ignatius was also founded on the fact that God gives special assistance to the immediate superior and his subordinate in particular cases, such as pertain properly and immediately to his office. Therefore, to seek to limit such cases, or to govern by general rules, would be to remove from him his essential role as superior, and consequently to impede co-operation with the special grace of God, which is more efficacious, as

---

[55] Although the word *noviço* is used here, it is not intended in the technical sense of "novice"; da Câmara was admitted into the Society 27 April 1545, and appointed rector two years later on completing his novitiate.

[56] See §269 with note.

[57] §269.

applying to a particular agent, than anything else. Moreover, how can the General, so far from the Province, react in time to the thousand affairs taking place there? And even if he does react, how can he possibly obtain information regarding all the details involved, which must be considered before a decision is made? How can the Provincial follow laws and general rules, when each day so many and such different circumstances arise, which totally alter the category of such affairs?

272   This is the reason why our Fr. Ignatius so often in the *Constitutions* defers to the judgement of the superior. He saw quite clearly that there could not be a universal rule in moral matters. Experience has shown, without doubt, that many important matters were not resolved because people were waiting for a reply from so far away; many matters have been resolved, but quite contrary to what would have been done if the overall superior had been present; in many other cases there were scruples, doubts and perhaps different interpretations, against blind obedience, because of the diversity of things, and owing to the presence of a precept and universal rule. Nor is it surprising that such inconvenient effects do follow, because both authority and knowledge are necessary for good government, and in this way the two parts are completely separated—since the overall superior, who has the power, cannot have the particular and practical information that is necessary, and the immediate superior, who has the knowledge and a hands-on experience of the affairs, does not have the power to settle them on his own.

There are other disadvantages on the part of individuals and officials, which are no less to be feared, such as the minimal obedience of the understanding shown to the overall superior. For it will often happen that the provincial gives orders to the rector contrary to what the latter can see with his own eyes, especially when one is aware of the difficulty of overcoming the natural resentment all men have against something which forbids or restrains them, or there is a lack of enthusiasm and a slackness in accomplishing tasks, as much through natural distaste, as through the frequent availability of an excuse not to do so, such as that one did not have permission or a commission from the provincial, etc.

Our Father Ignatius had clearly weighed up all this and that is why he considered it so important to leave the local superiors in as much liberty as possible, without prejudice to the possibility of certain persons being set necessary limitations at certain times and in certain places, but never by means of universal rules, which are a great obstacle to the subordination which should exist in the Society. If the provincial is restricted or limited in what pertains to his office, he then interferes in the office of the rector, and by the same token the rector in that of the minister, and so on, with the consequence that the order of government, which the Holy Spirit taught our blessed Father, is greatly disturbed.

273 6. Of the Germans[58] who have arrived, one can be received, although *he only wishes to enter to try it out,* [a] the second should go to work in the College, and the other is to be admitted to the German College.

[a] *he only wishes to enter to try it out*

Our Father wanted so strongly to receive Germans into the Society that he ordered even this one to be admitted on probation, although he had not decided to stay with us.

7, 8, 9, 10 March

274 Today, the 7th, Lorenzo[a],[59] nephew of Abbot Martinengo,[60] decided, in the course of making the Spiritual Exercises, to join the Society; he made vows, as also did the four brothers from Pesaro[61] here.

{a} *Lorenzo*

He is Fr. Lorenzo Maggio today,[62] provincial of Austria; he

[58] Identity unknown to the MHSI editors.

[59] Lorenzo Maggio, an Italian Jesuit born in 1531, and subsequently rector in Naples and Vienna, served as provincial of Austria for twelve years (1566-78), and as secretary of the Third General Congregation of the Society (1573), when he was one of the candidates to replace Francis Borgia as General, though finally Everard Mercurian, from the Low Countries, was chosen (as had been suggested by the Pope, Gregory XIII).

[60] Described below, §280.

[61] See §29, §268.

[62] Probably written in 1574 or 1575.

was secretary of the Third General Congregation, and received two or three votes for General.

275 1. Abbot de Salas[63] is to be granted everything he requested, except the obligation of preaching sermons, so that temporal goods do not appear to be exchanged for spiritual. But without making any contract sermons will be given much more often. As to Masses, they may be promised, because they will be said by clerics from outside [the Society].

276 2. Rodrigo de Dueñas[64] asks for twenty sermons a year in a monastery for nuns; the Father does not grant them, despite so many requests, supported with so many arguments, from the Canon of Toledo.[65] The Father's motive is that we might be left with only one preacher in our college at Medina, *who would be more effective*[a] preaching in another church of the town; finally the Canon has given way.

[a] *would be more effective*

Whatever motive of human respect or difficulty arose, our Father never hesitated from doing what he considered might be a greater service to God or of advantage to a neighbour. It often happened that there were in Rome one or two excellent apostolic workers, occupied in various tasks, of such value that it seemed neither the residence nor the College in Rome could continue to exist without them: despite all this, if the opportunity presented itself of working elsewhere outside the city to help souls more universally and with greater honour to God, the Father would break immediately with all the particular considerations of persons in the residence or in the College, and send the men there, and when the immediate superiors or others in the residence began to tell

[63] The abbot of the Monastery of Salas, near Burgos, Francisco Jiménez de Miranda, had promised to found and endow a Jesuit college in the city, on condition that sermons for the general public were to be preached by members of the Society.

[64] Also a benefactor, this wealthy businessman, who served as economic counsellor to Charles V, started the Jesuit college at Medina del Campo.

[65] In a letter written by Ignatius to Rodrigo de Dueñas (MHSI *Epist.* VIII, 566-67: No. 5267) and dated 18 March 1555, so only a few days after this entry, this canon is mentioned as Canon Guernica; his other names are not known.

him how much such persons would be missed, he would reply to them very gently, "What would we do if so-and-so or so-and-so died? Well, then, reckon that they are dead!," or something similar.[66]

It was not only in this but in many other things that he displayed the great zeal that Our Lord had given him for the common good. He often used to say. "It's certainly the case that, if I were to see someone received into the Society as a temporal coadjutor with talent that allowed him with study to help people spiritually[67] I would have serious scruples about not making him study." And that was why he made several men study, for example, Emerio;[68] our Father himself told me that he was accepted as a laundry-man, and having served some time in that duty, he made him learn Latin because he was convinced that he had a talent for preaching. And indeed he became, and still is, one of the preachers in Italy, where he has been very effective. Another example is Drusiano,[69] who was treated in the same way, and is now rector of the college at [Modena].[70] I am not sure if it was our Father or Fr. Laínez who ordered him to study.

277 3. As for the German priest who is in Vienna, and the other one who has already come to Rome, both ask to be received into the German College, but Father does not want to take them, lest the other Germans make one of them a leader, given the problem there is in governing them even now, when there is no one they can make a ringleader.[71]

[n.d.] The Father is always most solicitous for the good of the whole body even if that may be difficult for individuals. For this reason he usually dismisses anyone who is harmful to someone else in our house, sometimes very speedily, and even sometimes that very night.[72]

---

[66] This criterion of "the greater good" is presented in the *Constitutions* as the first principle for Jesuit superiors in the choice of apostolic activity: cf. Part VII, c. 2 [§618].

[67] The Spanish here (as in other places) says literally, "to bear fruit in souls," one of the favourite evangelical metaphors used by Ignatius for being spiritually effective.

[68] Emerio de Bonis (1531-1595), an Italian Jesuit, originally a lay-brother (1550); he became the official preacher in Perugia, but also worked in Naples, where he died.

[69] Drusiano Franco (1531-1588), another Italian Jesuit who joined as a lay-brother (1555); eventually he became vice-rector in Modena (not rector as da Câmara says).

[70] Da Câmara left a blank here; presumably he was uncertain about the place.

[71] See §251.

[72] See §§350, 396.

Our Father often says of these and similar cases, where someone does not behave well in the Society, that he would not dare to stay under the same roof with him for that night.

278 The Father is absolutely determined that when someone comes to call a priest to a dying person, the porter or the sacristan should ring the bell, as was said above,[73] and that all the confessors, even the minister, should come. The Father decided this after having called a consultation which was of a different opinion. He orders that it should be made the rule.

11 March

279 1. The Father has reprimanded me for my carelessness, and ordered that I should inform the porter of my whereabouts when I am not in my room, in the kitchen, in the servery or the refectory.

I have to remember how often the Father has reprimanded me for my negligence, and especially since I have been minister.

12 March

280 1. *Abbot Martinengo*[a] wishes to make the Spiritual Exercises, after his nephew Lorenzo[74] has made them. Vitoria[75] gave them to him, with constant instruction from the Father; I must get information from Vitoria.

I must recall the conversation that the Father had with the Abbot, and how insistent the Father was that he should not bring a servant

---

[73] See §224.
[74] See §274.
[75] See §§ 13-15. It may have been at this time that Fr. Vitoria wrote down, at Ignatius's dictation, the Directory to the Exercises that bears his name. See Martin E. Palmer, *On Giving the Spiritual Exercises,* St. Louis, 1996, pp. 15-28.

with him, though being the person that he is, and he succeeded in persuading him not to do so.

(a) *Abbot Martinengo*

Abbot Martinengo, the uncle of Lorenzo Maggio, was a nobleman, born in Brescia. He had an income of several thousand *cruzados,* had been papal nuncio in Germany, and was at that time president of the clerical chamberlains at the Pontifical Court. He wanted to make the Exercises in Rome, and though he was so distinguished, our Father would not agree that he should have any of his own servants during the Exercises, but only Lorenzo Maggio his nephew, who could serve him just like any lay-brother of the Society, since at that time he was determined to join it. Our Father ordered me to give him the Exercises and every day I was to go to the Church of SS. Giovanni e Paolo,[6] where the Abbot had withdrawn. I did this, but first discussed in detail with the Father the points that I had to expound, and the way in which he should be directed. With this opportunity, I asked the Father questions during these days, and he told me many things about the Exercises, some of which will be mentioned later.[77]

13 March

281 1. A Cardinal[78] sent to our Father a request for one of our fathers to come to Rome: he made this request with great insistence. The Father replied most courteously, as was his custom, but saying that he was not able to do anything without the Protector,[79] who had been informed about this business. The servant left very content. However, the Father gave this reply because he thought that probably he would be able to make the Protector adopt his point of view; and so it was not necessary

---

[76] This church on the Celian Hill had been entrusted to the congregation of the "Gesuati," a 14th-century foundation favoured by Popes Urban V and Nicholas V, which (despite the similar name) had no connection with the "Gesuiti." They were suppressed by Clement IX in 1668. Cf. Supplement 3, n. 1.

[77] See §§305, 311-313.

[78] His name is given a little later: Cardinal Giovanni Ricci de Montepulciano, mentioned above, §246.

[79] The Cardinal Protector: see §232, with note.

to explain the reasons to him. Indeed when Polanco began to suggest giving them to him, the Father would not listen to them, and said he would make Montepulciano, who was the cardinal in question, understand his point of view.

281b [n.d.] When something is asked of him (as he told me later when we talked about this business) our Father usually intuits immediately if he is to grant or refuse it: if he is not going to grant it, he prepares himself, while the person is speaking, to give him the sort of answer, and guide the conversation in such a way, that he will leave satisfied. One way is to transfer the business to a third party; another is to present all the difficulties that there are in the matter, and show how he is not able to undertake it. But he always replies courteously, displaying such love that those whom he sends away with a negative response, go content. Everything he says is founded on such reason that the other person can grasp it. It happens therefore very often that when someone comes to ask something for another with great insistence, he goes away so persuaded himself by the Father that not merely is he content with the negative reply, but he becomes an advocate against the other.

282 2. The Father added, moreover, that in this matter even if the Protector did not adopt his viewpoint, and other cardinals were to insist, they would never be able to make him alter his course.

282b [n.d.] Our Father is so constant in everything he undertakes that everyone is astounded. The reasons for this that come to my mind are the following: the first reason is that he reflects carefully on each matter before coming to a decision; the second is that he prays very much about each subject and is enlightened by God; the third is that he takes no decision with regard to matters that concern particular persons without listening to the opinions of those who are expert in the matter; he asks their opinion about nearly everything, *except for those things*[a] of which he has full knowledge.

He is also accustomed quite frequently to transfer the decision in matters where he does not have full knowledge, while giving some general principles.

   (a) except for those things

283 Our Father behaved in this way especially when it was a case

of dismissing someone from the Society. He would listen to the person reporting faults to him by virtue of his office, or on some other ground. Then, having been very well informed and quite certain about all the facts, he would spend a long time in prayer and reflection, and if he felt in the divine presence it was appropriate to dismiss the man from the Society, he dismissed him forthwith. And I do not recall that in these particular cases our Father felt the need to call a consult, in which he might have proposed, "So-and-so did this or that: the question is, should he for that reason be dismissed from the Society?", except in certain instances where for reasons of public knowledge and particular difficulties he did wish the case to be put to a judgement, and sentence to be given by some Fathers appointed for this purpose. Such a case, among others, was that of a German, who while a student in the Society in Vienna, Austria, laboured under the delusion that our Lord had communicated to him the spirit of St. Paul. He was in every other respect sensible and intelligent, but from this most evil starting-point the devil was dragging him to total disobedience. For he was saying that the authority the Society had to oblige him to obedience was derived from the pope as successor of St. Peter, and since St. Paul, whose spirit he possessed, was no less important than St. Peter, he was not obliged to obey the Society. This man finished his course in Vienna very peacefully, without giving any sign of anything strange, until at the end he came out with this. His superior, once he realised there was no cure there in Vienna, sent him to our Father in Rome. When the Father saw what type of case this was, he ordered six of us professed fathers to form a board, to listen to him slowly, and to come to a judgement. I remember that we all came together, and began to question him; he spoke very quietly and in good Latin with all the aplomb in the world, saying that there was nothing further to investigate here, since it was God who had given him the spirit of St. Paul, which of course He was well able to do, and he himself knew for certain that he possessed this spirit. The reasons and arguments we put to him were of no avail; he gave the same answer to all of them with great serenity and modesty, indeed in all the other matters he spoke and argued very correctly. When our Father saw this, he dismissed him immediately, with the support of the unanimous opinion of all of us.

14 March

284 1. As for Fabio,[80] who has spoken a little to his brothers in such a way as to upset them, I will not allow him to speak to them further, unless he goes to confession here in the residence.

> This man was the brother of Petronio and three other young
> men from Pesaro who had joined the Society, as was said above.

285 2. Someone went today to ask Father's permission to leave the Society; he gave as a reason that Father had told him that he was not suitable for it. The Father replied, "I remember having said to you, that if you were not willing to obey, then you were not suitable for the Society, and I say the same thing to you now, so go to confession, and then talk to Polanco." This was at 7:30 in the evening.[81] Later the Father learned from Polanco that, being very busy, he had not been able to speak to him, and he then told Polanco to talk to him. Polanco returned saying that the young man was determined to leave; no arguments had had any effect. The Father considered for a short time what he had to do, and then called for him, even though he was by now in bed like the rest of the house, and began to argue with him. I thought that the discussion would last all night, because Father had said we must be patient and the young man was very stubborn. Finally Father persuaded him to go to confession promptly there in his chapel; when the confessor had got out of bed, we were waiting while he made his confession, so that the Father could continue to argue with him, if he did not come back having given in, something that I never expected to happen. But instead he came and fell on his knees, begging pardon. Father asked him what penance he wanted to make. He said, "Whatever your Reverence wishes."—"The penance will be that you will not be tempted any more," said the Father (and so we all promised in his name, and he as well), "I will do penance for you every time I have pains in the stomach!"

I must recall the great charity Father showed in the details of this affair.

---

[80] Fabio was the fifth brother to the four mentioned above, e.g. §29.
[81] The text gives "one o'clock at night," the Roman time at that period.

286 3. Luís[82] may remain, since he is so necessary for setting up the pharmacy, provided that he is spoken to in the way he wishes and desires.

Father is very opposed to people saying one thing to him on one occasion and then later saying the opposite.[83]

4. Father decided that I should give the Exercises to Abbot Martinengo at the convent of SS. Giovanni e Paolo.[84]

15 March

287 1. I must recall what Father told me about the period when the Society was trying to get [papal] confirmation; Cardinal Ghinucci[85] opposed it even after the Pope [Paul III] had granted it, and a Bishop,[86] a Dominican friar, was upsetting everything; this friar later suffered many tribulations, including, it is said, much disturbance of the mind. At last, when the Father had received the Bull, he went to thank Ghinucci for advice he had given him, which he had given to hinder the process, but which *mutatis mutandis* [when what needed to be changed had been changed] the Father had followed; and thereby succeeded in reaching his objective.[87]

---

[82] A Portuguese Jesuit, Luís Quaresma, had been a pharmacist, he came to Rome to accompany Bernard, the Japanese mentioned above (§30), early in January (1555), but was dismissed from the Society in September; on the pharmacy, see §161.

[83] This remark can be understood as if Ignatius was the person who disliked people saying different things to him on different occasions (as the French and Spanish translators seem to take it) or as if the remark concerns Luis (the interpretation followed here).

[84] See §280.

[85] Cardinal Girolamo Ghinucci, as Secretary in charge of drawing up Papal documents, strongly opposed the publication of the bull *Regimini militantis ecclesiae*, which adopted the text of the five chapters submitted by Ignatius and the first companions outlining the essence of the Society of Jesus and officially approving the new order. The MHSI editors note that in one copy of the *Memoriale* the name of Card. Ghinucci is replaced by that of Card. Guidiccioni, who also began by opposing the papal approbation, but later changed his mind. The whole process, between the verbal approval given by Paul III in Tivoli (September 1539) and the publication of the Bull (September 1540) took a full year.

[86] The MHSI editors note that this person has not been identified.

[87] The advice may have been that Card. Guidiccioni (well known for his opposition to all new religious foundations) should be called in as arbitrator; see note above.

288 2. Father Polanco sent a message to the Father through Don Diego[88] that Cincinnato,[89] who is ready to go to the College soon, should go today, in order to make room for a novice who has just arrived. Father reprimanded him severely for his lack of consideration in such matters: no action should be taken precipitately, or just *depending on the circumstances;*[a] but only after deep thought and discussion.

[a] *depending on the circumstances*

Since our Father was guided in everything by reason, he was completely against taking action either because of human attachment, or because the opportunity arose by chance.

16 March

289 1. While the Father was talking to me, thinking that he understood what was on my mind, I spoke about it, and the Father reprimanded me. I must recall how many times Father has instructed me, in different ways, not to talk precipitately, but instead should never use words without first having thought about them.

290 2. Three of the boys[90] from Ferrara should go to eat tomorrow in the College, because the Abbot[91] takes his meals there. The other two are to stay here and can be told that they will go another day, so that they will not be disappointed.

Our Father usually takes great care not to offend anyone, and this applies to everything, even to these boys, who are novices in their First Probation; and so it can be said of the Father that he is naturally the most courteous and considerate of men.

Last Day of March

291 1. I was speaking about the students of the German College saying

---

[88] Diego de Eguía.
[89] See §29: one of the brothers of Petronius.
[90] Five young men had arrived from Ferrara on the 8th of this month to join the Society.
[91] Probably Abbot Martinengo; see §280.

that they declare themselves Theatines,[92] and say, "I'm a Theatine and you are not!" The Father reprimanded me severely, because they were not talking like this because they were Theatines. He said he had noticed that I greatly exaggerate things, and that was bad when I was reporting on a matter, because it destroyed my credibility, and that he was not joking when he said this, and he then dismissed me.

I have to recall how small an impression this made on me. The reason, I think, is the same which prevents me from appreciating the evil *of speaking too quickly.*[a] Yet, when I think of the evils which result from this, I think I do begin to have a desire to correct myself in this respect.

[a] *of speaking too quickly*

Our Father searched for many cures and gave me frequent advice. I remember that he entrusted me to Joan Cors,[93] ordering him to give me the penances that he thought necessary. Among other things, Joan made me admit my faults in public, and eat at the "little table" for a week. But when Fr. Ignatius saw that even with all this I did not mend my ways, he called for me one day and told me he had employed many remedies to make me speak slowly, and since none had any effect, it must be due to forgetfulness; therefore, in order that I should not forget, he thought it would be a good idea for me to have some tinkle-bells attached to my ears, so that when I spoke I should be reminded by their ringing of the need to speak slowly. At the time this was only a threat, but I think I gained some small benefit from it, as it was a penalty to fit the crime, and I am sure that if I had not departed shortly after for Portugal, I would not totally have escaped the bells.

Some Additional Things: 16-31 March

292 1. The Father ordered me to tell Bobadilla that two other people *must share his room,*[b] which was very small, and I was to come back to report Bobadilla's reply, and he replied that he was quite content.

---

[92] See §206 with note.
[93] This brother reappears below, §316.

(b) *share his room*

Fr. Bobadilla[94] lived in a room that was extremely small, and because of his various indispositions and needs he had talked of having a larger room. Our Father knew this, and in order to exercise his obedience and mortification, he ordered me to tell him what I am relating here.

19 March

293 1. Learning that there was slackness among the confessors he ordered me to give them the rule concerning confessions in writing, and to make it public.

> *Scribe's Marginal Note:* That is, to come to the porter's lodge when the bell rang for a sick person in danger, as has been said.[95]

294 2. Father had a very satisfactory conversation with Loarte: having reprehended him severely in such a way as to humiliate him and hurt his feelings considerably, he recognized his virtue. He told me not to oblige him to hear the confessions of Italians because Loarte said he could not understand them. And he added that there were some people who were scrupulous in one way and others in another, just as I had no scruples in speaking too fast.

> **295** Our Father often used to say that the Society should take particular care to mortify nobles and learned men, because if they were perfect they could perform great services for God, and if they were not, they would do great harm. He often repeated this saying to me, and I saw him put it into practice very effectively on certain occasions. When Fr. Nadal had finished his first visitation,[96] he returned to Rome in 1554 and brought Fr. Loarte[97]with him. Fr. Loarte was Spanish by birth, a priest, a good preacher and an academic;[98] he had taught theology for some years in Spain and was

[94] First mentioned in §23.

[95] See §§224, 278.

[96] This was the first Iberian visitation (Portugal and Spain), which finished in 1554.

[97] Gaspar Loarte (1498-1578), a Castilian disciple of St. John of Avila, joined the Society in 1553 and spent much of his life as rector of colleges in Italy and Sicily.

[98] As such he is often referred to as Dr. Loarte.

one of the most devoted disciples of Fr. Avila; he was a very prayerful man and dedicated to spiritual matters. He came to Rome while I was still minister. Our Father entrusted him to me and recommended me to mortify him greatly, something he had never asked of me with regard to anyone else, although at least a hundred had entered during that period. According to what Fr. Ignatius himself explained to me, he told him many good things about me, praising me and setting great store on what I could do to help him in spiritual matters; this was so that Loarte would hold me in esteem and would profit greatly from the penances and warnings I might give him. I accepted responsibility for him and treated him with all possible rigour, exercising it through people he was most likely to resent. I recall in particular that at that time we put a scrupulous novice, whom we dismissed shortly afterward, in charge of our practice sermons; he was to take special care of Fr. Loarte and order him to declaim. Once, as soon as he was in the pulpit, he made him come down and preach on his knees, kiss the floor and the feet of those present, talk first one way and then another, making him take back what he had said, and employing such devices that Loarte was at his wit's end, so that he made him start crying like a child. And when he asked him one day if he would like to visit the Station-churches with him, Loarte replied, "It's not necessary, because you give me a plenary indulgence here every day!"

I talked to him frequently[99] about the self-mortification and abnegation of the will, of the complete indifference and blind obedience which the Society sought. I often used the phrase current at that time: "It is necessary *to come to the point.*" One day when we were both discussing this, he asked me what it meant. I explained it by this comparison: "If a man is tied by a rope, and suspended from a hook in the ceiling, so that his feet still touch the ground, you cannot tell if the rope is strong enough to sustain him; but if one takes the ground from under his feet so that he is in mid-air, then you can properly test the strength of the rope: if it does not break, that is a sign that it is strong and can take any weight whatever. This is the way for our Father and the Society: as long as a man—although he is well attached [to the Society]—has not taken away and dug out from under him the soil on which he rests the

---

[99] The Portuguese phrase here, *a meude,* may mean "in detail" rather than "frequently."

feet of his attachments,[100] and on which he can in some way support himself, they do not consider him secure. But if when this is
done, and the man finds himself hanging in mid-air, the rope
holds, then the Father judges that such a man has reached "the
point" and that he is able to support any weight whatever. I said
these words with such decisiveness and efficacy that Loarte could
not hear them without bursting into tears and saying, "Poor old
me! I've got to be hanged!"

These exercises took up so much of his time that his complaint
was that after having received so many consolations in prayer
while still outside, he had not experienced any since he came into
our house. It needed our Father himself to speak to him quite
explicitly about spiritual matters, though he did this so very rarely
that, as he told me later, he had not had a spiritual conversation
with anyone but Loarte for many years.

296 Loarte returned amazed from his interview with Fr. Ignatius,
and greatly consoled and encouraged to confront all the tasks he
had in hand. When I asked him what he thought of the Father, he
replied, "The Father is like a fountain of oil." When I asked him
what he thought of me, he replied, "Your Reverence is all vinegar."

I reported to our Father in detail each day everything that
passed between the two of us, and I followed his instructions in
everything. I remember especially that when I told him of this
reply about oil and vinegar, he made a great joke of it, and
recounted it to various Fathers with signs of great satisfaction.

To conclude, he very much wanted to test this Doctor in all the
"experiments" of the Society. So when he sent Fathers Polanco

---

[100] The word in Portuguese is *affeyção*, translated into Spanish as *afición* and into
French as *affection*, however the English word *affection* has to be understood in the
Ignatian sense: "'Affection' is a key term in the language of the Exercises; it refers to the
many variants of love and desire, together with their antitheses, hate and fear. The affections operate on many levels, from that of quite transient feelings to the level where they
affect a person's ways of perceiving reality, making judgements, choosing and acting. The
Exercises have to do with the conversion of affectivity, with letting the Spirit enter into our
affectivity, change it, and act through it.... In English, this sense of the noun 'affection' has
been lost, and substitutes such as 'tendency', 'inclination', 'propensity', 'attachment' only
partly convey it." (Ivens, *Understanding the Spiritual Exercises*, p. 2.)

and Don Diego de Guzmán[101] on pilgrimage to ask Our Lord to grant health to Pope Marcellus II,[102] from whom he had high hopes for the reform of the Church, I also asked for permission to make a pilgrimage to Loreto, and I went and asked the Doctor if he would like to make the pilgrimage with me; I would ask permission for us both. He replied that he would like to go with me. Thinking that it was impossible for the Father to let me go (at the time the doctors were talking of sending me for a cure at the baths of Viterbo), I went back to find the Father, and when I told him that Loarte would like to go with me to Loreto, if his Reverence agreed, he was delighted. We both, therefore, took the road; during the pilgrimage Fr. Loarte suffered greatly, because he was not used to walking, and was not physically strong.[103] Shortly afterwards, our Father appointed him rector of the College at Genoa, after he had been for some time sub-minister at Rome.

20 March

297 1. N.,[104] the man who was tempted on the 14th, has been tempted again, and came today to talk to our Father. After a long conversation, he asked to go to Loreto. Father asked him what he wanted to gain from Loreto, and said that if he sought the merit from a pilgrimage, he himself would go in his place (the Father had already decided to go there next Easter[105]) and was willing to give him all his merit. In this way he satisfied and calmed him. He came to an agreement with N. that the latter should give him in writing the names of those he would accept as judges and by whose sentence he would abide. This was done, and after saying three Masses, we, six professed fathers of the Society, all together decided that he was not obliged to go to the assistance of his sisters and his mother, which was the business that misled him. As a result he calmed down and was consoled. I must remember to make a copy of the opinions of Fathers des Freux and Olave, which they gave in writing.[106]

[101] Diego de Guzmán (died 1606), also a disciple of John of Avila, joined the Society with Fr. Loarte and also spent much of his life in Italy, doing mainly catechetical work with children.

[102] Marcello Cervini, of whom so much was expected as a reforming Pope, reigned for only twenty-two days in April, 1555.

[103] Neither Loarte nor Polanco were able to complete the pilgrimage, and Ignatius had to write on 4 May to arrange help for their return to Rome.

[104] See §285.

[105] Ignatius was prevented from making this pilgrimage by the unexpected Papal conclave.

[106] Both the originals and the copies seem to have been lost.

298 2. So-and-so[107] seven or eight days ago called me and Botelho[108] into the garden, making serious complaints about the person who had spoken to me about his hundred thousand.[109] All these complaints were because I might think that he [So-and-so] had it in mind that our Father would like him to give them to Rome. He began to talk in an exaggerated way saying that he had never thought such a thing, or had occasion for it.

299 3. Our Father came to know that So-and-so had somehow raised the topic of the hundred thousand. He called together a large number of us and gave us a talk, and everyone said that there was nothing in it, except that So-and-so himself had said that he had suspected it. This matter has been written up at length by Polanco.[110]

300 4. When Father learned that Pope Julius [III] was ill, he offered up prayers for him. But he explained that he could not find devotion at first, and later he did, because of the many reasons that he sought and found for this, i.e. to ask that he should live, etc.

[n.d.] It appears that in every matter Father is moved by reason, and the feeling[111] and devotion always follow afterwards; he keeps this rule in everything and gives it to others. He says this is the difference between human beings and the other animals. This is the most outstanding characteristic of the Father, or one of the most.

21 March

301 Father always prays every day for the Pope, and now that he is sick he prays for him twice, and always with tears.

---

[107] It is likely that this was Teotonio de Bragança (see §150), wanting to speak with his countrymen, but the whole of this little incident (§§298-9) is far from clear in da Câmara's jottings.

[108] Miguel Botelho, a Portuguese Jesuit since 1544, had been called to Rome in 1545 and became a well-known preacher; he died in 1576.

[109] The currency in question is not mentioned.

[110] No such document has been found.

[111] The Spanish word here is *afecto* (translated into French as *sentiment*).

[23 March]

302 Today, 23 March, Pope Julius [III] died. Father gave orders to tell the Abbot,[112] but not to offer him advice. *The Abbot stopped his retreat*[a], which displeased the Father; it would have been greatly to the honour of God if he had left his office and all the rest to persevere in making the Exercises.

[a] *The Abbot stopped his retreat*

Abbot Martinengo abandoned the recollection of his Exercises to fulfil certain obligations, connected with the death of the pope, due to his post as president of the clerical chamberlains. This grieved our Father because the Abbot had nearly decided to join the Society, and therefore he would have preferred to see him break with his post and persevere in the Exercises he had begun. When he had fulfilled his obligations, he returned to them. But later, when Marcellus [II] was elected, a close friend of his who would, he hoped, make him a cardinal, he left the Exercises again. Recalling this, I remember our Father joking about it several times and saying to me, "Father, what is the news of your Abbot?" I used to reply, "Two popes against one abbot, two popes against one abbot, how could they not overcome him?" and so on. This reply greatly amused the Father.

303 The laymen[113] should not go to the garden *when there are outsiders present*[b] unless they are the sort likely to edify and are correctly dressed, etc.; this should be made a rule.

[b] *when there are outsiders present*

The nobles who come to listen to the sermons in our residence used to walk through the garden, which is the only way into the church and is above the lowest floor of the house. Our Father did not want the coadjutor Brothers, who sometimes go about there in just hose and doublet, to go out in the garden at that time unless they are suitably clothed.

---

[112] Abbot Martinengo; see §§280, 286.
[113] The comment by da Câmara makes it clear that the lay-brothers are meant.

304 Loarte went to make his act of humility in the refectory, confessing his temptations, and kissing feet, etc.; and this was on the orders of the Father.

APRIL

1 April

305   1. The Father talked to me about the Exercises of the Abbot.[1] What he said is as follows. First, in comparison with the rigour with which the Exercises were given at the beginning, now there is nothing; then, no one made them without fasting for some days (*nemine tamen persuadente* [despite the fact that nobody was using persuasion]). Now he would not dare to approve more than one day's fasting for someone who was robust, though he had no scruples about the past. All the first fathers made the Exercises with great exactness and in seclusion. The least abstinence they all undertook was three days without food or water, except for Simão,[2] who in order not to leave his studies and because he was not very well, did not leave his house, or undertake any of these extreme measures; instead the Father simply gave him the meditations, etc.

Favre made the Exercises in the [Paris suburb of] *Faubourg St. Jacques,* in a house on the left, at a time when people were crossing the Seine in carts because it was frozen. And although the Father took particular care to observe if his lips were sticking together, to know if he had not eaten, when he examined Favre he found that he had not eaten anything at all for six full days and he had been sleeping in his shirt on the logs which had been brought for him to burn, but he had never lit a fire; he was making his meditations in the snow in a courtyard. When Father learned this he said, "I'm quite sure you haven't committed any sin by doing this; on the contrary you have gained much merit. I'll come back before an hour and tell you what you have to do." Father then went to a nearby church in order to pray, and his desire was that Favre should fast

---

[1] Abbot Martinengo, once again; see §302.
[2] Simão Rodrigues, the future provincial of Portugal.

for as long a time as he himself had fasted, which he had almost done already. But even though he so desired this, after making his prayer he did not dare to allow it, and so he went back to light a fire for him and make him a meal.

306 Master Francis,[3] in addition to much fasting, *bound up all*[a] his body and his legs very tightly with a rope, because he was one of the best. jumpers on the island[4] in Paris, and tied in that way, unable to move, he made his meditations.

[a] *bound up all*

It seems that while he was meditating, thoughts of his earlier jumping and festivities on the island came to his mind, as these activities were something he naturally enjoyed; in order to overcome this passion at its root, he tied up his limbs, tormenting them with bonds, quite contrary to the agility and prowess of his jumps.

307 Pietro Codazzo,[5] to whom the Father has also given the Exercises, went for three days without eating, although he was a great eater and fond of comfort. At the time of Pope Clement[6] he was administrator[7] for someone who was himself administrator for the Pope himself. He stayed well *disposed,*[b] and some time later decided to enter the Society.

[b] *disposed*

He stayed well disposed, because although he did not enter the Society immediately, it was nevertheless from these Exercises that his decision to do so shortly after was born.

---

[3] Francis Xavier; for a full account of Xavier's period in Paris, cf. G. Schurhammer, *Francis Xavier*, vol. 1, pp. 77-273.

[4] More of the *Ile de la Cité* was then open ground and served the university students for sporting activities.

[5] A key figure in the early history of the Jesuits, Pietro Codazzo, an Italian canon from Lodi, joined the group of first companions in 1539, even before the official confirmation of the Society; he obtained permission from the Pope to transfer in 1541 the church of Santa Maria della Strada, which had been allocated to him, to the nascent Society, and also gave much material help in acquiring the first residence. He died in 1549.

[6] Clement VII (1523-34).

[7] The person who was administrator (in Spanish *governaba* is used in a technical sense) may have been Felipe Archinto, the Pope's vicar in Rome.

2 April

308 1. Father does not want anyone of the Society to arrange to hear the confessions of princes, or to make excuses for not hearing them either.

2. He would not approve of a royal confessor talking to the prince in confession about any of his affairs; he could however gather information from individuals so as to remind the prince at suitable times. Similarly the Father said, as he had on other occasions, that he had not thought it was good to decline hearing the confession of the King of Portugal.[8]

3. Father displayed a very great desire that I should not be careless, saying, "Indeed, how much I desire it!"

3 April

309 1. *A member of the Society,*[a],[9] who has received a revelation, as he thinks, was sent to Rome by his local superior, who had been unable to deal with him. The first thing the Father said was that he should be received as a guest, not as a member of the Society. After he had put his revelation in writing, and six of us had been ordered to examine it, we found that the revelation had come to him while he was making the Exercises, towards the end and before he had decided to enter the Society, where he was wanted because of his good qualities. Consequently he went to work in a hospital for six months, after which he joined the Society. The Father ordered him to sign a statement that he was prepared to abide by the judgement. And then the Father, after all of us had signed, agreeing to the judgement that had been given, added his own signature, saying that even before he had seen the judgement, he had thought that there was an evil spirit [responsible]. God willed that after this the poor soul submitted, although difficulties remain, because on the one hand he wants to believe in obedience, and on the other he cannot rid himself of

---

[8] Two years earlier Ignatius had written a letter reproving both da Câmara and his provincial (Fr. Mirón) for not accepting the duties of royal confessors; cf. *Select Letters*, No. 30, p. 248 [MHSI *Epist.* IV, 625-28, No. 3220].

[9] Jérôme Le Bas: this French priest was sent to Rome from Paris by Paschase Broët when he began claiming that it had been revealed to him that the son of Soliman the Great, Sultan of Turkey (1520-66), was the Anti-Christ, who would come in three months and ravage all Christian territories, thus making the further founding of colleges useless.

the impression he has that the revelation was genuine. The Father ordered the judgement to be delivered with all due ceremony, saying that was how the devil would like it.[10]

{a} A member of the Society

310 This was a French-speaking Flemish priest. The chief substance of his revelation concerned the bad things in France.[11] Our Lord willed to give him light by which to see his illusion. After the judgement I have described here had been pronounced, notwithstanding some difficulties at the beginning, and after he had submitted, our Father ordered him to enter with the Brothers, because until then he had been entertained as a guest. Our Father always displayed an aversion to prophetic revelations that had not been approved by the Church. The priest stayed in Rome for a few months obediently performing humble duties. I remember particularly that he was the best dispenser we had in my time. Our Father was so pleased with his probation that he sent him, a little later, to France as rector of a college. He died there, "showing great signs of virtue and giving great edification." I saw him myself[13] in his own college, giving great edification to those both inside and outside. This was for me a great example of how God favours those in the Society who reach a true obedience of the understanding. Indeed as I was the minister and spoke French, our Father put me in charge of the details of this affair. I used to visit this Father several times a day, and talk with him about the affair, and I seemed

[10] The text is muddled here with most of the sentence written in the margin (the MHSI editors wonder if the scribe forgot to add the words at the right place) and at the end the strange phrase, *que el demonio así se quiere,* which could mean, "that was how the devil appreciates himself".

[11] Perhaps a reference to the difficulties of the Society in France, but at the time Henri II was at war with Charles V over possession of parts of the Low Countries.

[12] A mistake here by da Câmara, as Le Bas's death took place in Rome in 1562, while he was engaged in further theological studies. However, he had been a successful rector in Billom from 1557 to 1560.

[13] In 1559, when da Câmara was returning to Portugal from Rome after the first General Congregation.

to be able to touch with my hand how violent it was for him to submit this business to the judgement of someone else. And I had to spend several days persuading him that he should, and could, do so in good conscience.

311 2. The Father judges that to persons who, it is hoped, will be able to follow the way of perfection, the Exercises should not be given *in an open form*[a] even though they ask for them like that.

[a] *in an open form*

I call those Exercises "open", when the person making them is not making a completely secluded retreat, but only employs a limited time for the meditations, and goes out to follow his normal activities.

312 3. In the Exercises nothing must be given in writing.[14] Again, the religious life in a particular form is not to be discussed, without having first put forward the Commandments and the Counsels in general, and the person has decided to follow the Counsels. For this reason, the Father said, when he learned today of someone who was not following this rule, that this person did not know how to give the Exercises.

313 4. Father said he wanted to compile a Directory on how to give the Exercises, and Polanco should ask questions about doubtful points at any time, because in matters relating to the Exercises he did not need to think a great deal before giving answers.

Our Father later wrote this Directory, and I brought a translation of it to this Province.[15]

4 April

314 1. The Father has taken great pains to free Mudarra[16] from the Inquisition. It was he who was the greatest opponent of the Society at the

[14] The one giving the Exercises should not need the text; however, Ignatius did recommend that the exercitant write down "on the spot in a very abbreviated form" what has been said to him at each visit: see Document 4, §14 in Martin Palmer, *On Giving the Spiritual Exercises*, p. 19.

[15] This is thought to be what appears as Document 1 in Martin Palmer, *On Giving the Spiritual Exercises*, pp. 7-10, with p. 31, note 5.

[16] Francisco Mudarra led a group of anti-Jesuit clerical agitators (all Spaniards) in Rome in 1538, in reaction to the criticism made by the first companions of his own

beginning; now he has fled from Rome, all his benefices, which were many, have been lost, and the thousands of ducats in his possession have been confiscated by the Inquisition. Father treated Miguel the Navarrese[17] in the same way; he also had persecuted the Society, but Father even received him in the residence, etc.

315 2. Father spent the best part of the day in learning how each priest gave absolution and penances, because even in this he wants uniformity.

316 3. It was proposed to the Father to make continual prayer for the papal election, and he did not agree as he did not want to set up rites,[18] nor that all should recite the litanies together. But he allowed them to be said, with two priests, by ten or twelve of those who had perhaps forgotten to make the prayer three times, as is ordered. And so some nights ago, when everyone was already asleep, he ordered the prayer to be said, because on that day they had not been started. Father himself says the litanies every night with Joan Cors[19] for this intention.

317 4. The man who was tempted before,[20] about whom I spoke, was once again tempted to join another religious order. Father talked to him at length, until the following agreement was reached: he should leave the decision in the hands of those who had considered it the first time, asking them—if they judged the Society was best for him—to give him a daily discipline every time he succumbed to the temptation, until he was at peace with himself; if they preferred to send him to the Franciscans, they should make the same recommendation to the Guardian.[21] This judgement was agreed, and he stayed in the Society.

Lutheran leanings; his accusations against the companions were examined and not only were they dismissed, but in consequence he had to flee from Rome, where he was burned in effigy.

[17] His full name was Miguel Landívar, and he came from Navarre to Paris as a servant of Francis Xavier; annoyed with Ignatius at the conversion of Francis, he first tried to kill him and then to join the group of companions in Venice (1537). Having failed there he moved in 1538 to Rome and soon began to spread calumnies about the group, to the point where Ignatius had a case brought against him and he was banished. See *Select Letters*, No. 10.

[18] The original Spanish reads, *por no hacer ritos,* and this has been understood in the modern Spanish paraphrase as, "in order not to establish customs" (in French, *pour ne pas établir d'usage*); but the reference seems to be a reaction against extra-liturgical practices.

[19] Already mentioned briefly above (§291), Joan Cors was a Catalan brother coadjutor who became a close personal assistant to Ignatius (see §327); he died in 1572.

[20] See §§285, 297.

[21] The title given by Franciscans to their superiors.

The Father had ceded his vote to the judges.

318 5. Even though it is a period of *sede vacante*[22] there may be tapestry hangings in the church, but the Father never wants silver there.

> There was doubt [about this], especially at that time of *sede vacante*, because while there is no supreme authority on earth, there are usually more robberies and libertinage.

319 6. Alms were given today to the College, but Father did not want to accept them. The Father has replied that when the person giving alms has no sons or other interest in the College it was licit to accept the gift. But he was of the opinion that small gifts should not be accepted, lest reputation be lost, and in order to maintain our credibility.

320 7. When a person who has interests [in the College] leaves a legacy to the College, it can be accepted.

321 I must recall how, when the Father learned from Fr. Nadal on his return from Spain about the opposition[(a)] to the *Exercises* there, and how Araoz[23] had emended copies [of the *Exercises*] in accordance with the Spanish, he regretted it very much, and greatly blamed Araoz for having done it, because the Latin text had been approved by the Pope. He said he himself would never defend the *Exercises*, but rather it was for the Church to defend them against their opponents.

[(a)] the opposition

> 322 When Fr. des Freux translated the *Exercises* from Spanish to Latin, for one of the rules[24] that the Father added to the *Exercises*, he used a word which caused concern in Castile that our Father

---

[22] The papal throne is empty, Julius III having died and Marcellus II not yet elected.
[23] See §39.
[24] These are the rules traditionally known as "Rules for Thinking with the Church" (*Exercises* §§352-70), though more properly entitled, "Rules to follow in view of the true attitude of mind that we ought to maintain in the Church Militant" (see M. Ivens, *Understanding the Spiritual Exercises*, p. 252). The rule that caused problems was number 14 (§366), where Fr. des Freux used a past subjunctive (*esset*) in place of a present subjunctive (*sit*) in translating a verb; the Latin could then be interpreted in an "unreal" sense, giving a loophole to the theory that one could be saved even if not predestined for this (a view which seemed to be proposed by one Dominican, Catharinus, and violently condemned by other Dominicans, led by Melchor Cano).

was following the opinions of Caterino[25] about predestination; and just as this opinion was very badly viewed in Spain, so was that rule. Fr. Araoz, to avoid such calumny and opposition, displayed the Spanish text and had the Latin corrected accordingly. Our Father greatly regretted this because of the great authority he wanted to be given to the Apostolic See and to whatever it approved.

One day Pedro de Zárate[26] was dining with our Father: he was a very devout man, and zealous for God's honour. At that time he was urging the Pope [Julius III], the Emperor [Charles V], and the King of Castile,[27] to found a convent at the Holy Sepulchre in Jerusalem: he solicited this with great diligence. When the conversation turned to the column to which Christ our Lord was bound for the flagellation—of which one half is in Rome and the other in Jerusalem—Pedro de Zárate said that in his opinion the column here in Rome was not a half of the original column; he had seen the part in Jerusalem, which was slimmer than that in Rome, and of different workmanship. Our Father replied with great gravity as follows: "I have certainly seen both the one and the other, and I would not dare to judge if there is any difference between them. If there were, I would rather hold the one here in Rome to be true, which the Church has approved, than the other which is there in Jerusalem among the Turks."

This was the way our Father felt.

323 8. Today Father said that Loarte[28] should be minister and subminister until after Easter, and then go to Genoa to take up his post.

5 April

324 1. I learned today that Fr. des Freux, when he was cook here, suffered with the flesh on his shoulder very badly grazed without

---

[25] Called "Caterino" by da Câmara, but usually known by his Latin name as Ambrosius Catharinus (or Politus), Lanciloto dei Politi, O.P. [1484-1553], a bishop since 1546, had published his *De praedestinatione* for the participants of the Council of Trent.

[26] An important friend and benefactor, this Basque was a knight of the Order of the Holy Sepulchre.

[27] Probably a reference to Philip II, though he became king of Spain only in 1556.

[28] See §295; he was to be rector in Genoa.

mentioning it. The reason was that he carried water and other heavy goods along with Antonio Rion[29] with a yoke on his shoulder.

6 April

325 1. Father's affection for music; and how he feared the Theatine[30] because of possible imposition of sung office.

326 2. The Father spoke today about offering prayers that (provided there was equal service to God) there should not emerge a Pope who would change the Society, since among the *papabili* there are some who it is feared may want to change it.

327 3. Joan Cors asks that everyone should weep for this intention three times a day, and if they fail to do so, should eat only bread.

Joan Cors, a Catalan, was a Brother of extraordinary simplicity and humility, so much so that our Father, when he was talking about someone, used to say: "If only he would never contradict anyone, and be like Joan Cors!" He looked after Father's room and therefore lived in the next room, where he spent all day. In order not to waste the time left over from prayer and the Divine Office, which he also said, he learned to make slippers and knitted socks, and he used to work at them continuously. I remember once our Father said to him, "Reprimand Martín[31] for this, wherever you find him, and do it angrily." He asked Martín afterwards if he had been reprimanded with a display of anger, and when he said. "No," Father called Joan Cors and said, "Didn't I tell you to give this reprimand angrily? Why didn't you do as I said?" He replied, "Father, I don't possess any anger." The Father then said, "What do you mean that you don't possess any anger?" "I vomited it all into the sea," he said, "coming over from Barcelona." This reply greatly pleased the Father, who appreciated his great frankness and simplicity.

328 Father summoned two fathers in the presence of the sacristan, *and presupposing the*[a] fault on their part, gave them a terrible reprimand; he

---

[29] See §109.
[30] Cardinal Carafa: see §93 with the notes there.
[31] Martín de Zornoza (§163).

threw them out and said it pained him in his heart[32] to speak in this way.

(a) *and presupposing the*

Although our Father was very inclined to impose ordinary penances, such as eating at the "little table" and other similar things, and did not wait for a fault to impose one, nevertheless, as I have already said, in order to reprimand someone and inform him of any fault, he always used to explain it to the person first, and enable him to understand, so that he would accept the penance for himself. That is why I have noted here the importance which he attached to the fault of these Fathers, which was that they did not come at once to hear confessions, given that without further preparation he reprimanded them as I have said.

10 April

329 1. *On the way of bringing together*[b] the confessors without any excuse, including the superintendent, the Flemings, and Bobadilla.

(b) *On the way of bringing together*

In order that no Father should find an excuse for not going to hear confessions during that period, which was Holy Week, Father proposed this: that first should go Fathers Bobadilla and Olave, the superintendent of the College, and also the Flemings, who as they did not understand colloquial Italian, could have more problems.[33]

14 April

330 *Concerning the two*[c] whom the Pope had asked for. Father wishes them to be *optimos super omnes* [the best of all]. Nevertheless there

---

[32] Literally "in his soul (*su ánima*)".

[33] An obscure passage; one suspects that it is linked with the reprimand given "on a presupposition" (§328). Were the Flemings—hesitant to hear confessions because they could not understand—being urged to learn the local language more enthusiastically? And were two of the busiest members sent first with them *pour encourager les autres?*

should be an election, not to please the Pope,[34] but rather to please some members of the Society.

[c] *Concerning the two*

As soon as Marcellus [II] was elected,[35] when our Father called on him, the Pope told him (even if he did not order this) that he would like to have two members of the Society with him in his palace, from whom he could take advice in everything that touched on reform. In addition, our Father's normal habit was always to avoid giving anyone in the Society the feeling that he was held in less esteem. This was the reason, it seems, that when the first fathers assembled to elect a general he decided not to vote for anyone in particular. His vote was that he would elect the one who had the most votes, but excluding himself.[36] And it is well worth considering this way of giving his vote, because it is known from him, and I have heard it from his own lips, that he had a very high opinion of several of these first members of the Society, and he mentioned to me by name some who, he said, had always been his pillars of support.

It was for the same reason, so we thought at the time, that he did not wish himself to choose the two Fathers the Pope asked for and so he put it to the vote.

The same process was adopted when he chose Fr. Nadal as Vicar General,[37] and in other particular cases, so that the temptation was removed that someone or other would be resentful against him for not being chosen; and when all was said and done, everything that the Father envisaged and wanted was arranged smoothly, because the qualities he required in the person to be elected could only be found in those he had seen to be most suitable.

---

[34] The choice of words may seem unfortunate. Ignatius did not intend to displease the Pope, nor did he give more importance to his fellow Jesuits over the Pope. The point here is that Ignatius chose a particular method for selecting Papal counsellors not because he knew the Pope wanted an election (he presumed that the Pope would not mind what method was used), but because he thought an election by his fellow Jesuits would cause the greatest satisfaction among them.

[35] The papal conclave finished on 9 April 1555.

[36] The various votes cast on that occasion (5 April 1541) have been preserved; that of Ignatius confirms what da Câmara says here: it is signed "Iñigo."

[37] November 1554. All the Jesuit priests in Rome at the time voted on this occasion.

15 April

331 1. The Father held a consult today; I must remember to obtain a copy of the points that the Father wanted to be discussed.

> This meeting was about the same election; I do not remember the points.

332 2. The Father spent some time in prayer, and although, given Juan[38] from Alba's latest temptations, which were submitted in writing, all of us, including Father, are left with little hope, the Father decided to help him and give him the Exercises. If he is left resigned, Father will give in to him and make him study.

> This is the same Brother coadjutor whose earlier temptations have been noted. I have already mentioned the heartfelt mercy and love our Father showed, and how he also presumed true resignation on the part of the one who was tempted, since otherwise, without feeling that, he would never have acquiesced to anything.

333 The Father ordered the holding of a consult on the two for the Pope. I must recall how Bobadilla conducted it on Father's orders, and how the latter was displeased with those who did not reply to the points proposed.

> Father Bobadilla,[39] one of the first companions of our Father Ignatius, is one of those of the whole Society, who has worked hardest for the Church of God in various missions, sometimes accompanying papal nuncios and legates, sometimes as nuncio himself to remote countries, and on the laborious affairs of reform. Nevertheless, as it did not seem that he ought to be one of those elected for the Pope because of his many infirmities, our Father wanted him to preside at the "consult" in which the election would take place, and for this reason he gave information beforehand on the attributes or qualities that those elected should possess. The "consult," therefore, was not concerned with the qualities they

---

[38] First mentioned in §236.

[39] First mentioned in §23. This eulogy of Bobadilla was written despite his "sedition" in 1557 at the first general congregation (see John O'Malley, *The First Jesuits*, pp. 333-35); despite his "many infirmities" he outlived all the first companions, dying in 1590.

should have, but what Fr. Bobadilla proposed was the following: "Our Father wishes that those who are to be with the Pope should have such and such qualities. His orders are that each member is to say who, in his opinion, combines all these, replying separately on each item, and then in accordance with that the election should be made."

Some of the consultors did not reply in the proper order to the points raised, which greatly displeased our Father.

16 April

334   After he had seen the votes, Father decided to keep Fr. Nadal.[40]

18 April

335   Father sent Polanco to the Pope with the reply, saying that he had taken the words of His Holiness as a command: after holding a consultation, Laínez had been selected for one of the posts, and for the other, four or five could be offered; when His Holiness ordered, he would go to give him a reply, and offer those to him so that he could choose.

22 April

336   1. Today Fr. Polanco and Don Diego left on pilgrimage to Loreto.

Our Father wanted some fathers to make a pilgrimage to Loreto for the restoration of health of Pope Marcellus, who became ill at this time. The first he sent were Fr. Polanco and Don Diego de Guzmán,[41] and a little later Fr. Loarte and myself.[42] For this reason I have nothing in this notebook from 23 April to 22 May.

---

[40] These words are interpreted to mean that his name was withdrawn by Ignatius from the list of possible nominees, because he wanted to "keep" (*tener*) him to work for the Society; however there is also evidence that Nadal was in fact elected with Laínez, so Ignatius may have decided to "keep" his name on the list. In any case, with the Pope's death the whole proposal was buried.

[41] See §296.

[42] See also §296.

337 2. Before Don Diego left, Father gave him a heavy penance with discipline, but later he changed it to a reprimand and a fault denounced by Giovanni Filippo.[43] The reason for this was that he persisted in asking to make the pilgrimage: one should not do more than make a representation and show one's inclination.

> With regard to this penance that our Father ordered Don Diego to make, I noticed that he wanted it to serve as an example, so that we could understand how, even in matters good and holy in themselves, one must observe and maintain complete indifference and obedience. In everything connected with obedience, our Father wished us to observe the highest exactitude, and even—taking a very particular point—that all should leave a letter of the alphabet unfinished.[44] For this reason when he summoned someone from the residence who was involved in ordinary and important duties, for example Fr. Polanco, he would often say: "Tell so and so to come here, if he is not busy at the moment: and if he is, to come a little later." If he did not qualify the message in some such way, he desired one to drop everything.

> I remember one occasion when he ordered me to be called when I was saying Matins. As I had nearly finished I answered Joan Cors, who brought me this message: "Please tell Father that I'm finishing Matins: would his Reverence like me to finish first, or to interrupt them?" But as Brother Joan was on his way, I began to fear about what might happen, and followed quickly on his heels. When I arrived at the door, Brother had just finished delivering the message to the Father, who was saying to him, "Go back immediately and give Luís Gonçalves a proper penance for not coming when you called him." I arrived behind saying, "I'm already here, Father!" To which he replied cheerfully, "Truly, you acted with good sense in coming quickly!"

23 April

338 1. Today Loarte[45] and I leave for Loreto: I must remember *how*

---

[43] See §116: Giovanni Filippo Vito was ordained priest later in this year, 1555, and was working along with Polanco in the secretariat. He died just three years later.

[44] Da Câmara has in mind here an example given in the *Constitutions* (6,1,1, §§435, 547) to illustrate how promptly one should obey.

[45] See §§296, 336.

he prayed, [a],[46] and other measures the Father took before giving us permission, and [how] all [was] for the Pope.

[a] *how he prayed*

I was at that time very indisposed, and the doctors prescribed that I should take the waters at Viterbo. That was the reason why the Father hesitated to give me permission to make the pilgrimage, until he came to a decision in prayer that I should make it. A factor that contributed greatly was the knowledge that Father Loarte had said that if I were to go on pilgrimage, he would accompany me, as I have related above.[47] I am certain that if I had not made the pilgrimage, and if I had gone (as I should have gone) with the intention of taking the waters, I would have died there. In fact I went to Viterbo the following September on Father's orders to hear the confession of one of Cardinal de la Cueva's[48] nephews, who was very ill and taking the waters there. And when the doctor advised me to take the waters for a few days, after only four or five days of doing so I became very ill and nearly in danger of death. That is why when I recall this prayer that the Father made when he granted me permission to make the pilgrimage, I remain convinced that by his intercession Our Lord granted me then my life.

339 2. Doctor Arce begged our Father very much that no others should go [on pilgrimage] and therefore these pilgrimages were commuted.

Our Father would have liked to send many more on pilgrimage but Dr. Arce,[49] who was a great friend of the community, was opposed to the idea, since he feared that with the heat many would become ill. Our Father agreed and he commuted the pilgrimages to visits to the Station[50] Churches and to the *Scala Santa.*[51]

[46] The Spanish text has simply *de la oración* ["about the prayer"].
[47] See §296. The Portuguese here, *como adiante contarey,* means literally "as I shall recount further on"; this may be simply a mistake, but it may indicate that the writing of the Portuguese commentary was not continuous. Instead da Câmara may have inserted comments on earlier points as they occurred to him.
[48] See §15.
[49] See §57; it should not be forgotten that the making of a pilgrimage involved considerable hardship.
[50] See §237.
[51] This pilgrimage site in Rome stands next to St. John Lateran and contains the steps reputed to be those down which Christ came after his condemnation by Pilate; devout pilgrims ascend the steps on their knees.

MAY

22 May[1]

340   1. Don Diego and I reach Rome on May 16.

Fr. Polanco,[2] who accompanied Don Diego, fell ill on the way to
Loreto. I left Fr. Loarte, who was also poorly, with him and came
back to Rome with Don Diego.

341   2. Juan from Alba settled down completely with the Exercises and
Father took away from him *[lacuna: the obligation?]* to write.[3] I must
recall how everyone thought it would be impossible for him to overcome
himself *et tamen vicit Patris constantia.*[4]

When this Brother joined the community he could neither read
nor write. He learned to read while he was working in the stables
looking after one of the animals. He used to read Isaiah frequently, and said he understood it; from here he was gradually drawn to
have temptations about his vocation, and said he wanted to study,
although he had been accepted as a coadjutor. It was on this occasion that our Father established the common rule[5] that no coadjutor should study on his own account or be taught to read and write
without permission of the superior.

[1] Da Câmara now resumes his notes which had broken off on 23 April. Unfortunately,
from this point onwards the only full manuscript (*Lusitanus* 109 [M] in the Roman Curial
Archives) has more and more lacunae (which are shown between square backets in the
text). The scribe of M may have found these in the original, or (more likely) may have
marked them to indicate that he could not read da Câmera's own hand.
   [2] See §296.
   [3] For light on this, see §332; Juan from Alba had been told to write out his problems.
   [4] Once again da Câmera's Latin takes over: "and yet Father's constancy triumphed."
   [5] In the General Examen, one of the documents placed by Ignatius before the text of
the Constitutions and intended to be presented to those applying to enter the Society, a passage directed to the Brothers (temporal coadjutors) urges them not to seek to pass to another grade, and adds, "Neither ought he, even if he does remain in the same grade, to seek
more learning than he had when he entered" (chapter 6, 6 [§117]). This rule remained

342 [n.d.] I must recall what Laínez told me, that the person who *[lacuna]* was already completely lost, talking to me of Father's fortitude in seeking means untiringly of helping a soul, and he never heard him.[6]

343 On Saturday [18 May] the Father said that if the Pope were to reform[7] himself, and his household, and the cardinals in Rome, he would have nothing else to do, and that everything else would take place subsequently.

344 [n.d.] When Father was asked about Jacomoe,[8] whose wounds shed blood, etc., he said that the devil often gave these external signs, whereas the Spirit of God properly works internally. As for this woman it has been learned now that it all was hot air.

This is the woman of Bologna whose story I have already told.

345 The Germans complained *to [the cardinal of] Augsburg*[a] about the "conversion."[9] Father ordered them to confess and receive Communion

in force until 1923 (General Congregation 27), when it was abolished. It was replaced with texts from later congregations such as, "In as much as brothers participate in the apostolic activity of the Society, according to the gifts received from God, they should receive appropriate theological instruction and adequate formation in what concerns their work" (Gen. Cong. 32, Decree 6, number 23). Cf. *Constitutions and Complementary Norms*, St. Louis, p. 151.

   [6] The lacuna renders this paragraph, and especially the last sentence, difficult to understand. However, it may help to recall the accounts, which may have come partly from Laínez, found in Ribadeneira's *Life* of Ignatius, (i) of the cold bath Ignatius suffered to persuade a youth to stop sinning, and (ii) of the Basque dancing that Ignatius indulged in to cheer up somebody suffering from depression (a passage omitted in the printed version of Ribadeneira); Ignatius himself in the *Autobiography* (§79) describes his efforts to help the student who had robbed him. See R. García-Villoslada, *San Ignacio de Loyola*, Madrid, 1986, pp. 343-5. See §375.

   [7] Clearly an important passage for understanding the attitude of Ignatius to Church reform (see also §§94, 330, 346b, 365): it is clear that he favoured reform "from below", rather than "from above", and does not seem to have hoped that much would be achieved by the Council of Trent, though ready to give it full support; on the other hand he considered it quite legitimate to call in the persuasive pressure of the secular powers to keep the Papacy on the right lines, as is clear from §§230-1 above; cf. John O'Malley, "Was Ignatius a Church Reformer?" *Catholic Historical Review*, 77, 1991, pp. 177-93; Philippe Lécrivain, "Ignace de Loyola, un réformateur? Une lecture historique des 'Règles pour avoir le vrai sens de l'Église'", *Christus*, 37, no. 147, 1990, pp. 348-60; Diego Molina, "San Ignacio y la reforma de la Iglesia," *Manresa*, 73, 2001, pp. 49-63.

   [8] Perhaps Giacoba Bartolini: see §197.

   [9] This is clearly a jargon term that was current at the time: to undergo a "conversion"

and put their complaints in writing. Some would not write, and he ordered that until they did so they should not be given anything to eat.

[a] to [the cardinal of] Augsburg

The Germans of the German College complained to the Cardinal of Augsburg[10] that our fathers were putting pressure on them to enter the Society. It was to clarify this matter that our Father ordered these measures.

346 [n.d.] I must record that the Father told me a long time ago that he would prefer those who had decided to "convert" not to reveal their intentions.

Today the Father sent Polanco there to talk to them.

346b [n.d.] Before it was known which *Pope was elected,*[b] the Father used to say he hoped the new Pope would do much good through rigorous action, and that he would reform the cardinals and even the *[lacuna]*. When he heard of the election the Father retired to pray and said he had felt very great joy, etc.; and I must remember what the Father used to say in the past.

[b] Pope was elected

It was Paul IV, who was the Theatine cardinal. One of the Fathers who came this year [1574?] from Rome, has just told me, that the opinion there is that a good part of the reform of the Church and of the Roman court, is due to him.[11] A detailed account has already been given about how deeply moved our Father was at the news of this election.[12]

347 The Father gives three rules for the Germans: (i) since they complain about *Kornelius*[c],3 putting pressure on them, each one should choose a

meant applying for entry into the Society, the implication being that this occurred because of excessive proselytism; see §19.

[10] Otto Truchsess van Waldburg; see §213.

[11] Paul IV had a short and stormy reign (1555-59) in which he attempted single-handedly to reform the Church; his two successors, Pius IV (1559-65) and Pius V (1566-72) restarted the Council of Trent, which seems to have been the decisive element in Catholic reform.

[12] See §93.

[13] Kornelius Wischaven: see §§82, 363.

regular confessor; (ii) they should be obliged to declare who is "converting" them, under penalty of fasting for three days on bread alone *[lacuna]*
and wine only once; (iii) all those studying grammar[14] should speak Italian
during the hour of recreation, and the remainder all the time.

(c) *Kornelius*

This was the confessor and Master of Novices of whom I have
spoken above: he heard the Germans' confessions and they complained about him.

[14] Grammar occupied the first grades of the curriculum; hence this rule applied to the
younger newcomers: see §§251, 363.

JUNE

3 June

348 Re: Don Giovanni,[1] who was tempted and then brought back by so many measures with tears and vows; later the Father absolved him from those and all others; he dismissed him and sent him to the Duke of Luna.

The Father said that care should be taken that the body of the Society is always clean, and for this the use of expulsions should be made easy, and thus he has done in [lacuna] now in dismissing men from the College on light grounds.[2]

The Father said that he always prefers with someone tempted to leave, rather than people getting to the stage of having to dismiss him or wanting to do so, not to send him away like that. Instead, efforts should be made to bring him in line and make him want to stay; and after that let him be sent away lovingly, as he did with Lazcano,[3] and now with Don Giovanni.

Because Giovanni Antonio[4] said that if Don Giovanni left he would go too, the Father ordered that he be dismissed; but as he made the remark *praeter tentationem, et hoc erat verisimile, imo certum,*[5] Father allowed some to plead on his behalf.

Those dismissed are: Don Giovanni, Pietro Faraone, Girolamo the Neapolitan, and Angelo.[6]

---

[1] Asdrubal de Luna, a Sicilian nobleman as brother of Pietro de Luna, the Duke of Bivona (called the "Duke of Luna" below), had entered the Society in 1550 but in 1554 suddenly decamped and returned to his family; after a change of heart he returned and was sent to Rome in 1555, where he took the name of Giovanni and joined the German College; before long he was expelled, along with a group of other students. He died assassinated in Palermo in 1582.

[2] For a corrective to this, see §405.

[3] See §61.

[4] Giovanni Antonio di Mauro, a Neapolitan, later expelled (see §404), but readmission was to be permitted if he showed signs of good conduct.

[5] Da Câmara slips into his Latin: "without being really tempted (and this seemed most likely, indeed certain)".

[6] Apart from the Neapolitan, the others were all Sicilians; the family name of Angelo was Joannis.

199

349 [n.d.] Fr. Laínez told me about the Father's simplicity towards the little shepherd when he made fun of him,[7] and later in Rome towards another man, the same thing happened: the Father stopped, and said to Araoz when he asked him why, "I feel very consoled when I see this brother consoled."

[4 June]

350 Father ordered Olave to give a sermon in the College on the theme: "he who judges, commits a mortal sin";[8] and [he said] that no mortal sin should be allowed in the Society if it is known outside confession; and [spoke] of the perfection the Society demands.

351 As one of those dismissed,[9] a wretched person, had jokingly told wicked tales about the others, based on suspicions which were in fact false, the Father ordered eleven men to receive the discipline, some because they simply believed the stories, others because they believed them and told them to other people. I must recall how the Father himself and Polanco explained the whole incident, and how much *[lacuna: severity?]* he has used for little faults.

[Up to 10 June]

352 1. Re: Vincenzo the Sicilian,[10] and how Father dealt with the payment.

I do not remember anything of this matter.

2. Re: Marco *[lacuna: expelled?]* because he was mischievous.[11]

3. Re: Vincenzo from Ravenna.

---

[7] One of the early Ignatian biographers, Giovanni Pietro Maffei (1585), claims this happened in 1537, when Ignatius and Laínez were travelling from Venice to Padua, but he must have got the account second-hand.

[8] Ignatius was clearly anxious to cut short speculation sparked off by the expulsions just noted, as becomes clearer in the next paragraph.

[9] Listed in §348.

[10] Thought to be Vincenzo Fieschetto, a priest who entered the Society in this year (1555), but was later expelled.

[11] No information available, but cf. §393.

This Vincenzo was an Italian of impressive appearance, who pretending to be a "Cardinal," one of those of Ravenna,[12] came to ask entrance into the Society, and in addition he asked Fr. Madrid for six ducats to redeem a bundle of expensive garments he had deposited in a certain part of Rome. Our Father did not want to give money to him, and he told Fr. Madrid to tell him that as he was to be a member of the Society, he should shave off the venerable long beard that he was wearing (it should be noted that at that time our Father and all the others used to shave; I can even recall that Martín[13] told me that when Fr. Ignatius ordered that they should all shave, he was the first to take a razor, without calling a barber to do it for him, and began to shave himself).[14] The good "Cardinal" did not agree, but he still managed to wrangle things in such a way that, even so, he deceived Fr. Madrid, getting 6 *cruzados* out of him. In fact the bundle consisted of nothing but old rags of no value.

353 [n.d.] Re: Fr. Favre's letter to Laínez about the *[lacuna: ways of dealing with heretics?]*.

I read this letter, which dealt with suitable means of converting heretics. It would be worth looking for and keeping.[15]

354 1.[16] Father did not approve of the agreement to act for the Inquisition, and he orders us to delay so that it will not be done; he judges it is not appropriate for the Society.

King João III had offered the Jesuit fathers in this province charge of the Inquisition in his kingdom. The fathers accepted it immediately, and then informed our Father. He was displeased that they had accepted the responsibility without ascertaining his wishes first, and he ordered them to suspend their acceptance until

---

[12] At that time the title "cardinal" was given to Canons of the Cathedral of Ravenna.

[13] Martín de Zornaza; see §163.

[14] Several attempts were made to prohibit the wearing of beards by the early Jesuits, as can be seen from letters of 1549 (MHSI *Epist.* II, 546) and 1552 (*ibid.*, IV, 460), but it may be significant that all portraits (though admittedly posthumous) of Ignatius (e.g. by Jacopino del Conte, Sánchez Coello, and the anonymous Flemish painter) show him wearing a short beard.

[15] The letter has survived (MHSI *Fabri Mon*, 399-402) and is available in English; see *The Spiritual Writings*, St. Louis, 1996, pp. 379-81.

[16] This number may indicate a change of date [11 June ?], but the MHSI editors note that the manuscript from this point onwards is inconsistent in dating and numbering.

they received his instructions.[17] Further on one will see the rest of what happened in this matter.[18]

355 [n.d.] I must remember to make a note of what Laínez so often told me about the Father, that he never speaks ill of others; also what the Father himself said [about this]; and the ways he looks for excuses for others.

356 Favre had scruples in Paris whether he should give the barber a *double or a liard*.[a]

> [a] *Double or a liard*
>
> This shows how greatly the early Fathers valued poverty. The *liard* is a French coin worth a little more than two *reis* in our cash, and a *double* a little less; Fr. Favre was doubtful if he should pay even this small sum, in the barber's shop where he had gone for a shave, while even the very poor pay at least a *liard* plus a *double*.[19]

357 1.[20] Re: the method used by the Father to forbid fasting; he always *leaves it to the individual*[b] except when he sees they are being excessive, or it is a novice; then he does not allow it.

> [b] *leaves it to the individual*
>
> Our Father wished, as I have already said, that as far as possible our actions should be free, gentle, and with our own divine light. Therefore he did not impose fixed norms with regard to fasting, but he would rein in those he could see would go to excess because of their great fervour, and spur on those slack and negligent, since, being novices, they were not likely to make so much effort.[21]

358 [n.d.] Father never gives credence to anything evil said about anyone, not even by Polanco. Just as in many other things he requires the matter

---

[17] For the letter from Ignatius on "the Society and the Inquisition"; cf. *Select Letters*, No. 36 [MHSI IX, 226-27], pp. 271-72.

[18] See §§368, 381.

[19] Even if the exact value of these ancient French copper coins now escapes us, da Câmara's explanation brings out the point of the story.

[20] Again a number that may indicate a change of date (probably in June).

[21] See §§212, 252.

to be put to him in writing, *[lacuna]*, he asks me to do so here, so that the person, with greater calm and without passion, may say what he knows or has heard.

The credulity that I am talking about here is the vice St. Bernard describes in Book 2 of his *De consideratione* (*ad Eugenium* [III]):[22] "There also exists a vice, from which if you feel you are exempt, among all those I know who have mounted the chairs [cf. Matt. 23:2], you will sit alone, in my opinion, for truly and exceptionally have you raised yourself above yourself, as the Prophet says[23] [cf. Lamentations, 3:28]. This vice is a facile credulity, and I have not found any great person sufficiently on guard against the ruses of this little fox. From this follow many acts of anger over nothing, frequent condemnations of the innocent, and rash judgements against the absent." *Haec ille* [these are his words].

Another reason why our Father asked for the fault that was indicated to be put in writing, it has been said elsewhere,[24] was that according to him the human tongue is naturally inclined to speak evil, etc.

359 [n.d.] When they tell him something evil, and have put it in writing, his custom is to show it to them and *to confront them*[a], and never to allow it to ulcerate without opening it, unless it is *ad tempus* [a temporary measure] for some cases that are very difficult to cure.

[a] *to confront them*

When a person accused by a *syndic* denied the fault which our Father saw was imputed to him in the writing, he would call for

---

[22] Da Câmara gives the Latin original: *Est item vitium, cuius si te immunem sentis, inter omnes quos novi ex iis, qui cathedras ascenderunt, sedebis me iudice solitarius, quia veraciter singulariterque levasti te supra te, iuxta Prophetam. Facilitas credulitatis haec est, cuius calidissimae vulpeculae magnorum neminem comperi satis cavisse versutias. Inde eis ipsis pro nihil irae multae, in[de] innocentium frequens addictio, inde praeiudicia in absentes.* Cf. J. Leclercq et al., eds., *Sancti Bernardi Opera*, vol. 3, *Tractatus de consideratione*, II, 14, p. 430.
[23] Bernard is quoting/adapting the Latin Vulgate here: *sedebit solitarius et tacebit quia levavit super se.*
[24] The MHSI editors note that they have not found another place in the *Memoriale* where da Câmara gives this reason; perhaps da Câmara means that somebody else has given such a reason and has in mind the famous diatribe against the tongue in the Letter of St. James (3:5-12), or he may be referring not to the reason for the custom but to the occasions when it has been mentioned: see §§215, 345.

the one who had made the accusation to confront the accused face to face, so that the accused would clearly recognize his fault. This is what I call "confronting". Our Father did this because in all things he wanted to proceed with great clarity in regard to all the parties involved.

360 [n.d.] Re: the matter of *Micer* Francisco: when he spoke about the *[lacuna]* and when he made the Exercises, the fact that he told his temptations to Benedetto; everybody thought he could have explained them to Father, and what else happened.

This *Micer* Francisco was the one whom I said earlier[25] that the Father dismissed from the Society; he was the only one who felt temptations against the Father himself, and he discussed them with Benedetto Palmio;[26] Benedetto hesitated to give an account of them to the Father because he had learned them in secret. He decided he should and ought to, and when he did, our Father had everything taken down in writing, so that with everything clearly laid out, help could be given to *Micer* Francisco.

361 [n.d.] Father Ignatius hardly ever looks at anyone in the face. He wants others to observe this rule rigorously, as he did with such as Olivier,[27] and with Giovanni Domenico[28] the Roman, and with Paolo[29] from Mantua.

---

[25] See §48, where a Francisco Marín figures; however if it is the same person here, this paragraph confirms that da Câmara's memory is playing him false about dates; another possibility is that he is referring to Francisco Zapata; see §51.

[26] First mentioned in §49.

[27] Olivier Manare (see §125): Manare recounts himself that Ignatius imposed on him the "penance" of daily examining his conscience to check whether he had peered too intently at the face of any superior, and of saying an Our Father and a Hail Mary; also in his future weekly letters to Ignatius he should mention if he was doing his "penance". The Latin text of this account has been published, MHSI *Scripta* I, 506-07; *Fontes Narrativi* III, 422-424.

[28] §181.

[29] Both he and Giovanni Domenico were sent to Sicily for their studies in 1554. Another example that shows how touchy Ignatius was on this point is found in the Preface da Câmara wrote to the *Autobiography;* he mentions there the rebuke he himself received, cf. *Autobiography,* p. 7, with reference to the Rules of Modesty, No. 2 (see §22). The practice probably stems from the court etiquette that Ignatius learned in his teens.

I have already mentioned[30] the rule that our Father wished us to observe with regard to looking at those with whom we are speaking. He wanted it observed to the letter, and imposed a penance on this account even on Fr. Olivier, a man of great modesty.

362 [n.d.] When he looks at someone, unless out of kindness in a conversation, he appears to pierce the person's heart, and sees all that is there. So sometimes he looks at one's face to observe the changes in one's features.

I can remember only once his looking at me in this way, and indeed his glance pierced through me as if he had just reprimanded me severely.

363 [n.d.] At Pentecost just passed [2 June], all the Germans chose Kornelius[31] of their own free will as confessor, and made their confessions to him.

Before this they were unable and unwilling to put up with the rule about Italian,[32] nor did they want to undergo the penance, and *Micer* André [des Freux] regarded the rule as impossible; but although he told the Father that no one would stay, the Father did not budge. On the contrary, he said that now they must be forced even more, because they were rising up with the support of the German cardinals they have here:[33] now they must be squeezed further, so that they will learn. *Factum est sic.* [So it was done.] Now they are all calm, even those they[34] wanted to expel because they were troublesome.

These are good examples of the success Our Lord granted to the constancy and to the measures employed by our Father.

364 [n.d.] I must recall the constancy of Father in everything he undertakes, and the reason for it, viz. that everything is carefully weighed up and recommended to God.

365 [n.d.] Re: a remark of Laínez, apropos of Pope Marcellus: the latter said that, as for his predecessors, they had begun by serving [others] and it

---

[30] §180.
[31] See §347.
[32] See §§251,347.
[33] See §345.
[34] Clearly the Jesuit staff of the college.

had been fruitless,[35] but that he wanted to try another way, i.e., by reforming himself, and afterwards, etc.

I noticed how the Supreme Pontiff gave his approval to a measure for a reform of the Church proposed and discovered by our Father.[36]

366 [n.d.] Re: the system our Father uses for a consult: he orders that the matter should first be discussed without coming to a decision; afterwards they should give their written opinion; then three Masses, etc.

367 [n.d.] Re: what Laínez said about when Bachelor Hoces died in Padua:[37] that the Father gave _[lacuna (two lines): signs of sorrow and joy?]_

[16-17 June]

368 Our vocation was to help souls by the way of humility, and therefore he did not consider we should accept the Inquisition; he expressed this view today in the consultation, in which he desired that all[38] should take part for three days without coming to a decision, and afterwards opinions should be given in writing.

369 Vincenzo the Sicilian[39] has gone to Naples and has written from there speaking badly of _[lacuna]_.

---

[35] This remark of Pope Marcellus II (_"habían començado serviendo y sin provecho"_) has puzzled da Câmara's readers: the French translator takes it to mean, "ils avaient commencé à suivre telle voie sans profit"; while the modern Spanish version gives, "habían comenzado preocupándose de los demás y sin provecho" ["they had started with care for the rest and without profit"]: this latter interpretation seems on the right lines—former popes had tried to reform other persons; Marcellus saw the need to begin with himself.

[36] See §343.

[37] This incident is mentioned in the Saint's _Autobiography_ (§98): "The pilgrim went to Monte Cassino [March/April, 1538] . . . and was there for forty days, during which he once saw Bachelor Hoces entering heaven, and at this had great tears and great spiritual consolation. And he saw this so clearly that, were he to say the contrary, it would seem to him to be telling a lie". Diego de Hoces had joined Ignatius when the latter passed through Spain on his way to Italy in 1537, and was accepted among the first companions. However, he died (1538) before their move to Rome and the official founding of the Society.

[38] Viz. all the consultors; from later remarks (§§380-3) it is known that there were six of them. From a letter of Polanco referring to this "consult" as still taking place the date of this entry can be established.

[39] See §352.

370 How members of the Society must read spiritual books and even *[lacuna]* and they should be asked how they reacted to them, if they have felt any *cooling of their vocation.* [a]

[a] *cooling of their vocation*

It was with reading stories of the saints of other religious orders that Fr. Ignatius prepared himself for Our Lord to do with him what he did. The same stories greatly helped the first fathers of the Society, as much for their own edification and desire for perfection, as for teaching their neighbour. I remember also that at the beginning of this province the brothers increased in holy emulation with the reading of these same things, and there was no one for whom such reading caused any temptation with regard to his vocation. On the contrary we saw that later, when such reading of the stories of the saints and of other religious orders was proscribed in this province, Our Lord allowed, almost immediately, a few months later, two well known members of the Society to leave and become monks.[40] One of these, after having caused a lot of trouble and public disquiet, finally persevered and still stays in his monastery.

[21-30 June]

371 Lazaro[41] asked for permission to go on a pilgrimage for three or four months to improve himself. The Father granted permission and was prepared even, if he wished it, to let him go free of his vows, but he did not wish it, and so he leaves today.

372 [n.d.] Our Father has ordered that no one should be called "Father" except superiors.

This has already been mentioned before.[42]

373 [n.d.] The Father reprimanded us because we were reciting office in the garden; he warned us not to do it again, saying we had been singing.

[40] The identity of these members of the Portuguese province is not known.
[41] A letter to the Rector in Florence (MHSI *Epist.* IX, 249) establishes that a scholastic of this name had set off for Loreto, at his own request, by 22 June. He was due to go on to Florence and then return to Rome, but nothing further is known about him.
[42] See §142.

He did not reprimand us for reciting our office in the garden but rather because we looked as though we were singing like friars.

374 [n.d.] I must recall what the Father said to us last *[lacuna: year?]*.[43] He was at table with Bobadilla, Salmerón, Simão and *the usual.* [a] When he found out that we were not well liked by the world, that is by some peo- ple, because they thought we looked like[44] hypocrites, *sic enim dicebant* ["so they said"], Father said, "Indeed, I would be very happy if we were more hypocritical than we are, because I do not know any hypocrites in the Society except Salmerón and Bobadilla." Father said this because he wants our external comportment to be very modest and very composed. And I must recall how many times he made this observation to me, and how he treated a large number to put them right.[45]

 [a] *the usual*

The usual ones were Frs. Nadal, Polanco, Madrid and myself. I have related this episode above.[46]

375 [n.d.] What Laínez told us about the Father in Barcelona, how he went into the water to help someone,[47] and he does *[lacuna]*.

It was for a similar reason that he walked from Paris to Rouen fasting.[48]

This case and the one above are related at length in the *Life of St. Ignatius.*[49]

---

[43] As Simão Rodrigues had left Rome by June of 1554 the missing word in the lacuna is probably that indicated; the episode has already been recounted, as da Câmara notes in his commentary.

[44] The original text has the unintelligible *no crymos hipócitas*, but the sense is fairly obvious.

[45] See, e.g., §361.

[46] See §23.

[47] This story has been mentioned in a footnote above; see §342, which strongly resembles the present paragraph. Ribadeneira says in his *Life of Ignatius* that this incident occurred not in Barcelona, but in Paris.

[48] This is the story told also by Ignatius himself in his *Autobiography*, §79.

[49] Da Câmara is referring to the monumental biography of Ignatius written by Ribadeneira (probably between 1553 and 1569) and published after many delays in 1572, but only in Latin. The original Spanish version was not published until 1583 (after the death of da Câmara).

376 [n.d.] About Don Diego,[50] how, in deepest winter, he walked with Ferrão from Paris to Navarre to find someone who had left.

I made a note of this here to show the zeal there was in former times for the things of the Society.

377 Neira[51] was telling the Father that he *had not spoken to him*[a] yesterday evening, because the Father had come back late and tired and [because he] had not spoken to the Pope. The Father replied: "I have observed this in you on other occasions; I will teach you how to speak to me. *Off with you! That's enough!*[b] Afterwards the Father said, "He thought my pulse would slow down because I had not spoken to the Pope!"

Our Father wants to be respected by all his subjects; likewise he wants this to be so for all superiors.

[a] *he had not spoken to him*

He said this to excuse himself for not having spoken to Father about a matter with which he had been entrusted.

[b] *Off with you! That's enough!*

378 This was the expression our Father used when he finally dismissed someone after giving him a reprimand.

Once our Father had sent me out with a very important message; when I returned with the reply, I went to his room to give it to him as usual. However, since he looked to me rather unwell and it did not seem to be the right moment, I waited for a short time to see if he would speak to me about it. Since he asked me nothing, I left him with others who were there with him, and went out intending to return and give him the reply. The same day, in the afternoon when I was in the garden, almost at the end of the recreation period, a very simple coadjutor Brother called Antonino came out to me and said, "Father Ignatius says that, since your Reverence is not

---

[50] Don Diego de Eguía; this incident is not recorded elsewhere. It may have occurred while he was briefly in charge of the scholastics in Paris in 1540.

[51] For the use of the nickname, see §262, there spelt "Neyra".

prepared to give him an account of the errand he had entrusted you with, would you give it to me and tell me in detail about the reply, so that I can take it to him." I did so, and came to understand the great simplicity our Father wished to be shown in matters of obedience.

379 Father always speaks with such careful thought that all he says can stand without any change.

380 Concerning the Inquisition,[52] Father told me today how he had felt, i.e., very unhappy at the beginning. Later having prayed *[lacuna]* he began to doubt, and was inclined *[to accept it ?]* on account of the labours and persecutions brought against the Society in Spain. So he put the matter for consultation *to six,*[a] and five were in favour, the sixth, Laínez, was against, but he gave in, and it was in this sense that Father had a letter written. I must remember to have a copy of the letter and of the opinions expressed.

> 381 Our Father experienced all these things and internal doubts on the occasion of the King of Portugal's conceding to members of the Society that they should be Inquisitors in this Kingdom. And as I say here, he finally inclined towards our accepting this responsibility on account of various persecutions that rose up against the Society in Castile precisely by means of, or on the pretext of, the Inquisition; it looked as if these persecutions would quiet down completely when people saw how the Society accepted the running of the same Inquisition in Portugal.

[a] *to six*

382 Of the six, I can remember five of our number: Frs. Laínez, Madrid, Olave, Polanco and myself.[53] I think the sixth was Fr. des Freux, although I wonder if it may have been Fr. Nadal, because I do not remember if he was in Rome.[54] The reason why Fr. Laínez

---

[52] See §368.

[53] Other sources (letters from Polanco and Ignatius) indicate that da Câmara's memory has played him false here: apart from Laínez, Madrid, Olave, and Polanco, the others consulted were Salmerón and Bobadilla; da Câmara himself was only called upon to give information, as he had been one of those in Portugal who had hastily accepted the King's offer.

[54] Indeed, Nadal was then in Vienna.

did not think the Inquisition should be accepted, was because of the great prestige enjoyed by the Inquisitors in Spain; this he thought, rightly, the Society should avoid because the nature of our order was to help souls in a spirit of humility. Nevertheless, he came over to the opinion of the majority, which was to accept, which our Father confirmed and therefore ordered a letter to this effect to be sent to this province,[55] as I have said above. I do not have the copy of this letter now, nor of the opinions given. By the time the letter arrived from Rome the discussion here had cooled so much, especially with the death of the Infante, Don Luis, who had wanted it very much, and with the illness of the Cardinal [Enrique], who had supported him in this respect, that nothing could be done.[56]

383 [n.d.] Father asked my opinion on two of ours who had been members and want to return, and he said later he had been more liberal than I, who did not want to have them back, had been.[57]

384 [n.d.] So far, Torres, the cook from Naples, has not been dismissed completely;[58] the Father agreed that he should make the pilgrimage to Florence or to Perugia, and should work there in a hospital this summer, and then return to his kitchen, if he brings a satisfactory reference. The Father did this because it was the opinion of Salmerón and two others.

385 [n.d.] About ten or twelve days ago Father told Olave that, to deal with N.[59] on serious matters, without his being able to say that he [Olave] had acted out of anger, he should never offer him any explanation of what he tells him, and that he should order someone else to give him any penances.

386 Juan from Alba[60] has lately reverted to his old ways and to telling the other coadjutors that they were not members of the Society, only the

---

[55] The letter has been preserved among the Ignatian letters (MHSI *Epist.* No. 5471, IX, 226-27; cf. *Select Letters,* No. 36, pp. 271-2).

[56] da Câmara's reasons for the collapse of this initiative seem questionable: of the two Cardinal Princes, Don Luis did not die until later, and Don Enrique argued against the transfer.

[57] Readmission is envisaged in the *Constitutions;* cf. part 2, ch. 4, §§231-42.

[58] Ignatius also wrote about Br. Torres to the Rector of Naples about this time (23 June 1555): MHSI *Epist.* IX, 252, No. 5490.

[59] Teotonio de Bragança; see §150.

[60] See §236; he later became a Franciscan.

priests were, etc. Father has handed the affair over to Madrid and Polanco. I have proposed various solutions to him, and so he has chosen to leave, absolved from his vows, and he left today.

387 [n.d.] *Giovanni Cocanaro,*[a] from Tivoli, should go ahead and carefully make the election[61] since he is so insistent, working on the supposition that he does not have a wife; and once he has taken the decision to join the Society, he should be told that the merit of the choice is enough, etc.

[a] *Giovanni Cocanaro*

This was a gentleman from Tivoli, married and particularly devoted to the Society. He was making the Exercises and had agreed with his wife that she should enter a religious order and he would live in the Society. Our Father did not want to receive him, but so that he should not be left unconsoled, without saying anything to him, he ordered that he should go ahead with the elections and the other parts of the Exercises, and that at the end he should be consoled in the way I have described.

388 [n.d.] Laínez much regretted the departure of Juan, the one from Alba, and showed *[lacuna]*, but when he understood the reason, viz. the bad example given to the other coadjutors, he thought it was valid.

389 [n.d.] The Father did not like the laymen [i.e. the Brothers] in the residence to be in long cassocks, and he has made it a rule[62] that they should be at least a hand's breadth, more or less, above the ground *[lacuna]* and with Polanco I should keep an eye on this, so that the change of ministers does not make this rule inapplicable.

Luis already *[lacuna]*.

390 *Micer Lorenzo,*[b] Dietrich, Stephan, Giovanni Antonio, Georgios the Greek, should go to the College to be examined.[63] And first Master

---

[61] In the Second Week of the Exercises (§§169-89); under normal circumstances the Exercises do not envisage a choice that would require a change to a previous "unchangeable choice" (Exercises §171), but the stratagem permitted by Ignatius in this case shows the degree of adaptation (Annotation 18, Exercises §18) that he was prepared to allow.

[62] Such a rule, stipulating that the cassocks of the brothers should be shorter than those of priests, was included among the rules of the Roman College.

[63] This examination is probably for entry into the Society, as stipulated in the title of

Polanco should go ahead to find out how they are to present themselves.[64] Georgios and Giovanni Antonio should go later.

(b) Micer Lorenzo

This was Lorenzo Maggio, whom I have already mentioned.[65]

391 [n.d.] Olave told the Father that Matthäus the German was not very obedient, and the Father asked him what he was giving him to eat; and Olave said, "They don't give him anything unless he does what he is told, dis- cipline, etc., but with great difficulty, and we are rearing a viper there." Father reprimanded him for having delayed so much in telling him, and he added, "I assure you, let me be the one who acts the inquisitor, and may he not be the only one to receive penance."

392 [n.d.] I must remember how, in most things, Father orders that he be reminded of them, but when it is a subject touching any of the brethren, he remembers of his own accord; also the great exactness Father wants in obedience.

393 Today Joseph left, who was also preached to by Juan from Alba; and it was not only to him, but to others who are staying, that he preached his ideas, such as Marco,[66] Matthäus, Luis,[67] etc.

394 Father said that it was a good *[thing ?]* to keep the house in peace, and he was determined *[to do so ?]* since there were no others *[lacuna]* with whom *[or, "which"?]* could be maintained the new *[Society?]*[68] which had cost so much.

the General Examen ("which should be proposed to all who request admission into the Society of Jesus") that precedes the Constitutions themselves; cf. *Constitutions*, p. 75.

[64] The Spanish word here, *apresentarse* ("to present themselves") is unusual, so much so that the MHSI editors suggested reading *aposentarse* ("to be lodged").

[65] See §§274,280.

[66] See §352.

[67] See §286.

[68] The word tentatively suggested by the MHSI editors here is "infirmary" (see §286); however, the context—the unrest caused by Juan from Alba (and the later comment [§402, with da Câmara's remark on the preoccupation felt by Ignatius for the "peace" of the residence])—suggest that a wider issue is at stake.

JULY AND BEYOND

2 July

395 Olave examined N.[1] on his poverty, and found he was far from the right path. Father made Olave write down all that was said by either side, and to read it to N, so that he could deny if that was how things had gone, and Olave was to sign it himself. The last word from Olave was that, if it depended on him, he would expel him from the Society.

3 July

396 The Father put the case to Laínez, Salmerón, and Madrid, whether he could dismiss someone from the Society because of a mortal sin *known through confession*[a] and they replied [Yes[2]], if the dismissal does not indicate a mortal sin in the Society, because there are many things which are not mortal sins for which members are dismissed, and beforehand the Father indicated that he had done this a few times.[3]

[a] *known through confession*

> Our Father's question was this: suppose that a mortal sin of a member of the Society is known in confession, and he has

[1] Once again, Teotonio de Bragança; see §385.

[2] Although missing, this word seems certain.

[3] Although St. Thomas and others maintained that knowledge acquired in confession could be used, provided there was no danger of breaking the seal of confession, a later Jesuit general, Claudio Aquaviva, ruled in 1590 that this was not to be done by Jesuit superiors, and Clement VIII extended this prohibition to all superiors of religious orders in 1594.

committed other faults, insufficient in themselves to provide ground for dismissal, but to which however the one dismissed can attribute his dismissal, in this case can the superior use the knowledge of the sin gained in confession to dismiss him because of that? As I say here, he gave them to understand, before having received their reply, that he had sometimes done so. In all this he showed the great purity he required of members of the Society, and how much he wanted fulfilled his frequent saying, "I would not dare to pass a night under the same roof as a member of the Society known to be in mortal sin."[4]

397 The Father asked if for mortal sins not known through confession, he could take advice: he was told he could, when there was doubt or when he saw that scandal might follow if he did not take advice.

4 July

398 Arnaud[5] in Venice has had some words with another: the school depends entirely on him alone, and he is a Master of Arts, etc., so much so that without him the school would disintegrate; some have interceded with the Father on his behalf, but all that one can get from him is that he should take a good dose of penances, and then be sent out on pilgrimage for three months, and come here. If he does not want to submit, they should dismiss him once and for all, and there is a fear that he will not agree.

399   Giovanni Filippo[6] brought 190 *[escudos]*[7] to the residence, which Silvestro from Pisa gave for good works, indicating 40 for the residence, or the whole sum, if that would seem to us well employed, indeed rather indicating a preference that we should take the whole sum. The Father did not want us to accept it, either for the residence, or for our College, or for the German College, or in Tivoli,[8] etc., and today distribution of the money has begun.

---

[4] See §350.

[5] Arnaud Conchus was from near Liège and entered the Society in Rome in February 1549, later studying for his M.A. in Louvain. In 1555 he was some thirty years old. He seems to have accepted the pilgrimage penance imposed on him (mentioned in several letters of this time: MHSI *Epist.* IX, Nos. 5499, 5515, 5578, 5772, pp. 265, 295, 402, 674).

[6] See §§116 and 337.

[7] A later Italian manuscript supplies the missing word.

[8] A college had been founded here in 1549.

Our Father was far removed from any sort of covetousness.

400 [n.d.] Olave asked the Father if, *his Reverence*[a] permitting, he could communicate with Polanco and Madrid about the suspension of lectures during the next two months. (Father had already dealt with Neyra[9] on the matter, whose opinion was *[lacuna]*.) Father answered sharply that nothing should be changed. I think that he grasps this matter, etc.

[a] *his Reverence*

> In his presence nobody addressed our Father with the title "Your Paternity", except for Fr. Olave, who sometimes inadvertently called him this, but I remember he was given penances for it. I have said "in his presence" because in letters some did address him as "Your Paternity".[10] I remember too that even Fr. Laínez we addressed as "Your Reverence" for a year or more after he had been elected General.[11] It was only after 1561 that the custom of addressing him as "Your Paternity" was introduced.

401 [n.d.] I must recall how Father maintains his gravity of manner with everyone.

10 July

402 Juan from Alba[12] asks to be received back again, and the Father has had a consultation held with all the laymen [i.e. the Brothers]. The conclusion of the majority was that he should be received, and this decision was to be conveyed to the Father. He replied that it was not appropriate, etc., and it was *to achieve this*[a] that he had ordered the consultation to be held.

[9] Fr. Ribadeneira: see §262.

[10] The aversion felt by Ignatius for the title "Paternity" cannot be explained simply by his general rule that in the Society the title "Father" should be avoided (see §142), since he allowed it for superiors (see §372); it may stem from his reading of Matthew 23:9 ("Call no man your father on earth").

[11] Laínez was chosen to act as Vicar General in 1556 on the death of Ignatius, but elected General only in 1558, when the First General Congregation could be held; from 1561 to 1564 he was absent from Rome on missions given him by Pope Pius IV, and it was then that the custom of addressing him as "Your Paternity" came in. He died 19 January 1565.

[12] See §386.

(a) *to achieve this*

The Father understood clearly that all the lay Brothers would share the opinion that Juan from Alba should be taken back, especially because they knew our Father had shown a special love for him. But after having heard everyone's opinion, he took this decision solemnly as he wanted to convince them that his only concern was for the tranquility of the house.

403 Re: Francesco from Ferrara and Thomaso,[13] who had talked in confession and aroused suspicion that they had broken the seal: the consultors to whom the Father entrusted the matter concluded that they should not be dismissed; the Father dismissed them, etc., and now he says, when there is talk of *[dismissals ?]*, "It is for you to receive, for me to dismiss."

404 Mariano,[14] a novice, and Giovanni Antonio,[15] a Neapolitan, who joined four years ago, were unsettled and the consultors did not want to dismiss them. The Father asked, "If they were now outside the Society and you knew them as well as you do, would you receive them?" They said, "No." The Father said, "Well, then, throw them out." And so they have gone today.

405 Laínez and Salmerón were discussing this affair, as well as the case of Thomaso and Francesco. Father did not want to explain his reasons to them, *unde patet*[a] ["from which it is clear"] that also in the case of those dismissed from the College, where the Father hides the reasons, it was for minor things.

(a) *unde patet*

When Father ordered the expulsion from the Roman College of those I have mentioned[16] and did not want to discuss his reasons for dismissing them, I thought to myself that they must be serious. However, when I saw that he would not disclose to Frs. Salmerón and Laínez the reasons why he had dismissed Thomaso and

[13] Both of these (one was from Ferrara, the other from Rome) had earlier been sent on pilgrimage (to Loreto and Perugia respectively), but seem to have returned to Rome by this date.
[14] A youngster of this name is known to have come from Loreto in May and returned home in August.
[15] See §348.
[16] See §348.

Francisco, which (as Minister of the residence) I knew were minor, I myself, in answer to my own argument, found that I had no reason to believe that the dismissal of those from the College was for serious reasons. And this is what I wanted to indicate here. However later I learned for certain that some of them had been expelled for very serious reasons.[17]

406 Salmerón[18] wanted to take to Augsburg the mule he had brought from Naples. Laínez agreed, but Father disagreed *omnino* ["totally"], unless he paid those in Naples for the mule using the funds of the legation.

407 Some people want to confer benefices *on the head of*[a] some of the Germans so that the College would have something to eat; the Father did not wish this to be on any of ours.

[a] *on the head of*

408 This expression "on the head of" is used when a benefice is applied to a house, but in such a way that a definite person from the said house is indicated.

409 Fr. Salmerón left *[lacuna]* for Augsburg and Poland.

[Some Time in July or August]

410 Olave has imposed a discipline on N.[19] because he had told Loarte that he was being persecuted because he did not censure N.[20] and he did not wish to undertake the penance. He ordered him to be confined to his room *[lacuna]* and the Ambassador[21] came to visit the Father and the

---

[17]As noted in the paragraph mentioned da Câmara gives a different opinion now (c.1574) from that held in 1555.

[18] Appointed to accompany the Papal Legate to Augsburg and Poland; see §§228-29.

[19] Once again, Teotonio de Bragança, as above (see §150), but a different person is indicated by this initial in the next line.

[20] Clearly Simão Rodrigues; a long letter from Polanco dated 26/29 August 1555 gives a full account of this case, which greatly helps to understand da Câmara's cryptic comments in this and the following paragraphs: cf. MHSI, *Epist.* IX, No. 5651, pp. 501-05.

[21]The Portuguese ambassador, Alphonso de Lancastre, to whom Teotonio had appealed.

latter told him that N.[22] should stay [as a guest?] until his case was decided.

411   The consultors met today and Laínez spoke openly about how unsuited N.[23] was for the Society, and the others followed him.

This month[24] *[lacuna]* there have been many things connected with this affair.

[n.d.] I must remember Father's constancy in not explaining himself further; (ii) his constancy in insisting on his going to confession, or persevering in the *[Society?]*, (iii) the manner and freedom with which he dispatched first Bobadilla, then Laínez to speak with the Ambassador; (iv) the mockery N.[25] made of everyone, and *maxime* ["especially"] of Laínez.

[Date and Month Uncertain]

412   The Father learned that *some thought*[a] it was necessary to have taken vows in order to attend the College, and he saw that there was a danger.[26] It was for this reason that *[so-and-so?]* had made them, and the Father showed that he greatly regretted this, and ordered that after this others should be sent who had not taken vows; and the first was, I think, Hermès[27] from Tournai.

[a] some thought

From time to time the Father ordered that some novices should leave the residence and go to study at the College. Fr. Polanco would ask the Master of Novices who he thought should go, and

[22] Teotonio.
[23] Teotonio.
[24] Either July or August, as the affair dragged on until Teotonio's departure, 8 September 1555.
[25] Teotonio.
[26] The danger was of misunderstanding the nature and purpose of the vows, as da Câmara's comment makes clear.
[27] This was Hermès Vinghenius, a medical student, who joined the Society in this year, 1555. After completing his theological studies in Rome he was sent to teach in Vienna, 1561.

he always selected those who had already taken vows of devotion. As this practice continued, without our Father's knowledge, some came to think that it was by the Father's order that no one should go to the College without having made these vows first. When our Father learned of this and understood the evil which followed, he gave the orders I describe here.

18 October

413 The Father explained how *[lacuna]* that if there was more talk than (*[lacuna]* . . . disgraceful), it was contrary to moderation and edification to talk in a loud voice in this house, and about Olave, I think that during a month he should not enter this house in *[lacuna]*. I must remember how much importance he gave to the fault and appointed two syndics to impose penances on everyone, including the Vicars.[28] No one should stop to talk in the corridor, except in a very low voice.[29]

---

[28] Those with the office of Vicar-General, such as Nadal and Laínez.

[29] There are signs in the *Spiritual Diary* of this hyper-sensitivity to noise on the part of Ignatius—cf. *ibid.*, (2 and 12 March 1544).

SUPPLEMENT 1

Making Peace between Pope and King[1]

Considering in the light of His divine goodness that ingratitude (*salvo meliori iudicio* [while recognizing that others may know better]), both in the sight of our Creator and Lord, and in the sight of those created beings capable of His divine and eternal glory, is one of the things most worthy of abhorrence among all the evils and sins that can be imagined, because it is a failure to recognize the benefits, the graces, and the gifts received, and thus is the cause, the principle, and the origin of all sins and of all evils; and considering on the contrary how greatly loved and esteemed, as much in heaven as on earth, is the acknowledgement of and gratitude for the benefits and gifts received, I thought it appropriate to remind you how greatly, after our entry into Rome, we were favoured whole-heartedly and continually in all sorts of ways by the Pope, from whose Holiness we received special favours, while at the same time—as is well known to all of us in the Society, but more clearly to you, given that you were present there—how great are our obligations to the king, who is both your lord and ours in Our Lord.

First, in view of the many spiritual graces that God our Creator and Lord has seen fit to grant him, desiring to exalt him in everything for His greater service and praise out of His usual kindness, looking upon him with infinite love, like a creator on his creature, given that though He is infinite, He made Himself finite and wished to die for His creature.

Second, reflecting on who we are and from where we have emerged, that God Our Lord should have so ordained that such a noteworthy prince should have paid such attention to us that, whether of his own

[1] This is part of a letter (Letter 38 [MHSI, *Epist.*, I, pp. 192-6], 18 March 1542), from Ignatius to Simão Rodrigues, which da Câmara wished to be added to his *Memoriale,* as he mentions above (§146); it deals with the hoped-for reconciliation of Paul III and João III of Portugal, after a quarrel concerning Miguel da Silva, Bishop of Viseu, who had fled Portugal and was made a cardinal in Rome. The matter was settled in 1545, when the bishopric of Viseu was ceded by the King to Cardinal Alessandro Farnese.

volition, *immediate*, or because of those close to him, *mediate*, without ourselves having thought of it *penitus* [at all], nor striven for it, and before the Society had been confirmed by the Apostolic See, he requested with so much insistence from the Pope some of ours for his service in Our Lord, and that at a time when there were considerable suspicions about our teaching he showed us his favour in so clear a way.[2]

Third, after your arrival there (you will be better informed about all the details even though nothing was withheld from us), [the King] treated you with such affection and love, also with financial subsidies that are not so customary from all royalty, offering you *ex abundantia cordis* [out of the abundance of his heart] for the great affection he has for us, to found a college and build some houses for this Society, which is so unworthy before our Creator and Lord in heaven and before such a prince on earth; and in addition, somewhat later, receiving under his patronage all whom we sent from here in order to study over there.

I wanted to remind you of all this in order that you there, and we here, all striving for the same purpose of serving ever more our Creator and Lord, while being completely faithful and utterly grateful to the persons to whom—under God's divine and supreme goodness—we owe so much, we (I say) should endeavour (with all the strength that is granted us from above) to accept our part of the spiritual and bodily problems which in opposition the enemy of human nature tries to place in great number between so eminent and such important persons.

And since you will be well informed there, as we are here, of what has occurred or is still occurring, it only remains, as we are all—both you there and we here—so indebted and under such obligation, that we should all, with great diligence, seizing our spiritual arms, for we abandoned the temporal arms for ever, insist in making prayer continuously every day, and also with special intentions during our Masses, begging and supplicating God Our Lord that He might deign to intervene with His hand and His great grace in an affair of such great difficulty, which is so worthy to be greatly recommended to His infinite and supreme Goodness. And although I for my part, thanks to His divine grace, am completely convinced that our Enemy will not emerge triumphant from this

---

[2] Ignatius and the first companions reached Rome in 1537, and already in the summer of 1539 João III was making enquiries through his Ambassador about the possibility of some of them going out to the Portuguese possessions in India.

business, still it would be no small harm and cause turmoil in many persons if the situation were to continue as it is, even if only for a few days.

However, during a long discussion of this matter with the Cardinal of Burgos[3]—as someone exceptionally a patron to us and defender of us in all our affairs—the Cardinal made some remarks, which confirmed what I was feeling and caused great spiritual consolation in my soul, viz., "So-and-so was speaking to me and said, 'It is said or inferred that the King of Portugal is abandoning his obedience to the Pope.'" At which the good Cardinal replied with great warmth, unable to contain himself, "Who says this? Even if the Pope were to trample the King of Portugal under his feet, he would not do this. Do you really think that people there are like the people here, or that the King there is like the King of England,[4] who was already half outside before he made his declaration? You must not think such a thing about such a Christian prince, one of such good conscience!"

Although I would have liked to write a letter to the King, I have held back, partly because I can see myself and how inadequate and unworthy I am to do this, partly because you yourself are over there and I feel I am excused from doing so. It is for you then to offer our complete reverence and to speak on behalf of us all, as much as for yourself. However, should you think otherwise, I would not wish or desire to be found wanting, in even the smallest thing, with respect to Our Lord.[5]

[3] The Dominican, Juan Alvarez de Toledo, known by the name of his episcopal see, Burgos, was made a cardinal in 1538 and appointed to examine the *Spiritual Exercises*.
[4] Henry VIII: his Act of Supremacy, 1534, followed his earlier rejection of Catherine of Aragon, against the wishes which Pope Clement VII made clear in 1529.
[5] There is a further paragraph in the original letter, but this is to give information about the movements of other Jesuits known to Fr. Rodrigues, and da Câmara omitted it.

SUPPLEMENT 2

Refusing Bishoprics for Jesuits[1]

The fact is—as I think you had gathered before your departure from here—that the King of the Romans[2] sent his confessor, the Bishop of Ljubljana,[3] to deliver a letter from him to Fr. Claude Jay of our Society, who was resident at the Council of Trent; Fr. Jay joined the bishop in Venice, so that they could make the journey together, and they met and talked with each other for two or three days. When Master Claude opened the letter from the King he saw that it contained nothing else but a request, made with great charity and out of the best of loving intentions, asking him to accept the bishopric of Trieste, which was then vacant and which lies on the border of Venice and Slovenia, an area with many inhabitants and a bishopric with an annual revenue of two thousand ducats. However Father Jay, even though the confessor did all he could to persuade him to accept such a dignity, became convinced that it was a greater service to the Lord not to receive it and decided that he would act accordingly; so he wrote to the King to excuse himself as best he could.

Three months after this we had wind one day, thanks to *Micer* Bernardino Maffei, Secretary to His Holiness, that a new attempt was under way to make the said Father a bishop. Therefore early the next day Fr. Master Ignatius went off to the Palace and had a conversation with the Secretary; the latter read him a most pressing letter that the King of the Romans had written to the Pope [Paul III], where he dwelt on three main points: the first was that since the See of Trieste was vacant, he had

---

[1] This is an extract from a letter (Letter 153 [MHSI, *Epist.* I, pp. 460-670, 2 March 1547]) written by Fr. Bartolomeo Ferrão, who was at the time acting secretary to Ignatius, to Fr. Miguel de Torres (see §7n); da Câmara wanted it to be added (as he mentions above, §147) as an example of Ignatius's opposition to the appointment of members of the Society to bishoprics.

[2] Ferdinand I, brother of Charles V and later Holy Roman Emperor; see §18.

[3] Then known by its German name, Laibach; the bishop (1543-58) was Urban Weber (or *Textor*).

selected Master Claude Jay for it, as there was great need for a perfect pastor in that land, where so many errors and vices abounded, and he could see nobody else who would be better suited than Fr. Jay, with whose great goodness and knowledge he was acquainted as he had spoken with him and heard many of his sermons, in Germany, etc., and whom he praised with great conviction. The second point explained how when he had written to the said Father by means of his confessor in order to get him to accept the bishopric, he had offered his excuses out of humility. The third point, in view of this would His Holiness kindly order him in virtue of obedience, as it was such a just and necessary matter, to accept the bishopric because of the great spiritual fruit that would come as a consequence of his person, given that he was so outstanding in life and teaching. Each of these three points was dilated upon to such an extent that the letter resembled one of the major supplications that it is the custom to present in the *Signatura*.

When Fr. Ignatius had seen this, he went from our house to that of Don Diego Lasso, the Ambassador of the King of the Romans; the Ambassador showed him a letter from the King his lord, some of it actually written in his own hand, in which he charged him with the greatest insistence to work with all care and diligence so that he might settle the matter of the bishopric, in accordance with the request that he had sent to the Pope; our Father said to the Ambassador that, while maintaining good relations with the King his lord, still would he refrain from seeing this matter to its completion because such conduct would cause less harm to the Society than would be caused if the bishopric were to be accepted. The Ambassador then replied, after having made many other gracious remarks, that if Master Claude were to decide not to accept the bishopric and the Pope did not excommunicate him, he himself would be leaving Rome!

When he realized that the matter was very serious and had spoken once more with *Micer* Bernardino Maffei the Father found that three cardinals, who were experts in negotiations, had seen the King's letter to the Pope and had come to the conclusion, moved by holy and good intentions, that the matter should take a different course. Although the Supreme Pontiff was ready, at the Ambassador's request, to order a brief to be published, which would have commanded Fr. Claude to accept the bishopric, these cardinals were saying that to avoid further excuses it would be better if His Holiness first made him a bishop and later sent the afore-mentioned brief. The Secretary pointed out that with this, all the cardinals, in his opinion, would be opposed to us, and that if any were to be in our favour, they would be the cardinal of England,[4] and the one who had been Master of the Sacred Palace,[5] because both of them had also refused bishoprics.

However our Father, after talking with one of the cardinals, and then with some of the others, and not finding what he wanted, made up his mind to go to the source and talk to the Pope, so that his conscience would not accuse him of not having made every possible effort in this matter. When he did this, he explained very humbly and at length the whole matter to His Holiness, demonstrating with many arguments that such an appointment would not be good for the Society, nor for the good of souls. The first reason, based on the nature of the Society, took this form: this Society began with a lowly spirit of humility, and as long as it was inspired by this spirit it is quite obvious how greatly Our Lord has seen fit to work on its behalf until now; consequently if in the present circumstances it were to abandon its starting principle and its first dedication, and proceed instead with a quite contrary spirit—as would be the case if it accepted and climbed in dignities—it is quite obvious that it could not maintain itself in its peace and good works, but rather would head into the utter ruination of itself.

The second reason: given that there are so few professed fathers in this Society, it is inconceivable that with the acceptance of this dignity the Society will not be dragged to destruction; since if Fr. Claude were to accept the bishopric mentioned, another professed father would do the same, and then another would follow him, *et sic de caeteris* [and so for the others], until none would be left. There is a corroboration of this: during the past seven years, four bishoprics have been offered to four of ours, and if any one of these had agreed, the others would easily have followed, *quod Deus auferat* [may God impede this]!

A third argument, this time aiming at the good of souls: with such a move there would be great harm to the good of souls and to the universal advantage of the neighbour; because in the final outcome Master Claude could only help those souls that he had in his bishopric, if he were to accept this; but if that were not the case, he could help many cities,

---

[4] Reginald Pole, a cardinal since 1536.

[5] Tomás Badia, O.P., who had been Master of the Sacred Palace from 1529 until his appointment as cardinal, 1542; he died later this year (1547).

provinces and kingdoms bear great fruit in the Lord—because even if in one place the word of God is not received, in another it can be well sown and bear a hundred fold,[6] as has been demonstrated by what individuals of this Society have been able to do, *Domino cooperante* [with God's help] in parts of Italy, Spain, Germany, Hungary, Portugal, and the Portuguese possessions in the Indies.

In the fourth place, given that the Society is held in high repute and veneration in the Lord in all parts, principally because it has proceeded in this spirit of humility and simplicity and quite alien to covetousness, there is no doubt that if now it were to accept dignities it would thereby cause greater scandal, disedification and malicious rumours everywhere that this was known, than would be the good that might be done in one particular bishopric.

Fifthly: this acceptance of the said dignity could cause another grave harm to the Society, viz., seeing that there are round about two hundred novices and students who have left all worldly things and have deliberately chosen to enter this Society with poverty, chastity, and obedience, it could happen that many of them, being scandalized by our accepting bishoprics and altering our founding principle, would turn back; others would have the opportunity to remain or enter into the Society with the *arrière pensée* or the hesitancy that they in their time might become bishops, and thus the enthusiasm for the Society could be changed into division and ambition.

While alone with His Holiness in this first audience and also while in his chamber after the meal, our Father laid great emphasis on this and on many other arguments. Eventually, when our Father thought that he had made his case completely, the Pope replied with great charity and with esteem for his arguments and long speeches, and praising the Society, but nevertheless he stopped short over one matter, which he felt was stuck firmly in his mind, viz., that what the King had done in arranging a bishopric for Master Claude had been done by the Holy Spirit; and he quoted texts in favour of this, like, *Cor regis in manu domini est* ["The heart of the king is in the hand of the Lord" (Prov. 21:1)], etc., and that this was what His Holiness felt to be the case here.

---

[6] An allusion to the parable of the sower: cf. Mark 4:3-20 and parallels.

Finally, after a very long discussion, Fr. Ignatius said to His Holiness that if this bishopric were accepted, it would cause such great scandal and murmuring that members of the Society would no longer be able to speak to His Holiness or to the cardinals and other people in authority without people saying that they were acting out of ambition, seeking and angling for similar dignities, and that His Excellency Juan de Vega[7] and Madama[8] had already appreciated this scandal and were therefore intending to speak about it to His Holiness.

Then the Pope replied that the Father should leave him and pray about this case, and that he also would give it further thought. So he left, after having asked for certain favours that His Holiness granted him, and went off once again to search for all possible means to prevent what has been mentioned, not finding a moment's rest until he had first obtained what he wanted. Later he spoke with His Excellency Juan de Vega and obtained that the Emperor's secretary[9] should use his means to speak to the Pope and deal with the matter in our favour. In spite of this, although he carried out his ambassador's role with all the warmth that he could, the reply from His Holiness was no more favourable than that which he had given to our Father, or rather he found the Pope more inclined to give the bishopric to Fr. Claude. When Master Ignatius saw this, he decided to undertake the holy Stations,[10] with the help of *Micer* Pietro Codazzo[11] and of anyone else he could find, visiting and talking to as many cardinals as he could, because a consistory was expected in three or four days at which the question was due to be discussed.

The diligence shown by Fr. Ignatius over this business is quite incredible: it was not enough for him to spend the whole day working at it, but at night he would go to speak to three cardinals, each living a good mile from one another, as happened with Cardinal Gaddi,[12] who lives in Montecitorio, and Cardinal Salviati,[13] who resides in the quarter near the Palace. So great was his diligence, that, *Domino cooperante* [with the

---

[7] See §74.

[8] Margaret of Austria, daughter of Emperor Charles V, and thus niece of the King of the Romans, and wife of Octavio Farnese, the grandson of Pope Paul III.

[9] The person in question is thought to have been Pedro de Marquina: see §74.

[10] The Spanish here, *tomó por estaciones santas*, seem to be a figure of speech; in the same way that pilgrims visited the Station churches of Rome, Ignatius organized pilgrimages to the houses of the different cardinals.

[11] See §307.

[12] Nicolà Gaddi, created a cardinal in 1527; he died in 1552.

[13] Giovanni Salviati, a cardinal from 1517 to 1553.

Lord helping] half of the cardinals became of our opinion, and all were in our favour. Leaving aside the first, the others who wanted the bishopric to be accepted were motivated by the judgment that bishoprics ought to be given to men who were good and had sufficient learning, and they said that ours would be of this sort, and for that reason we certainly ought not to refuse bishoprics. A high proportion of them held this opinion, even those who have most love and affection for us in the Lord.

There was not a cardinal left who had not been spoken to about this matter on our behalf, except for two: the reasons for these were that one of them had been given the duty of speaking in favour of the bishopric at the consistory, and there was thus nothing to be gained; and in the case of the other, he had originally out of his own devotion renounced a certain bishopric, and later once again accepted it.[14]

In this situation, seeing that we were surrounded on all sides and that the consistory would be held on the following day, with the Pope holding fast to his opinion, our Father found a solution by visiting Madama and getting her to write a note to His Holiness in which she begged him kindly to avoid dealing with the subject at the appointed consistory, and to wait until Her Excellency[15] and Juan de Vega would have written about it to the King; and if in that case he were not to desist and His Holiness gave the order, the Society would accept the bishopric. The letter was sent that same Thursday, on the eve of the Friday when the consistory was to be held, and the Pope replied to Madama that he was pleased with it. However, as the cardinal who was to propose the subject was not aware of it, he did bring the matter up on the following day; however it went no further because one of those who supported our view intervened with good arguments that he had brought with him. Later Fr. Ignatius had letters written to Juan de Vega, to Madama, and to Cardinal di Carpi, our protector,[16] and to the King, and he himself also did so[17] on behalf of the whole Society, and this with so many reasons and laments that we have always had good hopes of a successful outcome.

----

[14] Probably a reference to Cardinal Carafa, the future Paul IV; he had renounced the bishopric of Chieri in 1524, and then taken it up once more in 1537.

[15] In the Spanish it is not clear if *Su Excelencia* here (and similarly the initials *S.E.* in the MHSI *Epist.* edition] refer to another person ("His Excellency") or to Madama herself; but the latter is more likely as a little later Ignatius is said to have written letters only to her and to the Ambassador, Juan de Vega.

[16] See §20.

[17] Letter 149 addressed to King Ferdinand I (MHSI *Epist.*, I, 450-453), which is a relatively short letter (about three pages).

In the same way he gave instructions that those of ours who are at the Council,[18] and Master Bobadilla, wherever he may be, should write, and make anyone else they can in Trent write to His Majesty about this case; but bearing in mind that in the Council there was only one prelate they could ask to write, as there also different opinions were held about the matter.

Even after all these measures had been taken here, Don Diego Lasso was still pressing as much as he could to prevent delay in satisfaction being given to the request made by the King his lord; and therefore he arranged that at the next consistory, which was one week later, the cardinal appointed should deliver his proposal. However by the grace of God this was prevented as it had been previously, because His Holiness declared that he wanted to keep his promise to Madama and wait for a reply from the King. This arrived here just a few days ago, with the King instructing his Ambassador not to insist further with the business, as he judged that this would be for the best. For this reason the order was given in the residence that Masses and the *Te Deum Laudamus* should be celebrated *in gratiarum actionem* [in thanksgiving] for our having escaped such a tribulation and pestilence. Certainly we all thought that it would be the equivalent of having our faces covered or blackened, if such a bishopric had been accepted.

May infinite and never-ending thanks be given to God Our Lord for this!

---

[18] Frs. Laínez, Salmerón, and Claude Jay himself were all at the Council of Trent this year.

SUPPLEMENT 3

The Troubles in Paris

At one point [see §149] da Câmara seems to have envisaged adding the text of the Latin Responsio *drawn up in Rome (January 1556) in reply to the Decree of the Faculty of Theology of the University of Paris against the Society of Jesus, presumably because this would cast further light on his notes and remarks. However, he subsequently crossed out the marginal note [§149], and also the Supplement, even if some lines of the latter can still be deciphered. The full text of the* Responsio *was published in an early edition of the Ignatian Letters (Cartas de San Ignacio de Loyola, vol. 5, Madrid 1889, pp. 494-512), and is also available as Letter 56 in the Fifth Appendix of MHSI Epist. XII, pp. 614-29. The part crossed out is a reply to the objection that the Society has appropriated a name which is* insolita *(in the pejorative sense of "contrary to custom").*

This title is not very *insolita*. Indeed there are in Italy some congregations that have the same name, as there are religious called "Gesuati".[1] There is also an order the "Soldiers of Christ," nor is there any reason why anyone should be more offended by our tide.

---

[1] Founded by Giovanni Colombini (1304-67) towards the middle of the 14th century, they bore a close resemblance at first to the Franciscans but excluded priests; they expanded rapidly in a very disorganized fashion without written rules; in the 15th century some conventions were established, and further developments occurred in the 16th and 17th centuries, but in 1668 Clement IX ordered their suppression: cf. art. "Jean Colombini de Sienne," *Dictionnaire de Spiritualité,* VIII (1974), cols. 392-404. See §280 footnote.

INDEX

338, 340; *Memoriale* 9-10, 12,
256b*, 265, 338n; minister 37,
39, 134-35, 161, 218, 251, 279,
295-96, 310; 405; motivation 3-
6; notebooks 12, 31-32, 87,
192n, 265-66, 336; personal
memories 23, 35, 83, 93, 100,
150, 179, 237b, 280, 298, 362,
383; preface 1-12; Portugal 197,
253, 271; Ribadeneira's help 31-
32, 34; short sight 55, 110n.,
251; testimony of older Jesuits
20, 22, 40, 46-47, 93, 100, 191,
256b, 259, 271, 305, 330, 333,
370 (cf. Laínez, Nadal, Polanco,
Ribadeneira); vainglory 111;
vinegar to Ignatius's oil 83, 296;
cf. secretary
Canisius, St. Peter 131
Cano, Melchor 162n., 221n., 322n.
capelo 102, 212
captives, redemption of 120
Carafa, Card., cf. Paul IV
Cardinal: 16, 20, 48, 68, 71, 72,
149, 193, 204, 230-32, 239, 265,
269, 302, 343, 346b; cf. (persons)
Badia, Carafa, Carpi (card.
Protector), Cueva, Enrique,
Gaddi, Ghinucci, Guidiccioni,
Guise, Luis, Morone, Pole,
Pozzo, Ricci, Salviati, Silva,
Toledo, Truchsess; (title)
Ravenna
Cardoner 137n.
Carmelites 239n.
Carneiro, Melchior 52,123
Carpi, Cardinal Rodolfo Pio di
20, 67, 232, 281-82, Sup. 2
Castello Branco 117, 126
Castile 118, 163, 231, 257n, 322, 381
castro 174
casuistry 50n., 69n.
Cataluña/Catalan 165, 327
Catechumens, House for 20, 240n.
Caterino/Catharinus, cf. Politi

Celso, San (church of) 5 ln.
Cesari, Ottaviano 67, 70
chamberlain, papal 280, 302
chapel 93, 17, 128, 179, 194, ora-
tory-chapel of Ignatius 106,
175, 179*, 285
Charles V (Emperor) 15n., 18n.,
47n., 70, 132, 142n., 163,
231, 276n., 310n., 322, Sup. 2n.
chastity 56, 58, 59*, 60
chestnuts 189
Chieti Sup. 2n.
Chronicon (Polanco) 46n., 65n.,
127n., 164n.
Church (in general) 30, 239, 310,
321-22, 333, 365
Church of Rome 118, 251
church of the Society in Rome, cf.
Strada, Santa Maria della
Cincinnato 29, 75, 101, 268, 288
clavichord 178
Clement VII (Pope) 307, Sup. 1n.
Clement VIII (Pope) 396n.
Clement IX (Pope) Sup. 3
coadjutor Brothers (sometimes called
"laymen") 106, 142*, 158*, 236,
276*, 303, 327, 332, 337, 341*,
378, 386, 388-9*, 402; cf.
Glossary
Coconaro, Giovanni 387
Codazzo, Pietro 307, Sup. 2
Cogordan, Ponzio 191, 193, 216.
Coimbra 8, 30, 40, 65n., 121-23, 271
colleges 76, 87, 93, 117, 138*, 157,
206; German College 16-19, 76,
83n., 84-85, 138n., 176, 178,
185, 212-13, 238-39, 246, 250-
51, 273, 277, 291, 345-47, 363,
399, 407; Roman College 49-50,
53-55, 64, 74n., 83n., 125n., 130,
133, 135, 142-44, 172, 176, 185,
212, 230, 232, 234, 239, 246,
273, 276, 290, 319, 348, 350-51,
389n, 390, 399, 400, 405, 412;
cf. Coimbra; Evora; Florence;